BOOK

OF

FIRST

SAMUEL

Pastor Palmer's Pen
(First Samuel)

Chapter One

WE CAN GO FROM PRESSURE TO PRAYER TO PRAISE

1 Sam. 1:1-28

Intro:
1. One day Linus and Charlie Brown are walking. Linus says, "I don't like to face problems head on. I think the best way to solve problems is to avoid them. In fact, this is a distinct philosophy of mine. No problem is so big or so complicated that it can't be run away from!"

2. That will work if you're a cartoon character, but if you're a real person you cannot avoid problems! But you can run to God when the pressure comes.

3. We can go from Pressure to Prayer to Praise – part 1

I Sam. 1:1-28

I. First, Hannah's Pressure. 1:1-8

A. Her *Husband.*

1. He was a *Priest.*

Ramathaim Zophim – elsewhere called Ramah was about 15 miles north of Jerusalem.

an Ephraimite – relates to the territory in which they lived not their tribal origin. They were Levites thus did not have an appointed portion of land but lived among the other tribes. I Chron. 6:16,22, 33-35

Today all believers are priests (I Pet. 2:5,9/ Rev. 1:6; 5:10), but in the O.T. only those from the tribe of Levi were.

2. He was a *Polygamist*. 1:2a

Polygamy is the practice of having more than one wife at a time. God's Word teaches that marriage should consist of one man and one woman (Gen.2:18, 24/Mt.19:4-6).

The Bible records the evil effects of polygamy as in the life of Abraham (Gen.16:4-16); Jacob (Gen.35:22; 37:18-28); David (2 Sam.13:1-29; 15:1ff), and Solomon (I Ki.11:1-12).

What apparently happened was the same thing that happened to Abraham and Sarah. She could not have a child so he married Hagar with the purpose of giving Abraham a child. Hannah is the first wife; she could not have a child so he married Peninnah.

He should have sought God's will not another wife (Gen. 25:21).

3. He was a man of *Praise!* 3

Is not that grace? Here is a man who had disobeyed God's Word and yet worships the Lord through the sacrifice [Jesus].

Maybe you have a terrible sin in your past; you can confess it as sin and get preoccupied with praising God through Christ.

Thomas Merton, "If I make anything out of the fact that I am Thomas Merton, I am dead. And if you make anything out of the fact that you are in charge of the pig barn, you are dead. Quit keeping score altogether and surrender yourself with all your sinfulness to God who sees neither the score nor the scorekeeper but only his child redeemed by Christ."

4. A *Provider*. 1:4-5, 8

He provided her with, not only food, but love and encouragement! But notice he could not take the place of God! No human being can do what God can do. Gen.30:1-2
It is not enough to see the problem we must also see the right solution.

During WWII the British navy was frustrated by the threat of German submarines. They couldn't locate them, one officer offered this solution, "Once you bring the ocean to a boil, the submarines will be forced to the surface. Then you can knock them off!"

He was then asked, "But how does one boil the

ocean?" He replied "I don't know. I just give the ideas, I don't implement them."

Hannah was frustrated, but Elkanah's solution was worthless! Ultimately only God, not man, can solve our problems.

B. Her *Headache*. 1:2, 6-7

1. Peninnah's provocation was *Unbearable.*

Provoked her severely – lit. "Provoked her to anger, indeed provocation." It means to be irritated to the point of anger.

to make her miserable – lit. "to cause her to tremble."

2. Peninnah's provocation was *Continual.* 7

You got any headaches? Maybe an ex-husband or wife; a rebellious child; an unprofessional teacher at school; perhaps your boss is a jerk; or you have a neighbor who is up every night with loud parties;

C. Her *Heartbreak*. 2b, 6b

had no children – this was the worst thing that could be said of a woman in that day. It went against God's mandate to be fruitful and multiply; it meant that the Messiah could not come through her; it meant a lack of needed manual laborers; it meant that people thought one was cursed by God, since children were considered a blessing from God.

Hannah is having a bad life! Her husband can't help, her life is one headache and heartbreak. She reminds me of Charlie Brown who is talking with Linus. Linus says, "Charlie, you look kind of depressed." He says, "I worry about school a lot. I also worry about my worrying so much, that my anxieties have anxieties!"

But did you notice verse 5b? The Lord has closed her womb! It was God who gave her a husband, it was God who allowed her to have that thorn Peninnah, and the heartbreak of barrenness was from the Lord's hand also!

Margaret Clarkson, "The sovereignty of God is the one impregnable rock to which the suffering human heart must cling. The circumstances surrounding our lives are no accident; they may be the work of evil, but that evil is held firmly within the mighty hand of our sovereign God…All evil is subject to Him, and evil cannot touch His children unless He permits it. God is the Lord of human history and of the personal history of every member of His redeemed family."

We must see God's invisible hand behind everything in our life. Her pressure, what should she do with it?

II. Next, our pressure should take us to God in *Prayer*. 1:9-28

A. First, her *Desperation*. 1:9-10

God always meets us at the point of our desperation.

- Hagar was treated harshly by Sarah causing her in desperation to flee into the wilderness where she meets God. Gen.16:21

- Jacob was desperate when he was about to meet his brother Esau, but it was there that God blessed them. Gen.32

- Joseph was crying out in desperation as he was lowered into that pit by his brothers, but it was the pathway to the throne of Egypt.

- Moses, after killing a man, spent 40 years of desperation, but it guided him to God's burning bush.

- The Book of Judges is a cycle of how desperate people cried out to God and repeatedly received deliverers.

Bill Stafford, "Oh thank God for holy desperation. Did you know that God never met a man that He couldn't get desperate? Go through the N.T., and see that every man and woman that Jesus healed or saved were desperate people. The only people that God couldn't work on was people like the rich young ruler. Too proud, too self-sufficient, too able – rich, young, in need of nothing! And he went away lost. I wonder if we can get desperate enough to let God do something in our lives?"

B. Furthermore, her *Devotion*. 1:11

I will give Him to the Lord – this was not a self-centered act, but a mother who was willing to give her son. Why do we want our prayers answered? For God's glory or for our personal pleasure?

3 You ask and do not receive, because you ask amiss, that you may spend it on your pleasures. Jam. 4:3

Spurgeon, "Mothers wish to keep their children about them. It is natural that they should wish to see them often. But Hannah does not seek him for herself, but for her God. Her heart longs not to see her boy at home but to see him serving in the house of the Lord.
Our hardest lesson is to learn to give up what we most prize. This is real self-denial."

C. Next, her *Distraction*. 1:12-16

1. Eli's *Hostility*. 12-13

Goulburn, "This was not the first time, nor will it be the last, that God's true servants have been mocked and falsely accused for actions which have been really pious and devout. If you resolve to be a Christian, indeed you must be prepared to be misunderstood."

2. Eli's *Hypocrisy*. 14

Here is a man who is going to face a premature death because he did not restrain his wicked sons. 2:22-25, 29-30; 3:13

3. Hannah's *Humility*. 15-16

There is no anger just a straightforward and gentle explanation of the truth.

D. The *Divine Direction*. 17-18

1. The *Messenger* – Eli was God's spokesman in spite of his apparent failures. God has been known to speak through murderers like Moses; adulterers like David; Christ deniers like Peter; Liars like Abraham; etc.

2. The *Message* – may God grant your petition. She took this as a promise from God, and it was.

3. The *Miracle* of faith. 18

She immediately went from sad to glad! She is still barren; nothing has changed except God's promise. That is how faith operates. Heb. 11:6

How can she change when she is still barren? Because faith's object is not our self but God Himself. Rom. 4:20-21

Manley Beasley, "Faith is acting as though a thing is so, in order for it to be so, because God said it is so. Which comes first, believing or receiving? Believing, anyone can believe after they have received!"

It's not enough to have God's promises, we must act upon them.

E. Finally, the *Dedication*. 1:19-28

1. *Source* of the child. 19-20

2. *Sequence*. 21-23

3. *Sacrifice* of the child. 24-28

It's not enough to make a commitment but we must also follow through with them! 2 Cor. 8:10-11/Heb.10:38

Con:

1. Do we have any pressure? Do we know

why? It is designed to drive us to God in prayer. 2. Some automobiles are equipped with motors of 325 horsepower. I read the increase of power is produced when the cylinder head is ground, the result is an increase in the compression ratio, thus greater horsepower.

The principle is the greater the pressure, the greater the power – likewise God uses adversity in our lives, pressure, to drive us to appropriate His power.

Chapter Two

HANNAH'S HYMN OF PRAISE

1 Sam. 2:1-10

Intro:

1. J.I. Packer wrote, "I've experienced God's presence most powerfully in worship, often during the singing, I suppose because when we sing to him, we are looking hard in his direction."

2. Hannah's Pressure caused her to look *hard in God's direction* with Prayer and Praise.

Trans: We have seen her Pressure, which lead her to Prayer, and now her Praise to the One who answered her Prayer.

As one put it, "Hannah has left her little boy at the Temple now and has gone her way without the pitter patter of little footsteps at her side. They are now a shadow of the past. Little fingers no longer find warmth in her hands as she journeys back to her home. She has kept her vow to God and given her son, her only son, to the Lord for service in God's work. Her dedication, devotion, and sacrifice moved the heart of God because this is exactly what God was going to do for you and me when He gave His only son Jesus to die for our sins. Think, how would you feel if you were Hannah at this point. You would reason this mother would probably be very sad, feeling sorry for herself, down, depressed, and distraught. Not Hannah! She is like a button that popped on the belly of a fat man. She is bursting at the seams with joy, not sadness."

I..FIRST, SHE EXAULTS THE LORD'S WORTHINESS. 1-5

A. A very *Brief Resume.* 2:1-3

1. His *Strength.* 1

Then Hannah prayed and said, "My heart exults in the LORD; My horn is exalted in the LORD, My mouth speaks boldly against my enemies, Because I rejoice in Your salvation – This is the fifth time we are told she prays. She was a great example of a prayer warrior.

Hannah turned to the Lord in her despair over her barrenness. Other women in that day turned to fertility figurines. Hundreds have been found in Judah and were prayed to by many women seeking to get pregnant. It is also interesting that she did not focus on Samuel but on the Lord.

Matthew Henry, "What great thing she says of God she takes little note of Samuel, she overlooks the gift and praises the giver. There may be other Samuels, but no other Jehovah."

Ryan King, "notice what she does not talk about. She doesn't focus on her son, what he looks like, or the color of his hair. She skips the gift and simply praises the giver. Often we do the opposite: we focus on the gift and the give the Giver a passing glance."

To have your "horn exalted" meant to receive new strength from God and be especially helped by Him at a time of crisis. The Bible does not distinguish between horns and antlers, so horn refers to pointed bony structures on the heads of male sheep, goats, deer, cattle, oxen and so forth. These horns were basically for defense. The horns were used for carrying oil, and to make trumpets, and are symbolic of strength.

The NIV Application Commentary, ""It appears to be a metaphor in which the horns and head of an animal are held high as a symbol of triumph and power (Dan. 8:3, 5, 9)."

It was God's strength that enabled her to become pregnant and deliver her from her barrenness. As one put it:

"Her horn was exalted; that is, a new power had come into her life. She had been lifted out of weakness, far above the infirmities of her flesh, and now she exulted in a new strength in the Lord. When we have placed our all on the altar, God will be sure to put a new power into our lives."

2. His *Separation*. 2a

"There is no one holy like the LORD, Indeed, there is no one besides You, Nor is there any rock like our God – God is in a class all by Himself.

In the myths, the assembly of the gods was called, "sons of the holy one." El, the high god, is the head of this assembly, but Baal has a prominent position. He is even depicted as standing beside El. The goddess Anat declares: "Mightiest Baal is our King, our judge, over whom there is none. It is as if Hannah is directly countering this claim. Hannah calls the Lord, "holy" and affirms that he is in a class all by himself.

Sproul, "The primary meaning of holy is "apartness" or "otherness." When we say that God is holy, we call attention to the profound difference between Him and all creatures. It refers to God's transcendent majesty."

Origen noted, "What it means to say "There is none besides You," I do not understand. If it had said, "There is no God but you" or "There is no creator but you" or had added something like this, there would be no problem. But it says "There is none besides You," this is what it seems to me, to mean: none of those things which are, possess their existence, by nature. You alone, O Lord, are the One to whom, Your existence, has not been given by anyone. Because all of us, that is the whole creation, did not exist before we were created; thus, that we are, is [due to] the will of the Creator. And because there was a time, when we were not, it is not wholly right, if it is said of us, without qualification, that we exist…For the shadow is nothing, in comparison with the body; and in comparison with the fire, smoke too is nothing."

Of course, this is not to forget the secondary meaning of holiness as moral purity. Moreover, a holy God demands a holy people (1 Pet. 1:14-16).

This is one of the most neglected truths among God's people today. But it is a clear requirement for the Christian who lives in fellowship with God. What is holiness? John Ryle gives the following descriptions:

- Holiness is the habit of being of one mind with God, according as we find His mind described in Scripture. It is the habit of agreeing in God's judgments, hating what He hates, loving what He loves, and measuring everything in this world by the standard of His Word.

- A holy man will endeavor to shun every known sin, and to keep every known commandment. He will have a hearty desire to do His will, a greater fear of displeasing Him than of displeasing the world.

- A holy man will strive to be like our Lord Jesus Christ.

- A holy man will bear much, forbear much, overlook much, and be slow to talk of standing on his rights.

- A holy man will follow self-denial. He will labor to mortify the desires of his body, to curb his passions, to restrain his carnal inclinations, lest at any time they break loose. He knows his own heart is like tinder, and will diligently keep clear of the sparks of temptation.

- A holy man will desire, in lowliness of mind, to esteem all others better than himself. He will see more evil in his own heart than in any other in the world.

- A holy man will follow spiritual-mindedness. He will endeavor to set his affections entirely on things above, and to hold things on earth with a very loose hand…He will aim to live like one whose treasure is in heaven, and to pass through this world like a stranger and pilgrim traveling to his home.

Holiness is for the preacher to practice what he preaches and for the congregation to practice it as well. Calvin was right when he said, "It would be best for a preacher to fall and break his neck as he mounts the pulpit, if he is not himself going to be the first, to follow God in living his own message." And it is not a mere outward conformity to some rules but an inward focus. Packer notes:

"Holiness has to do with my heart. It is the center and focus of one's inner personal life: the source of motivation, the seat of passion, the spring of all thought processes and particularly of conscience. Holiness starts inside a person. A holy person's aim, passion, goal, and drive is to please God, both by what one does and by what one avoids doing. We must labor to keep our heart actively responsive to God."

This is not legalism; it is the saved sinner's response of gratitude for the grace he has received.

Charles Wesley wrote:

"O for a heart to praise my God, A heart from sin set free;
A heart that always feels Thy blood, So freely shed for me;
A heart resigned, submissive, meek…
Where only Christ is heard to speak, Where Jesus reigns alone;
A heart in every thought renewed, And full of love divine,
Perfect and right and pure and good,
A copy, Lord, of Thine."

Holiness is as one put it, "The essential problem is "a self that has not learned to die. But a true surrender to Christ shrinks our inflated ego to its proper size in relation to Him and our fellows, and imparts reality to our lives." If God's holiness does not affect ours, something is amiss (Titus 2:11-14/Eph.4:21-24; 5:25-27). It is the breastplate in the armor that the Christian is called to wear in order to counter the devil's attacks (Eph. 6:14).

Let us never forget that we are still a work and progress and we all fall woefully short. Let us also not blur the distinctions between justification and sanctification. One rightly notes:

"As far as concerns the making atonement for our sins, and the consequent pardoning and justifying of our person, the work is entirely and exclusively God's. We contribute nothing to our new relationship with God save our need of it. We get into God's favor, not by paying our way, but by accepting His gift of a blood-bought amnesty. However, in sanctification, which is the work of God within us from which our holiness flows, we are called to cooperate actively with God."

This may seem to be taking too much time on this point, but in light of the making light of this truth today, it is both needed and worthy of the space.

3. His *Stability*. 2b

Nor is there any rock like our God – a rock speaks of something that is immovable and fixed.

Evans, "God frequently compares Himself to a rock because He is a shelter, defense, refuge. He is likewise spoken of as a rock because in ancient days they oftentimes made rocks their habituation. They dwell in His love and in His attributes, and find them the place of abode. But He also bears the name of a rock because He is the shade of His people."

Augustus Toplady was traveling when a violent storm came up and forced him to take shelter in the clef of a great rock. As he reflected upon his situation he looked down and saw a playing card that someone had left there. On that card Augustus wrote these words:

"Rock of Ages, cleft for me,
Let me hide myself in Thee;
Let the water and the blood,
From Thy riven side which flowed,
Be of sin the double cure,
Cleanse me from its guilt and power.
Rock of Ages, cleft for me.
Let me hide myself in Thee."

4. He is *Smart*. 3

Boast no more so very proudly, Do not let arrogance come out of your mouth; For the LORD is a God of knowledge, and with Him actions are weighed – God knows all things, the schemes and dreams of the wicked are laid bare before His eyes.

Wiersbe, "The Lord is also "a God of knowledge", so people had better be careful what they say and how they say it. There's no place for pride and arrogance when you stand before a God who knows you through and through, everything you've thought, spoken, and done. God heard all of Peninnah's haughty words spoken against Hannah, and He also heard Hannah's prayer from her heart. God is omniscient and knows all things, and He is omnipresent and beholds all things."

Hannah rejoiced that the Lord "weighed" the words and deeds of the arrogant. Hannah wisely left judgment to God as she expressed confidence in God that He would act on behalf of the disadvantaged and oppressed.

Trans: God's Strength, Separation, Stability, and Smarts – just a very Brief Resume of God.

William Sangster told of an invalid girl who lived in a box. She said, "In this position I can only look up. On those nights when I can't sleep, I play with the stars."

William asked, "How can you play with the stars?" She said, "I pick out the brightest star I can find and say, "That's Mummy." I pick out another and say, "That's Daddy." Another and say "That's brother." Then she said, "But, there are never enough stars to go around!"

In the same way we can never say enough about God – it might be enlightening some night to go outside and just lie down and look up at them. Pick out a star and say, "That one is God's *self-existence*; that one is His *sovereignty*; that one over there is His *immutability;* that one His *holiness;* there is His *Omniscience*; and there His *Omnipresence;* and there His *Omnipotence;* that one His *faithfulness;* there His *longsuffering;* that one His *grace*; that one His *mercy;* there is His *love;* if we really knew all that there is about this infinite God, there would never be enough stars to go around!

B. Her *Breath-taking Response.* 4-5

1. *Strengthened.* 4

"The bows of the mighty are shattered, But the feeble gird on strength – praising God brings about supernatural strength.

"...the people who know their God will display strength..." Daniel 11:32

The Hebrew is lit, "but the stumbling they gird on strength."

- Jonah stumbled, but got back up to go to Nineveh and preached the greatest revival in history.
- Peter stumbled, cursed the Lord, but got back up to be greatly used of God. At Pentecost, three thousand were saved.
- Jacob stumbled by being a deceiver and disobedient at times. God worked in his life and he became the father of the twelve tribes of Israel.

God is an expert at picking up pieces and helping us get back up on our feet. He can strengthen the stumblers and use him for His glory.

2. *Satisfied.* 5

"Those who were full hire themselves out for bread, But those who were hungry cease to hunger. Even the barren gives birth to seven, But she who has many children languishes – God brought her from barren to blessed.

The truth in this statement is reflected in the fact that Hannah bore five more children (v. 21).

Trans: God alone can Strengthen and Satisfy. This He will do for every believer regardless of our lot in life or how long we live. As one put it:

"Lord, it belongs not to my care,
 Whether I die or live;
To love and serve Thee is my share
 And this, Thy grace, must give.

If life be long, I will be glad,
That I may long obey;
If short – then why should I be sad
To soar to endless days?"

All of this caused Hannah to break out in a song, Bill Arnold notes, "Sometimes you just have to sing! Hannah had to sing!...Whether it is the Scripture choruses many of us use in modern churches or the great classic hymns of the Christian faith, such singing of theology helps shape our thinking and prepares us for the day when we just cannot help ourselves, and we too have to sing."

II. NEXT SHE EXAULTS HIS *WORKS.* 2:6-10

A. His *Providential Control.* 6-8

6 *"The LORD kills and makes alive; He brings down to Sheol and raises up.* 7 *"The LORD makes poor and rich; He brings low, He also*

exalts. ⁸ "He raises the poor from the dust, He lifts the needy from the ash heap To make them sit with nobles, And inherit a seat of honor; For the pillars of the earth are the LORD'S, And He set the world on them – the point is that God is the one in control of every aspect of our lives. Everything from life to death and everything in between, in the myths Baal engages in a struggle with death; space he goes down to the grave, is pronounced dead, and later returns to life. In stark contrast, the Lord is sovereign over death. He can kill and make alive.

Hughes, "Hannah's grasp of reality was extraordinary. We occasionally hear it said that the Old Testament had no concept of resurrection from the dead. Hannah did! The Lord changes life to death, and death to life. When we think of life and refuse to think of death, or when we think of death and ignore the God who raises the dead, our understanding is a distortion of the reality… God determines these things. They are not under our control at all. Nor are they under the control of others, or of social and economic forces. The government does not determine them, nor does the stock market….let me ask you, do you see life as Hannah did? It is a searching question if we consider it honestly. What is your attitude to the various forms of human power? Do you see wealth as a means of security? Do you fear being weak or poor? Do you mind being unimportant? What do you think about life and death? Do you think that you have the power to hold on to life and avoid death? Most people seem to live as though they do. There is a natural, understandable, defensible human answer to each of these questions. And there is an answer that comes from actually believing in the God of knowledge. As we listen to Hannah's prayer we must ask, where is the Lord, the God of knowledge, in our real thinking about life?"

Spurgeon, "Here the agency of God, in life and death, is clearly revealed to us. How well it is to discern the Lord's hand in everything. Our Puritanic forefathers spoke of God as restraining the bottles of heaven, or sending a gracious rain; as sending forth the wind, or hiding it in his storehouse; but we have grown so wise, that we begin to understand how the rain is formed, and we talk about the winds as if we had been into the chambers from which they come howling forth, and had discovered all the secrets of the universe. We ascribe events to second causes, to the laws of nature, and I know not what. I think it were better far, if we would go back to the good old way of talking and speaking of the Lord as being in everything. While we do not deny the laws of nature, nor decry the discoveries of science, we will suffer none of these to be hung up as a veil before our present God. O foolish wisdom, which widens the distance between me and my heavenly Father! O sweet simplicity of love, which sees the God of love in every place, at every hour! I need no telescope to see my God with; behold, O sons of men, He is here; and my heart joyfully perceives Him. God is in life and death, in sickness and in health. This, surely, will soften the pains of sickness, and produce the joys of recovery. If you look upon sickness and restoration as merely the products of natural causes, you will not feel humbled when you are stretched upon the bed nor grateful when you walk out again and breathe the fresh air; but if you see God's finger in touching your bones and your flesh, you will be humbled under the chastisement; and if you discern His hand, in restoring your youth, like the eagle's, you will be able, like David, to say, *"Bless the Lord, O my soul, and forget not all his benefits."* Let others forget God if they will, that is the attribute of the wicked; but let his saints remember Him, and let them speak well of His name, and have it in their mouths all the day long."

A. His *Protective Care.* 9

He keeps the feet of His godly ones, But the wicked ones are silenced in darkness; For not by might shall a man prevail – He is with us every step of the way!

The Bible says several things about our steps:

- God has determined an *Exact* Number of them— Job 14:16.

- He *Enlarges* them for Stability— Psalm 18:36.

- He *Establishes* our Steps— Psalm 37:23, 24; 40:2

- He Directs our Steps— Proverbs 16:9.

[11] "I am no longer in the world; and *yet* they themselves are in the world, and I come to You. Holy Father, keep them in Your name, *the name* which You have given Me, that they may be one even as We *are.* John 17:11

[3] But the Lord is faithful, and He will strengthen and protect you from the evil *one.* 2 Thessalonians 3:3

[24] Now to Him who is able to keep you from stumbling, and to make you stand in the presence of His glory blameless with great joy, Jude 24

We find a wonderful list of God's Nevers:

- Breaks his covenants (Judges 2:1, II Sam. 23:5, Isa. 55:3, Matt. 26:28)

- Suffers the righteous to be moved (Ps. 55:22, 121:3, 125:1, 2; II Tim. 2:19)

- Leaves nor forsakes His own (Heb. 13:5, Matt. 28:20, Deut. 31:6)

- Permits them to be overcome (Prov. 10:30, Isa. 26:3, 4; Rom. 8:37)

- Lets them be ashamed (Joel 2:26–7, Ps. 71:1, II Tim. 1:12)

- Allows them to perish (John 10:28, 6:35, 11:26; 3:16; Jude 24–5)
- Will let His kingdom be destroyed (Dan. 2:44, II Peter 1:10–11, Heb. 12:28)

What we have in Christ is nothing short of amazing! Here Hannah speaks of Providential control and Protective care. That is more than enough to put a smile on our face. The only problem we have is failure to believe it.

George Walker discovered gold in South Africa, the gold vein was 50 miles long and served as the world's leading gold source for the next 30 years. And yet old George sold his gold discovery for less than 50 dollars! George did not realize what he had – do we?

B. His *Prophetical Conquest.* 10

1. *Judgment* on *Men.* 10a

Those who contend with the LORD will be shattered; Against them He will thunder in the heavens, The LORD will judge the ends of the earth; - soon, and very soon the world is going to face a time of unprecedented judgment.

For then there will be a great tribulation, such as has not occurred since the beginning of the world until now, nor ever will. Matthew 24:21

The horrifying time is further, described in some detail in Revelation 6-16, where the seal, trumpet, and bowl judgments exhibit the escalating intensity of God's wrath upon sinful, rebellious mankind.

2. *Establishment* of the *Messiah.* 10b

The LORD will judge the ends of the earth; And He will give strength to His king, And will exalt the horn of His anointed – this king is none other than the Lord Jesus Christ. He will return at the end of the Tribulation Period and set up His kingdom.

Chisholm, "Samuel's birth is a turning point in Israel's history. Hannah's deliverance from her own press condition foreshadows what God will do for the nation in the years that immediately follow."

Philips notes, "The golden age has come. The armies of the nations have been disbanded, and the great military academies have fallen into ruin and decay. The machinery of war has all been smelted down and converted to the implements of peace. Jerusalem has become the world's capital. The throne of David is there, and the twelve apostles are there judging the twelve tribes of Israel, for Israel rules the world, The millennial Temple has been built, and the nations of the earth come there to worship the living God. Prosperity is evident from pole to pole and from the new river, which now graces Jerusalem, to the ends of the earth. Poverty is unknown. Every man has all that heart can desire. There are no prisons, no hospitals, no mental institutions, no barracks, no saloons, no houses of ill repute, no gambling dens, no homes for the aged and infirm. Such things belong to a past and lesser age. The bloom of youth is on everyone's cheek, for a man is a stripling at a hundred years of age. Cemeteries are crumbling relics of the past, and tears are rare. The wolf and the lamb, the calf and the lion, the cow and the bear, the child and the scorpion, all are at peace. Jesus has come, and the Millennium is here. The golden age, so frequently heralded by the prophets of Israel's past, has dawned at last, and the earth is filled with the knowledge of God.

Jesus is Lord, and He rules the nations with a rod of iron. His reign is righteous, and the nations obey. The principles of the Sermon on the Mount are the laws of the kingdom, and men obey them because infractions are not allowed. Sin is visited with swift and certain judgment. The golden age will dawn at last and the earth will be filled with the knowledge of the Lord, form sea to sea, from shore to shore."

Con:

1. I hope our Pressures in life has caused us to look hard in God's direction through Prayer and Praise.

2. Spurgeon, "Praise should always follow prayer. Has the Lord been gracious to you and inclined His ear to the voice of your

prayer? Then praise Him as long as you live. Deny not a song to Him who has answered your prayers and given you the desire of your heart. To be silent over God's mercies is to incur the guilt of shocking ingratitude, and ingratitude is one of the worst of crimes."

Chapter Three

THE SIN OF HONORING CHILDREN MORE THEN GOD

1 Sam. 2:12-17, 22-25, 27-36; 3:13

Intro:

1. Jones, "That we can be too kind and indulgent to our children "is the simple, yet important lesson taught, by the history of Eli. Having been too fondly indulged in the days of their youth they gradually lost respect for parental authority which is of great importance to the welfare of a child. Let those parents, whose besetting sin, like that of Eli which tempts them to make a practice of excusing their faults and allowing them to have too much of their own way, remember that, they are certainly exposing themselves and their children to the chastening hand of God. And if they do not turn out immoral then they are likely to turn out proud, self-centered, ungrateful, disrespectful, and inattentive. Be

sure such a sin will find the incautious parent out. God says so, who shall contradict it?"

2. It is time that children quit acting like parents, and parents quit acting like children!

I. FIRST, THEIR *SINFUL CONDITION.*

A. Eli's *Sons.*

They were *Worthless.* 2:12a

Now the sons of Eli were worthless men – lit., "sons of Belial. It means to be worthless. Deut. 13:13; Judg. 19:22; 1 Sam. 1:16; 2:12; 1 Kgs. 21:10; Psa. 101:3.

Because of their wickedness, these sons were worthless and useless in the service of God. They were serving themselves and Satan.

In the Allegheny Mountains, a huge eagle was shot by a hunter. When the eagle was examined, the hunter was amazed to find that one of its claws was held firmly in a strong steel trap from which dangled a five foot chain. The chain was not heavy enough to prevent the eagle from flying, but the additional weight did weary the majestic bird and brought it down within the reach of the hunter's rifle.

Christian's entrapped by known unconfessed sin are brought low making their service ineffective and basically useless.

2. They were *Without* any regard for the Lord.

they did not know the LORD - Here were sons of a true believer and were even serving in God's house as priest! Yet, they did not know the Lord. That does not mean they did not know *about* Yahweh (obviously they did) or that they were ignorant of his mighty acts according to Israel's creed (surely they were not). Rather it means that they 'had no regard for' (RSV) or that 'they cared nothing for Yahweh' (JB). The Lord and His works didn't matter to them, had no influence over them.

There is a danger of becoming too familiar with things, according to the Associated Press, the North Carolina state medical board suspended the license of a neurosurgeon in Wilmington, North Carolina, after an investigation turned up remarkably casual behavior on his part during brain surgery. The investigation revealed that in the middle of one surgery, as a patient's brain was exposed, the neurosurgeon left the operating room for twenty-five minutes to go and have lunch. While he was having lunch, no other physician was present in the operating room to care for the patient. I wonder how many unbelievers who have been in church all their lives have become so familiar with the worship service that it means virtually nothing to them at all.

3. They *Withheld* the offering that rightly belonged to God. 13-17

[13] *and the custom of the priests with the people. When any man was offering a sacrifice,*

the priest's servant would come while the meat was boiling, with a three-pronged fork in his hand. ¹⁴ Then he would thrust it into the pan, or kettle, or caldron, or pot; all that the fork brought up the priest would take for himself. Thus they did in Shiloh to all the Israelites who came there. ¹⁵ Also, before they burned the fat, the priest's servant would come and say to the man who was sacrificing, "Give the priest meat for roasting, as he will not take boiled meat from you, only raw." ¹⁶ If the man said to him, "They must surely burn the fat first, and then take as much as you desire," then he would say, "No, but you shall give it to me now; and if not, I will take it by force." ¹⁷ Thus the sin of the young men was very great before the LORD, for the men despised the offering of the LORD – God's Word was clear.

- All of the fat belonged to the Lord (Lev. 3:16-17). It was to be given to the Lord first, as a reminder that the entire offering belonged to the Lord.

- Then, the priest would get his portion, the breast and the right shoulder (Lev. 7:29-34).

- Last, the family who brought the peace offering would enjoy the rest of it, symbolizing their fellowship with the Lord.

Dale Davis, "Worship is a farce at Shiloh. A worshiper brings his offering and here comes the priest demanding some raw meat BEFORE the fat was offered to the Lord; If one protested they were intimidated or slapped; Later as the family sat down to enjoy the meal here comes a thug with a three-pronged BBQ fork! He plunges it into the pot and takes it to the priest!"

Like people today who rob God's offering by taking that which is rightly His and using it to gratify themselves. How many today give God their leftover's, and not of their first fruits!

Tozer shared this:

"Somebody else came in with a machine that takes wastepaper and crushes it into a bale. He said, "You announce to your audiences, 'Bring all your wastepaper to church.' We'll bale it and you can sell it and have money to pay the preacher and keep the church and your missionary program going." I said, "Mister, over there's the door. I want you to get to that door just as fast as you can. I don't want my board to know that I even talked to you. If they even found out that I'd let you even make a proposition like this to me, they'd be on my neck. In this church, we go down in our pants pocket, pull the money up, take it out and put it silently in the plate. That's how we get our offerings. We don't bale wastepaper." Can you imagine when God sent His only begotten Son, the best He had, and

His Son gave His blood, the best He had, and the apostles gave their lives, the best they had, we'd bring God our wastepaper?"

4. They were *Wayward.* 22

Now Eli was very old; and he heard all that his sons were doing to all Israel, and how they lay with the women who served at the doorway of the tent of meeting – woman served at the tabernacle (Ex. 38:8) and apparently these boys committed fornication with them.

Today people offer a host of reasons why it is all right to have sex outside of marriage:

When researchers at the University of Texas at Austin asked 2,000 people why they have sex, there were plenty of answers—237, to be precise. The most popular answer given by those surveyed was that they felt an attraction for the other person. Others said sex was a chief way to feel closer to someone else or to show someone how much they are loved. Many simply said they had sex because "it feels good" and "it's fun."

Most of the answers were expected, but researchers also received quite a few unexpected reasons for sexual behavior. The more startling included:

• "[I wanted] to boost my social status."

• "[I had sex] because my partner was famous."

- "[I wanted] to get a raise or promotion."

- "[I wanted] to change the topic of conversation."

- "[I wanted] to return a favor."

- "Someone dared me."

- "I wanted to punish myself."

- "I lost a bet."

- "I had sex to keep warm."

- "[I had sex] because my hormones were out of control."

- "[Sex] seemed like good exercise."

- "I wanted to give someone a sexually transmitted disease."

But God's Word offers only one reason why it's wrong – it is sin against God (Gen. 39:7-9/1 Thess.4:8).

5. They *Withstood* parental advice. 22-25

23 He said to them, "Why do you do such things, the evil things that I hear from all these people? 24 "No, my sons; for the report is not good which I hear the LORD'S people circulating. 25 "If one man sins against another, God will mediate for him; but if a man sins against the LORD, who can intercede for him?" But they would not listen to the voice of their father, for the LORD desired to put them to death – it appears that part of the problem was that Eli neglected the wood shed when they were little. You cannot wait until your kids are teenagers to start making them obey.

Cuyler, "At the 11th hour he rubs open his sleepy eyes to see what he ought to have seen 10 hours before. He had two faults. One was that he rebuked his sons too late. The other was that of having postponed his correction until his sons became hardened in vice, thus his words of review were weak as water."

But that does not excuse these boys' sins!

Trans: If you are indifferent to your parents, ignorant of God, indulgent or self-centered, involved in illicit sex, and insolent you are headed for a collision with God. The Titanic not long ago was making a lot of headlines, "it was billed as "The ship that God himself couldn't sink! That is until it had a head on collision with a huge iceberg – and it lost! So will all who head butt with God.

B. Furthermore Eli's *Sins*.

1. There was a lack of *Discipline*. 2:27-29a 3:13

27 Then a man of God came to Eli and said to him, "Thus says the LORD, 'Did I not indeed reveal Myself to the house of your father when they were in Egypt in bondage to Pharaoh's house? 28 'Did I not choose them from all the tribes of Israel to be My priests, to go up to My altar, to burn incense, to carry an ephod before Me; and did I not give to the house of your father all the fire offerings of the sons of Israel? ^{29} *'Why do you kick at My sacrifice and at My offering which I have commanded in My dwelling, and honor your sons above Me, by making yourselves fat with the choicest of every offering of My people Israel?'* - The phrase, "kick at my sacrifice" means to show scorn at God's sacrifice. How? By not removing his sons from the priesthood.

Liddon, "Eli only talked to his sons, and we can understand how he may have persuaded himself that talking was enough; just leave it alone, surely as they grow older they will straighten out. This is what weak people do. If Eli had not been blinded by his misplaced affection for his children, he would have known that outward circumstances do not improve the heart, and getting older has nothing to do with getting better."

Prov. 12:1; 13:1; 13:24; 19:18; 22:15; 23:13; 29:17.

Billy Graham described the time when his two-year-old son spit at him in a fit of anger. Graham said, "I don't know where he learned such an ugly habit, but one thing I know for certain, it's a good thing that he didn't later in life take up chewing tobacco because after what I did to him, he'll never spit again!"

According to a survey conducted by Columbia University's Center on Addiction and Substance Abuse (CASA):

"Almost one in five American teens say they live with 'hands-off' adults who fail to consistently set rules and monitor their behavior. These youth are at a four-times greater risk for smoking, drinking, and illegal drug use than their peers with 'hands-on' parents."

In a survey of 1,000 children in the age group of 12- to 17-year-olds, it was found that:

"Teens who believe their parents would "not be too upset" if they used marijuana are more than three times as likely to use drugs than those who believe their parents would be "extremely upset." Likewise, teens with parents who are "very unaware" of their academic performance are almost three times more likely to engage in substance use than their peers whose parents are "very aware" of their school performance.

Joseph A. Califano, Jr., president of CASA, remarked that, "Mothers and fathers who are parents rather than pals can greatly reduce the risk of their children smoking, drinking, and using drugs." In addition, he notes that "the family is fundamental to keeping children away from tobacco, alcohol, and drugs."

2. Misplaced *Devotion.*

and honor your sons above Me – By not restraining the sin of Hophni and Phinehas, Eli had shown preference for his sons above the Lord.

Spurgeon, "Oh, take heed, dear friends, that you do not despise God. Eli, who was God's high priest, fell into this sin because he thought more of displeasing his sons than he did of displeasing his God. He said to himself, "I cannot speak sharply to Hophni. He is my eldest son, and a man of ripe years. He does behave very badly; but what can I do? I fear I must speak a word to him, but I will do it softly. And Phinehas—Phinehas has some fine points about him. I think he will come right by gentle means, I must not say anything sharp to him." Now in this he honored his sons with a false honor, and did not truly honor the Lord. I sometimes tremble myself lest I deal too gently with some here present; and I would pray to be forgiven when, in tenderness of heart, I have not liked to speak sharply upon evil things which I know must grieve the Spirit of God in some that are the Lord's people. I would to God you would take more care of yourselves, and watch yourselves, and not grieve the spirit of your minister by things that are not consistent with the will of God, and the holiness of Christ. Do see to it, beloved members of this church, that you do not dishonor my Lord. Do not bring me under this great temptation to speak timidly about these things. We can easily do it, you know; and so can you when you see sin in a brother and do not rebuke that brother when you ought to do so, or when those that are put by God under your own care are allowed to sin with impunity. God help us to be found honoring him, for if we do not rebuke sin, we shall be dishonoring him, and that may spoil our life as sadly as Eli spoiled his."

Trans: Eli's sins were lack of Discipline and misplaced Devotion. In reality his sons were more important to him then God. Davis notes:

"Hence the man of God rebukes the sin of *sweet reasonableness* in Eli, the willingness to tolerate sin, to allow God's honor to take a back seat, to prefer "my boys" to "my God." But *sweet reasonableness* really smells [to high heaven!].

How easy to practice a gutless compassion that never wants to offend anyone, that equates niceness with love, and thereby, ignores God's law and essentially despises His holiness. We do not necessarily seek God's honor when we spare human feelings."

Of course, like all truth, this must be balanced lest we become harsh and unreasonable. Eph. 6:4.

II. FINALLY, THE *SAD CONCLUSION.* 30-36

A. They would be *Lightweights.* 30

³⁰ "Therefore the LORD God of Israel declares, 'I did indeed say that your house and the house of your father should walk before Me forever'; but now the LORD declares, 'Far be it from Me—for those who honor Me I will honor, and those who despise Me will be lightly esteemed – to esteem lightly means that they would be insignificant. We can also lose rewards and end up lightly esteemed not only in time but in eternity: 1 Cor. 3:12-15/1 Jn.2:28/2Jn.1:8/Rev.3:11).

B. There would be no *Longevity*. 31-33

³¹ 'Behold, the days are coming when I will break your strength and the strength of your father's house so that there will not be an old man in your house. ³² 'You will see the distress of My dwelling, in spite of all the good that I do for Israel; and an old man will not be in your house forever. ³³ 'Yet I will not cut off every man of yours from My altar so that your eyes will fail from weeping and your soul grieve, and all the increase of your house will die in the prime of life - The judgment of untimely death followed the descendants of Eli. Eli's sons died in the flower of their manhood (4:11). Later, Saul massacred the priests at Nob (22:16-19).
C. They would *Lose* their lives and *Leadership*. 34-35

³⁴ 'This will be the sign to you which will come concerning your two sons, Hophni and Phinehas: on the same day both of them will die. ³⁵ 'But I will raise up for Myself a faithful priest who will do according to what is in My heart and in My soul; and I will build him an enduring house, and he will walk before My anointed always. - This prophecy was fulfilled beginning with Hophni and Phineas. They were killed by the Philistines (4:11). More of Eli's house were slaughtered by the command of Saul because he felt they favored David (1 Samuel 22:17, 18). Eli's priestly line ended in 1 Kings 2:26, 27. Abiathar, the last official representative of Eli's house conspired against King Solomon. Solomon deposed and disgraced him. Solomon replaces him with Zadok from Aaron's son Eleazar (1 Kings 2:35). Eli was from Ithamar.

D. They would *Lack* food. 36

[36] *'Everyone who is left in your house will come and bow down to him for a piece of silver or a loaf of bread and say, "Please assign me to one of the priest's offices so that I may eat a piece of bread."'* – they would reap what they had sown, they had deprived the Lord of the food [fat] that rightly belonged to the Lord, so they would be deprived of food as well. Gal. 6:7
Trans: All of this was due to the fact that Eli failed to obey God and remain a father to his boys. Paul Harvey wrote these words:
"At a time when being a Buddy to one's son is popular, I am going to stay a Father. In days when woman's rights, civil rights, people's rights, and children's rights have made it wrong for fathers to speak with authority, I am

going to stay a father. If a gap exists between my sons and daughters and myself, I am going to work hard to understand, but I am also going to be understood! And if old fashion things like prayer, Bible study, worship and faith in God ever seem to my children to be out of it, square, or whatever – I trust God's help to have faith enough to yet pray for them, and I pledge with Job to offer additional sacrifices for them. I will answer their questions about the facts of life, but at nudeness and lewdness I refuse to wink. Drinking and smoking are out of place and unwanted in my house as are profanity or the plague. I want my children to know that I make mistakes, that I am foolish, proud, and often inconsistent. But I will not tolerate that as an excuse for sin. Others may let the offspring in the house determine the foods, the music, the spending of the household, but I am going to stay a father."

Con:

1. Honoring our children over God is a sin – in fact honoring anybody or anything over God is a sin.

2. Whatever the cost we must choose to Honor God, because those who Honor God are honored by God.

3. This verse played an important role in the life of Eric Liddell, son of James Liddell, Scottish missionary to China. While in a boarding school in Great Britain, Eric excelled

in his studies and sports. He was involved in Christian activities and was faithful in Bible studies and church attendance. When he went to the university, he joined the track team and won an abundance of medals and trophies for his great running speed. He was considered a national treasure of Scotland and his career was followed all the way to the 1924 Olympics. His fame and faith opened doors of opportunity to tell others about Christ. This faith was tested at the Paris Olympics when his favorite race, the 100 meter sprint was scheduled for Sunday. Eric had a conviction about not competing on Sunday for it was the Lord's Day.
In spite of pressure and criticism, he did not run this race, but instead entered a race that was on a different day, the 400 meter race, and the world watched and wondered at this unusual young man. In the dressing room just before the race, he was given a note which said, "In the old book it says 'He that honors me I will honor.' Wishing you the best of success always." Eric was very familiar with 1 Samuel 2:30. He smiled and made up his mind that, win or lose, he would honor God and that he did. Eric won the gold medal in the 400m and set a world record, honoring God and being honored by the Lord who gave him the ability to run as swift as a stallion. Honor God beloved, and He will honor you and your faithfulness to Him. In due season we will reap if we faint not.

Chapter Four

HOW TO FIND AND CONTINUE IN GOD'S SPECIFIC MINISTRY FOR YOU

1 Sam. 3:1-21

Intro:

1. Woodford, "We may define a call, as an inward conviction of the soul, that such and such, is the will of God, accompanied with, an irresistible desire, to obey the conviction." (Eph. 2:10)

2. God, not only calls us to salvation, but to a particular place of service – a work, a selected ministry.

I. FIRST, ONE MUST BE *SAVED.* 2:11

Then Elkanah went to his home at Ramah. But the boy ministered to the LORD before Eli the priest - all things indicate that Samuel was saved at a very young age.

Testimony abounds of children being saved – Matthew Henry was saved at the age of 11; Polycarp at the age of 9; Jonathan Edwards at the age of 8; Richard Baxter at the age of 6; W. A. Criswell at the age of 8; and Stephen Oldford at the age of 7. The average Southern Baptist Missionary is saved at eight years old.

Spurgeon, "When the child knowingly sins, he can savingly believe."

Point: Eph. 2:8-9 comes before verse 10! Eli's sons, while they were active in the House of God, in reality they did not have a God-given ministry because "they did not know the Lord."

On May 7, 1824, Beethoven made his last public appearance in Vienna. At the conclusion, Caroline Unger one of the soloists, took him by the arm and turned him around to see that the crowd was giving him a standing ovation. He never heard the applause because he was stone deaf! He was making beautiful music but was not experiencing it himself. Some work in the local church and do some good things, and are even used by God to influence others for Christ, but they themselves never have experienced salvation.

II. FURTHERMORE, HE *SERVED* BEFORE HE KNEW HIS PROPHETIC CALL. 2:18; 3:15a

Now Samuel was ministering before the LORD, as a boy wearing a linen ephod

So Samuel lay down until morning. Then he opened the doors of the house of the LORD... - Notice Samuel did what he could, he opened and closed the doors of the tabernacle; no doubt trimmed the lamps; and many other things like that.

Many people refuse to do anything unless it is something spectacular. Or unless they know exactly what God is calling them to do, but even if you're not sure of your exact calling, you can still serve the Lord, until you are sure.

It is in serving God that we often find our calling – remember it is easier to steer a moving object then one that is stationary.

Leadership Journal carried a true story about a B-17 bombing run over a German city during World War II. A Nazi anti-aircraft hit the gas tank of one of those bombers. No explosion! They later, upon examining the gas tank, discovered 11 unexploded shells in the gas tank. The shells were empty, therefore they did not explode – one of the shells contained a note: "This is all we can do for you!" But it was enough.

It is enough to be involved in serving the Lord, in a general way, until we find our specific calling. We can do the general will of God, which opens the door for us to understand, the specific word of God. For example: We are commanded to be Saved; Surrendered to the Lordship of Jesus Christ; Spirit filled; progressively Sanctified; and Submissive to delegate authority. These things will keep us more than busy – if we walk in the light that we have God will give us more light.

III. THIRD, HE WAS *STRENGTHENED* BY OTHERS.

A. First, you're *Parents.* 2:19

19 And his mother would make him a little robe and bring it to him from year to year when she would come up with her husband to offer the yearly sacrifice - who knows you, better than your parents? Many times they can see things that you cannot see. Clearly his mother, Hannah, knew what God had in store for Samuel long before he did.

B. Furthermore, you're a *Preacher.* 3:1, 9

^{1} Now the boy Samuel was ministering to the LORD before Eli. And word from the LORD was rare in those days, visions were infrequent...^{9} And Eli said to Samuel, "Go lie down, and it shall be if He calls you, that you shall say, 'Speak, LORD, for Your servant is listening.'" So Samuel went and lay down in his place - few people will spend as much time in prayer for you, as your pastor. Your pastor may be as carnal as Eli was! But, God still used Eli, as He does all delegated authority. 1:17; 2:20-21; 3:1, 8-9.

C. Finally, through various *People.* 3:20

All Israel from Dan even to Beersheba knew that Samuel was confirmed as a prophet of the LORD - notice God's people recognized Samuel's gift. The phrase, "Dan to Beersheba" was used to refer to the whole land of Israel. Dan is located in the far north of Israel, and Beersheba is in the South.

Trans: God often speaks to us through Parents, Preachers, and other People. God usually confirms His decision through others.

IV. FOURTHLY, HE WAS BEING *SANCTIFIED.* 2:21, 26

21...And the boy Samuel grew before the LORD...26 Now the boy Samuel was growing in stature and in favor both with the LORD and with men - even before he knew specifically what he was supposed to **do,** he was **being** what he was supposed to be. What we are is far more important than what we do. God's call for us to be Saints is more important than his calling for us to serve (2 Pet.3:18).

Arthur Schopenhauer a German philosopher was in a greenhouse concentrating on one of the plants. One of the attendants asked him, "Who are you?" He looked at him and said slowly, "If you could only answer that question for me, I'd be eternally grateful!"

What we are as believers are people who are Forgiven, Righteous, a New Creation, Blessed with all spiritual blessings, Children of God, members of His Body, sheep of His fold, a branch tied into the Vine, living stones of His temple, and much much more. But only as we grow into Christ likeness do we begin to see what we are called to do.

V. FIFTH, HE WAS *SUMMONED.* 3:1-4

If you are Saved, Serving as you can, Strengthened by others, and living a Sanctified life, you will be Summoned.

A. The *Abominable.* 3:1

1 Now the boy Samuel was ministering to the LORD before Eli. And word from the LORD was *rare **in those days**, visions were infrequent* - keep in mind that "those days" were the dark days we looked at in the book of Judges (Jud. 17:6). The reason for this was related to Israel's sin. There is clearly a connection between the rarity of the word of God and the sin of the priesthood. As predicted several centuries later by Amos, there would be a famine of God's word, so it was in the days of the judges.

[12] "People will stagger from sea to sea And from the north even to the east; They will go to and fro to seek the word of the LORD, But they will not find *it*. Amos 8:12

Today in America, the word of God is always Available to us, but unfortunately most have not Availed themselves of that Word. When was the last time we saw, our political leaders, seeking God in prayer and searching God's Word for guidance on what to do? When people live in disobedience, God stops speaking, to them. But if one is obedient to God, then God will definitely have a message for that one. Sin keeps us from listening to the Word of God. Reminds me of, a Dennis the Menace, cartoon. Dennis runs into Mr. Wilson's house and sees him sitting down and reading a newspaper. Dennis greets him, "Hello, Mr. Wilson." But Mr. Wilson does not respond. So Dennis says it a little louder, "Hello, Mr. Wilson." Again no response. So Dennis yells out, "HEL-LOOO, MR. WILSON!" Still Mr. Wilson does not answer. So as Dennis is leaving he says, "Well, then, goodbye, Mr. Wilson." Mr. Wilson replies, "goodbye, Dennis." Dennis then says, "There's nothing wrong with his hearing, but his listening is not so good."

The result of not listening to God always causes us society to go downhill (Prov. 29:18/ Psa.66:18).

B. The *Available.* 3:2-8

1. His *Excitement!*

*² It happened at that time as Eli was lying down in his place (now his eyesight had begun to grow dim and he could not see well), ³ and the lamp of God had not yet gone out, and Samuel was lying down in the temple of the LORD where the ark of God was, ⁴ that the LORD called Samuel; and he said, "Here I am." ⁵ Then he **ran** to Eli and said, "Here I am, for you called me." But he said, "I did not call, lie down again." So he went and lay down. ⁶ The LORD called yet again, "Samuel!" So Samuel arose and went to Eli and said, "**Here I am**, for you called me." But he answered, "I did not call, my son, lie down again."* – Eli was "very old" (1 Samuel 2:22). His failing eyesight was, no doubt, part of the physical deterioration that accompanies old age.

We have several things in this passage:

- The lamp of God – it is the golden lampstand found among

the temple furnishings in the holy place. It was positioned by the veil that separated the holy place from the holy of holies (Ex. 25:31-40). A lamp was kept burning in the tabernacle from evening until dawn (Ex. 27:21).

- The temple of the Lord – was a portable tabernacle, also called "the house of the Lord" (3:15); "the Tent of Meeting" (2:22); and "My Dwelling" (2:32). See Exodus 26.

- The ark of God – it was a chest made of acacia wood overlaid with gold, which symbolize the Presence of God with Israel (Ex. 25:10-22). Above it were two cherubim that looked down on the mercy seat.

What a contrast with the sons of Eli – while they were lying down with the women in the tabernacle; Samuel was lying down before the Presence of the Lord!

Notice also that Samuel ran to Eli! He says, "Here I am!" Obviously Samuel lived in the "ready zone!" That should be our attitude also, Here I am! This reminds us of Abraham (Gen. 22:1,11); Jacob (37:13); and Moses (Ex.3:4). Likewise we should be eager to do God's will.

2. His *Experience* – none! V.7

⁷ Now Samuel did not yet know the LORD, nor had the word of the LORD yet been revealed to him. ⁸ So the LORD called Samuel again for the third time. And he arose and went to Eli and said, "Here I am, for you called me." Then Eli discerned that the LORD was calling the boy - when it says that Samuel did not yet know the Lord, it is not the same thing as when it says the sons of Eli did not know the Lord. In this context, it means that Samuel had not yet had any direct revelation from the Lord. He had not yet learned how to get a word from God. Notice there are three kinds of people in most churches today:

- Those who are lost and do not know the Lord.
- Those who are saved but do not know how to get a Word from God.
- Those who are saved and know how to listen to God.

Samuel at this stage, lacked knowledge, but not a hunger for God. If we are available to God, we will soon learn how to get a word from God.

C. He was also *Agreeable*. 9-10

⁹ And Eli said to Samuel, "Go lie down, and it shall be if He calls you, that you shall say,

*'Speak, LORD, for Your servant is listening.'"
So Samuel went and lay down in his place.
¹⁰ Then the LORD came and stood and called as at other times, "Samuel! Samuel!" And Samuel said, "Speak, for Your servant is listening."* - Eli told him how to articulate what was already in his heart. He had a heart that was ready to obey God!

- His Lord – "Speak LORD"

- He was Lowly – "your servant"

- He was Listening – "is listening."

¹⁰ *The LORD then stood beside Samuel and called out as he had done before, "Samuel! Samuel!" "I'm listening," Samuel answered. "What do you want me to do?" 1 Samuel 3:10 (CEV)*

Notice how persistent God is, the verb *call* occurs 11 times in verses 4-10. God is relentless in getting our attention, He does not give up! If we really want to hear from God we will sooner or later get a Word from God!

Also notice it is God who always makes the initiative – we do not come to God, it is God who comes to us!

D. God's message was *Audible.* 11-14

¹¹ *The LORD said to Samuel, "Behold, I am about to do a thing in Israel at which both ears of everyone who hears it will tingle.* ¹² *"In that day I will carry out against Eli all that I have*

spoken concerning his house, from beginning to end. ¹³ *"For I have told him that I am about to judge his house forever for the iniquity which he knew, because his sons brought a curse on themselves and he did not rebuke them.* ¹⁴ *"Therefore I have sworn to the house of Eli that the iniquity of Eli's house shall not be atoned for by sacrifice or offering forever."*
– God repeats the truth that he will punish Eli's house because of their sin.

Repentance is not always an option, as we will later see with Saul (1 Sam. 15:28-29). Kent Hughes notes:

"Eli was not an excessively wicked man. His various failures, such as his mistaking Hannah's prayer for drunken mumbling, his inability to curb his sons, and his slowness in recognizing that God was speaking to Samuel, are all readily attributed to his advancing years. We can think of plenty of excuses for Eli, for he was (we might feel) no worse than any of us. And there are things about Eli that we admire…[It was] the sons of Eli, who treated with contempt, the very provision God had made for the forgiveness of sins (see 1 Samuel 2:17, 29). This had frightful consequences: "Therefore I swear to the house of Eli that the iniquity of Eli's house shall not be atoned for by sacrifice or offering forever" (v. 14). Do you understand the horror of those words? If the gracious provision God has made for the forgiveness of sins is spurned, scorned, disdained, despised, there is nothing left but the fearful prospect of judgment. This now makes sense of the disturbing words of 1 Samuel 2:25: "But they [Eli's sons] would not listen to the voice of their father, for it was the will of the Lord to put them to death." The sons of Eli had passed a point of no return. They had sinned with such high-handedness that they were beyond the pale. The New Testament recognizes the same reality. If you trample the Son of God underfoot, if you treat with contempt the death of Jesus for your sins, what hope do you think there is for you? There is no sacrifice left to atone for your sins if you have discarded the death of Jesus (cf. Hebrews 10:26-31)."

In the Old Testament, ears were said to "tingle" when they heard a message of approaching judgment (2 Ki. 21:12/Jer. 19:3).

Also note, God does not speak to us today in an audible voice but through the written word of God, and, of course, by the Holy Spirit's still small voice.

F.B. Myer, "Let us not seek revelations through dreams and visions, but by the Word of God. Nothing is more harmful then to contract the habit of listening to voices and dreams. It is best to take in hand and read the Scriptures reverently, carefully, and thoughtfully, crying, "Speak Lord for your servant hears."

VI. SIXTH, HE *SUBMITTED* TO GOD'S MESSAGE. 15-18

15 So Samuel lay down until morning. Then he opened the doors of the house of the LORD. But Samuel was afraid to tell the vision to Eli. 16 Then Eli called Samuel and said, "Samuel, my son." And he said, "Here I am." 17 He said, "What is the word that He spoke to you? Please do not hide it from me. May God do so to you, and more also, if you hide anything from me of all the words that He spoke to you." 18 So Samuel told him everything and hid nothing from him. And he said, "It is the LORD; let Him do what seems good to Him." - Submitting to God's word is not always pleasant because He often asks us to do and say things we do not want to say and do. Samuel did not want to confront Eli. We may not want to confront our self centered ways, or a particular person, or even exercise a certain gift.

When I first started preaching I was terrified of speaking before people. And I have never enjoyed confronting people with God's Word. All they do is leave the church, but I still have to share God's Word without apology. Sharing God's word is both joyful and painful because we have to tell the good bad news as well as the good news; we have to tear down as well as build up (Jer. 1:5-19).

You have to appreciate Eli's godly response:

- Recognition – "It is the Lord" (Job 1:21)

- Resignation – "let him do" (Mt.26:39)
- Realization – "good to him" (Rom. 8:28).

I think one man had it right, "This may have been Eli's finest moment, as he acknowledged and accepted the rightness of God's judgment. His words were not unlike the one who, many years later, after God's judgment had finally fallen on Jerusalem, said, "The Lord is in the right, for I have rebelled against his word" (Lamentations 1:18)."

We ought to listen and take to heart whatever God has to say to us. Years ago, the brokerage firm E. F. Hutton had several television commercials. People in a crowded room, or a restaurant, or some other location were all talking about financial investments. Then somebody said, "Well, my broker is E. F. Hutton, and E. F. Hutton says…" Immediately everybody stopped speaking, and became completely silent as they all stretched to hear what he said next! That's the way we should respond to God's word. God's word is the only thing that is really eternal and lasting (Isa. 40:8/Lu.21:33/Mt.5:17-18). It alone can transform a life. The philosopher Emile Caillet was born in a small village in France near the end of the 19th century. He had no tolerance for God or anything supernatural. He was a soldier in World War I and after seeing his friend shot, he later said:

"The moment came when I was overwhelmed by the inadequacy of my views. What could be done about it? I did not know. Who was I, anyway? Nay, what was I? These fundamental questions of human existence remained unanswered." Then one night a bullet hit Emile also, after nine months in the hospital he was discharged and resumed his graduate studies. But he had to admit that the books no longer seemed like the same books... He writes:

"During long night watches in the foxholes, I had in a strange way been longing – I must say it, however queer it may sound – for a book that would understand me. But I knew of no such book."

Then one day his wife came into possession of a Bible, he was 23 years old and had never seen a Bible. He decided to read it; here is how he describes what happened next:

"I literally grabbed the book and rushed to my study with it. I opened it and "chanced" upon the Beatitudes! I read, and read, and read – now allowed with indescribable warmth surging within me...I could not find words to express my awe and wonder. And suddenly the realization dawned upon me: This was the book that would understand me! I continued to read deeply into the night, mostly from the Gospels. And lo and behold, as I looked through them, the One, of whom they spoke, and acted in them, became alive in me."

We never outgrow the Bible! If we neglect it as believers our spirits will soon shrivel and an inner emptiness will be felt. John Wesley noted:

"I am a spirit come from God and returning to God; just hovering over the great gulf, till a few moments hints I am no more – I dropped into an unchangeable eternity! I want to know one thing, the way to heaven – how to land on that happy shore. God Himself has condescended to teach the way: for this very end He came from heaven. He has written it down in a book. Oh give me that book! At any price give me the Book of God! I have it. Here is knowledge enough for me. Let me be "a man of one book.""

VII. FINALLY, HE *STAYED* IN THAT CALLING. 19-21

19 Thus Samuel grew and the LORD was with him and let none of his words fail. 20 All Israel from Dan even to Beersheba knew that Samuel was confirmed as a prophet of the LORD. 21 And the LORD appeared again at Shiloh, because the LORD revealed Himself to Samuel at Shiloh by the word of the LORD – Samuel goes from being a priest to, also having, a prophetic ministry. The phrase literally, "none of his words fell to the ground," means that what he said came to pass. This is the way that Israel distinguished a true prophet from false ones (Dt. 18:18-22). The Lord does not permit his word to fail (Josh. 21:45; 23:14/ 1 Ki. 8:56).

Notice that Samuel continued to grow, continued to be what God wanted him to be and thus continued to do God's will. The sad fact is that many people who discover what God wants them to do, no longer seems to have time to be what God wants them to be. In other words ministry soon overshadows intimacy – and they no longer have time to spend alone with God. The focus is always upon the Lord being "with us." The words, "the Lord appeared again at Shiloh" is in a tense in the Hebrew which speaks of continual action. Yahweh was appearing in Shiloh.

- Isaac – experienced the Lord being with him (Gen. 26:3).
- Jacob – knew it as well (31:3).
- Joseph – it is said repeatedly that the Lord was with him (Gen. 39:2-3, 21, 23).
- Moses (Ex. 3:12).
- Joshua (Josh. 1:5)
- Gideon (Judges 6:16) and
- David – experience the presence of God (1 Sam. 16:18; 18:12).
-

And the list could include every true man of God! Being and doing is a lifelong calling…

Jim Elliott, "One does not surrender a life in an instant. That which is lifelong can only be surrendered in a lifetime. Maturity is the accomplishment of years...hence; the fullness of God's Spirit is not instantaneous but progressive, as we attain fullness of the Word which reveals His will."

Con:

1. How To Find And Continue In God's Call For Us: Be sure you're **Saved**; **Serve** Him in what you know until He makes it more clear; allow *others to* **Strengthen** you – don't turn a deaf ear to your Parents, Pastor, or godly People; keep *Being* **Sanctified**, always remembering that Being is more important than Doing; get into His Word with ears that are ready to be *Submissive*; and He will one day give you a specific *Summons*; and then be prepared to *Stay with it* till the Lord Jesus comes.

2. God has a special call for all of us, a work, a ministry – find it and abide in it.

Spurgeon, "Everything around you is arranged for the production of good works in you. When God made Adam, when did he make him? Only after, He had a place for him to live in. When the Lord God created you in Christ Jesus, He had prepared for you a position of service and usefulness, exactly fitted for your capacity... Rest assured that divine wisdom has not only prepared you for this hour, but this hour for you."

"I am only one, but still, I am one.

 I cannot do everything; but still, I can do something;

 and because I cannot do everything,

 I will not refuse to do, the something, that I can do."

Chapter Five

THE PATHWAY TO GOD'S ABSENCE

1 Sam. 4

Intro:

1. Augustine a fourth century philosopher wrote of the momentary pleasure that was offered to him, with only one condition, that he would forfeit the pleasure of seeing God." He responded immediately with the words, "No pleasure is worth that loss!"

2. The essence of sinful pleasure is that it disrupts our fellowship with God, all or awareness of his manifested Presence – and the truth is, no pleasure is worth that loss.

I. FIRST, THEY DID NOT *CONSULT* GOD'S WORD. 4:1a

Thus the word of Samuel came to all Israel - since Samuel is God's prophet to Israel, God's Word is available to all who will avail themselves of it. The problem is, Israel did not inquire about God's will through Samuel.

America is a nation literally full of Bibles; God's Word can be found throughout the land – in local churches; in bookstores; on TV and the radio; on the Internet; etc. But I wonder how many people actually are reading the Bible these days?

Swindoll, "If I could have only one wish for God's people, it would be that all of us would return to the Word of God, that we would realize once for all that His Book has the answers."

People don't like to consult the Bible, they prefer their own way and rules to God's.

An article on CNN reported on two atheists who wanted to rewrite the Ten Commandments. The article begins with this question:

"What if, instead of climbing Mount Sinai to receive the Ten Commandments from God, Moses had turned to the Israelites and asked: Hey, what do you guys think we should do?"

That was the idea behind the "10 'Non-Commandments' Contest," in which atheists were asked to offer modern alternatives to the famous Decalogue. The contest even offered

$10,000 for the best ideas. The article summarized the list this way:

"There's nary a "thou shalt" among them—nothing specifically about murder, stealing, or adultery, although there is a version of the Golden Rule, which presumably would cover those crimes. If they lack faith in the divine, the atheist "non-commandments" display a robust faith in humankind, as if Silicon Valley had replaced Sinai."

Here are the winning "Ten Non-Commandments":

1. Be open-minded and be willing to alter your beliefs with new evidence.
2. Strive to understand what is most likely to be true, not to believe what you wish to be true.
3. The scientific method is the most reliable way of understanding the natural world.
4. Every person has the right to control of their body.
5. God is not necessary to be a good person or to live a full and meaningful life.
6. Be mindful of the consequences of all your actions and recognize that you must take responsibility for them.
7. Treat others as you would want them to treat you, and can reasonably expect

them to want to be treated. Think about their perspective.

8. We have the responsibility to consider others, including future generations.

9. There is no one right way to live.

10. Leave the world a better place than you found it.

II. FURTHERMORE, THEY DID NOT *CONFESS* AND FORSAKE SIN. 1b-3a

A. The *Enemy.* 1b-2

...Now Israel went out to meet the Philistines in battle and camped beside Ebenezer while the Philistines camped in Aphek. ² The Philistines drew up in battle array to meet Israel - the Philistines had settled along the S. W. Coast of Palestine and were one of Israel's greatest enemies.

B. The logical *Expectancy.*

When the battle spread, Israel was defeated before the Philistines who killed about four thousand men on the battlefield – when we do not pray, or get a Word from God, and tolerate sin we can expect the enemy to prevail! Not only did they not deal with the sin of the priesthood, but they failed to consecrate themselves before going into battle, which was standard procedure for the Israelites (Josh. 3:5).

Hal Lindsey, "the attitudes of the flesh are all the ideas, plans, schemes, imaginations, and good works which proceed out of the human mind without the Holy Spirit being the source of them. They can be either good or bad, as the worldview sets things, but in God's estimation they're all unacceptable, because the flesh is the source of all of them, not the Spirit. Such ideas originate with self not with the Spirit; self-confidence and self-reliance are two notable traits that the world applauds but God says, they indicate a reliance on the flesh rather than on the indwelling Holy Spirit."

C. The Elder's *Inquiry*.

³ When the people came into the camp, the elders of Israel said, "Why has the LORD defeated us today before the Philistines? – they asked the right question but did not wait for the answer!

They should have consulted with God's prophet Samuel, notice that Samuel is completely absent from this battle and he will remain completely out of the picture until we get to chapter 7. Today we have God's full and final prophetic written Word to consult. It is not enough to ask questions, we must also find the right answers by seeking God through his Word. If they had waited they would have realized that sin needed to be confessed and forsaken before going to battle. The problem is not sin, but not bringing it into the light and coming clean about it.

Josh Shaw, cornerback and captain for the University of Southern California's football team, recently sprained both of his ankles.

According to the original story on ESPN, Shaw saw his nephew struggling in a pool and "jumped from a second-floor balcony onto concrete below and crawled into the pool where he was able to help his nephew to safety." His coach, Steve Sarkisian called him a hero saying, "That was a heroic act by Josh, putting his personal safety aside. But that's the kind of person he is."

But the story made headlines. Why? Because he lied about how he injured himself. But the pressure caused Josh to come clean – because of his cover up he's been suspended from the team indefinitely and is still being considered a suspect in a burglary and domestic dispute. God is about to put the pressure on Israel in order to confront her with sin.

III. THIRD SOUGHT TO *CONTROL* GOD. 3b-

A. Their *Manipulation.*

Let us take to ourselves from Shiloh the ark of the covenant of the LORD, that it may come among us and deliver us from the power of our enemies." - Instead of following the ark, they are now seeking to manipulate the ark and to make it follow them.

Stephen Andrews noted, "The Israelites misunderstood the purpose of the ark of the covenant. The ark was the symbol of God's presence with his people. The ark was not God. Nor could the Israelites manipulate God or guarantee His presence by moving the ark wherever they pleased."

We must never think that God's presence and power can be controlled by us.

Robert Bergen, "this might have been an attempt by the elders to twist God's arm into helping them instead of trying to find out the reason for God's displeasure."

Chisholm, "God's powerful presence is closely associated with the ark (Ex.25:22/Num.10:33-36/2 Sam.6:2), and the ark seems to have played a key role in the defeat of Jericho (Josh. 6:6-13)… So one can see why some might think of it as a guarantee of victory, but such a notion is fundamentally pagan. The Lord cannot be manipulated or coerced into intervening for his people, and we should not view the Lord as being like a rabbit's foot or a four leaf clover."

Bill Arnold, "They presume they can reverse the horrible events of that day by treating the ark of the covenant as though it were a magic wand… But the sins of Eli are not being addressed and God cannot be manipulated… What they failed to realize is that if God's will is defeat for His people, 1000 arks would not bring success… They have, in a sense, precluded God's blessings because of their sins."

B. Their *Maneuvering.*

1. Go to *Shiloh* and get the ark.

⁴ So the people sent to Shiloh, and from there they carried the ark of the covenant of the LORD of hosts who sits above the cherubim; - Shiloh is the modern day *Seilun*, located about 9 miles north of Bethel. Since the days of Joshua, Israel has worshiped there. It was there that the tabernacle was set up (Josh. 18:1).

The ark of the covenant was a chest of acacia wood overlaid with gold (Ex. 25:10-22; 37:1-9). Two cherubim hovered over the top of the mercy seat (1 Sam. 4:4). It symbolized God's Presence with Israel, and was kept in the holy of holies behind a curtain (Ex. 26:33).

2. The *Sinful* sons of Eli still not removed.

and the two sons of Eli, Hophni and Phinehas, were there with the ark of the covenant of God - the problem with Israel was that Eli's sons were there with the ark, as in the case of Achan all Israel would have to suffer because of their sins (Josh. 7:8-11).

3. The empty *Shouting* of Israel.

⁵ As the ark of the covenant of the LORD came into the camp, all Israel shouted with a great shout, so that the earth resounded- shouting is no substitute for real substance! Emotions will never take the place of obedience. Job 20:5/Prov. 14:13/Isa. 16:10

People who shout praises to God while they are persisting in rebellion against God have misunderstood grace. Rom. 6:1

Reminds me of three zoology students who were sent to different parts of the world to study spiders. The first went to Africa and reported a spider that climbs trees; the second went to South America and told of a poisonous type of spider; The third student went to Australia. They did not hear from him for five years! He finally returned with a cart full of a particular type of spider that he was studying. He was excited, shouting about his discoveries. He called together all of his professors and put a spider in the midst of them. He looked at it and yelled, "Walk!" And sure enough, the spider walked around in a circle and stopped! He then said to the spider, "Walk Two Circles!" And he did! He picked up the spider started pulling off its eight legs, one at a time. He put it down and cried "Walk!" Nothing happened. He bent down to the spider and yelled at the top of his voice, "Walk!" Rubbing his hands together in excitement he said, "See there! That proves my theory! Spiders without legs are deaf!"

Getting all excited about the Lord does not prove that the Lord is all excited about us!

C. Their *Massacre.*

1. The *Dread.*

⁶ When the Philistines heard the noise of the shout, they said, "What does the noise of this great shout in the camp of the Hebrews mean?" Then they understood that the ark of the LORD had come into the camp. ⁷ The Philistines were afraid, for they said, "God has come into the camp." And they said, "Woe to us! For nothing like this has happened before. ⁸ "Woe to us! Who shall deliver us from the hand of these mighty gods? These are the gods who smote the Egyptians with all kinds of plagues in the wilderness - at first it looks like, even if they disobeyed God, they would get away with it. They did not seek God's Word through His prophet; nor had they sought God in prayer; and they have not cleansed the sinful priesthood – but look! The enemy is terrified!

Sin is deceptive! How many live in it and think that because God has not yet judged them, He will not judge them.

2. The *Determination.*

⁹ "Take courage and be men, O Philistines, or you will become slaves to the Hebrews, as they have been slaves to you; therefore, be men and fight." - the only explanation of this strange turn of events is God. Usually when people are frightened they run – but here God apparently put a resolve in their hearts to fight even harder.

3. The *Defeat.*

¹⁰ So the Philistines fought and Israel was defeated, and every man fled to his tent; and the slaughter was very great, for there fell of Israel thirty thousand foot soldiers.

Lutzer, "Have you ever said to yourself, "there I got away with it. Everyone said I'd get in trouble if I did it, but I've done it, and the Lord is still blessing me. I know he understands." I have counseled men who are immoral and think that just because God was not smiting them with judgment, they rationalize that he understood, and possibly even winks at their lifestyle. It is possible to compromise moral principles and still appear to have God's blessing. A car salesman tells a lie and still makes a profitable sale; a waitress does not record her tips and thus has more money; somebody falsifies a job application and still gets the job; but you can be sure eventually that God will step in (Eccless. 8:11). The bottom line is that we cannot Control God. There are few things more foolish and childish then trying to manipulate God. I have shared this before but it illustrates the point. A small boy was writing a letter to God about the Christmas presents he wanted. He writes:

"I've been good for six months now." But after a moment's reflection he crossed out "six months" and wrote "three." After a pause, that was crossed out, and he put "two weeks." There was another pause, and that was crossed out too. He got up from the table and went over to the little nativity scene that had the figures of Mary and Joseph. He picked up the figure of Mary and went back to his writing and started again: "Dear God, if ever you want to see your mother again…"

IV. FOURTH, THEY LEARNED GOD ALWAYS *CONFIRMS* HIS WORD. 12-18

11 And the ark of God was taken; and the two sons of Eli, Hophni and Phinehas, died. 12 Now a man of Benjamin ran from the battle line and came to Shiloh the same day with his clothes torn and dust on his head. 13 When he came, behold, Eli was sitting on his seat by the road eagerly watching, because his heart was trembling for the ark of God. So the man came to tell it in the city, and all the city cried out. 14 When Eli heard the noise of the outcry, he said, "What does the noise of this commotion mean?" Then the man came hurriedly and told Eli. 15 Now Eli was ninety-eight years old, and his eyes were set so that he could not see. 16 The man said to Eli, "I am the one who came from the battle line. Indeed, I escaped from the battle line today." And he said, "How did things go, my son?" 17 Then the one who brought the news replied, "Israel has fled before the Philistines and there has also been a great slaughter among the people, and your two sons also, Hophni and Phinehas, are dead, and the ark of God has been taken." ¹⁸ When he mentioned the ark of God, Eli fell off the seat backward beside the gate, and his neck was broken and he died, for he was old and heavy. Thus he judged Israel forty years - God's word is always reliable, sooner or later it will be fulfilled. It is the death of Eli's sons which is the real reason that God allowed Israel to be defeated.

Dale Davis, "In Israel's defeat the Lord was defeated; He was it appears a loser! But, if we look carefully, a strange twist happens here. It is on this very day that seems to dishonor the Lord, that the Lord was in fact beginning to protect His honor and to restore it. The Lord may be despised in Philistine for a while [wait until the next chapter], but he will be no more despised in Shiloh! With the death of Eli a whole new era will pass away! The slate of old leadership will be cleared for Samuel, the man the Lord has called."

A lot of times God looks like he's being defeated, but when all is said and done it will be victory and glory to Him. Years ago a flag at half mast was an acknowledgment of the enemy superiority. It was put at half mast to give room for the victors flag to be put on top of the pole. As time progressed it was used as a symbol of honor to those who died. In chapter 4 God's flag appears to be flying at half mast but as we progress into chapters 5 and 6 we will see that His flag is really flying at half mast to honor His name.

V. FINALLY, THE *CONSEQUENCES* OF SIN WAS THE LOSS OF GOD'S PRESENCE. 19-20

A. Their *Refusal.*

- They did not consult God through the *Prophet.*
- They offered no *Prayer* to God.
- They *Permitted* sin to go unchallenged.
- They did not *Purify* themselves. Josh. 3:5

B. Therefore there was a *Removal.*

1. The *Delivery.*

[19] *Now his daughter-in-law, Phinehas's wife, was pregnant and about to give birth; and when she heard the news that the ark of God was taken and that her father-in-law and her husband had died, she kneeled down and gave birth, for her pains came upon her* - what should've been a joyous occasion will become a time of grief and sadness.

2. The *Death.*

[20] *And about the time of her death the women who stood by her said to her, "Do not be afraid, for you have given birth to a son." But she did not answer or pay attention* - the giving of life will be the cause of her death.

3. The Declaration of a *Departure.*

a. Of the *Shekinah* Glory.

²¹ And she called the boy Ichabod, saying, "The glory has departed from Israel," because the ark of God was taken and because of her father-in-law and her husband. ²² She said, "The glory has departed from Israel... - The word Ichabod means "No Glory" or "Where is the glory?"

This is a Hebrew word. Shekinah means, "that which dwells." It refers to God's presence appearing in a visible or special way. The word is not found in the Old Testament, but was introduced into the Jewish religious vocabulary by rabbis of a later era. These rabbis spoke of the Shekinah in order to encourage Israelites to have a higher idea of God. They wanted people to think of him as a dazzling light or a shining presence, rather than as a human-like figure with physical features such as hands, arms, eyes, mouth and the like. The Shekinah became particularly associated with God's glorious presence, as seen in the tabernacle and later the temple (Exod 40:34-35; 1 Kings 8:11; Ezek 44:4). It also referred to other displays of God's glory or to the reality of his presence among his people (Num 14:10,22/ Isa 60:1-2/ etc.).

b. Of the *Symbol* of God's Presence.

for the ark of God was taken - the ark is a symbol of God's manifested presence (Ex. 40:34/Lev. 9:23-24). It would be more than

20 years before David would rescue the ark out of obscurity in Abinadab's house in Kiriath-Jearim and restore it to its central role in the worship of the sovereign God of Israel.

Life without the manifested presence of God is not really living but merely an existence. There is a frog in central Australia, it's called the *water-holding frog*. Living in the desert where it rarely rains, this frog when it does rain, leaves its underground home and absorbs the water. It the bloats up like a huge balloon. It eventually goes back to its underground hole and becomes very still, it does not move for up to five or six years – until the next good rainfall. Then repeats the process. I would say that those frogs merely existed, and so is the person who does not enjoy the reality of fellowship with God's manifested presence.

Con:

1. The Pathway to God's Absence – Refuse to Consult God through His Word and prayer; refuse to Confess and forsake sin; and try to Control God;

2. But before long we learn with Augustine – "No pleasure is worth the loss of not experiencing God."

3. Many years ago, when I was just a kid our family went to Niagara Falls – it was spectacular! To hear 500,000 tons of water rushing over Niagara Falls every minute, gives you goose bumps.

Back in March 29, 1948, people within the sound of the Falls were stunned by the silence. The falls suddenly stopped and people who live by the Falls thought that the world was coming to an end. For some 36 hours they were beside themselves!

What had happened was heavy winds had set the ice fields of Lake Erie in motion. The tons of ice jammed the Niagara River entrance near Buffalo and the flow of water stopped.

God's Presence is like Niagara Falls – He is Awesome! He makes your heart run a little faster, you almost find yourself shaking with excitement. But sin that is un-dealt with, is like that ice, it shuts down the flow of His power and Presence. I would to God that we were beside ourselves when we perceived that we have blocked Him and grieved His Spirit.

Chapter Six

WHO IS ABLE TO STAND BEFORE THIS HOLY LORD GOD (6:6)

1 Sam. 5-6

Intro:

1. According to the Wall Street Journal, guys who use the online dating site *Tinder* have a fondness for taking their picture with tigers, hence the name "tiger selfies."

According to the *Journal*, some users of the site estimated that one in every 10 guys on the site had a tiger picture. Well, the New York legislature doesn't want you putting your life in your hands so you can show everyone you're buddies with tigers. According to one article:

"State Rep. Linda Rosenthal...who sponsored a bill that passed this week, pointed to New York's history of tiger attacks—seven over the past 15 years, according to her office—as evidence the ban is in the public's best interest." Ms. Rosenthal said, "There is no safe or humane result when direct contact with wild animals is allowed. The bill bans "hugging, patting, or otherwise touching" tigers at fairs or circuses. "Getting caught doing so will cost you $500—which is still probably less than the hospital bill you could incur from trying to snuggle with a 500-pound jungle cat."

It is important that one knows how to properly relate to a tiger, it show the ignorance of people, when a sign has to be put by the tigers cage – "Don't pet the Tigers!" And it is important that we know how to properly relate to God! He is holy and must be treated so.

I..FIRST, THE *SUPREMACY* OF GOD. 5:1-5

A. The *Trophy*. 1-2

¹ Now the Philistines took the ark of God and brought it from Ebenezer to Ashdod. ² Then the Philistines took the ark of God and brought it to the house of Dagon and set it by Dagon – they "took the ark" just like the Israelites who "took the ark into battle." Both soon learned that you don't take the ark, it takes you! No one controls God; it is God who is in control of everything and everybody. When will we learn that we do not carry God, it is God who carries us!

The name Dagon comes from the word *"dagan"* meaning *"corn"* or from the word *"dag"* which means *"a fish."* He was an emblem of earth's fertility. His image consisted of a man to the waist with the lower part of the body being the tail of a fish, like a mermaid. Dagon also represented the fruitfulness of water... life springing up out of water. We have our Dagon today in America called "Evolution" which claims that life or man came out of the ocean and evolved.

In the Philistines mind, their victory on the battlefield indicated that their God had defeated the God of Israel. And by putting the Ark of the Covenant in the temple of Dagon, they were saying that Dagon was superior to Yahweh. No doubt the ark was placed at the feet of Dagon. They would soon get an education related to Who's who.

B. The *Testimony*. 3

When the Ashdodites arose early the next morning, behold, Dagon had fallen on his face to the ground before the ark of the LORD… - When the Philistines got up the next morning they had their Wheaties, the breakfast for champions. But when they went into the temple, Dagon is bowing down before the ark! God is giving them a testimony to His supremacy over Dagon.

The expression "had fallen on his face to the ground" refers to an act of submission (Gen. 44:14/Josh. 5:14; 7:6/Jud.13:20/ Ruth 2:10/ 1 Sam. 28:20/ 2 Sam. 1:2; 14:4, 22/ 2 Ki. 4:37/Job 1:20).

C. The *Tragedy*. 3b

So they took Dagon and set him in his place again - apparently they did not get the message! And what kind of God is it that you have to set up?   Isa. 49:18-10

Dale Davis noted the contrast, "not only does the episode teach the Philistines the supremacy of Yahweh over Dagon, but instructs Israel that God's supremacy is utter independent of His people. The Lord is not like Dagon, a helpless god needing to be cuddled, protected, and sustained by worshipers…And what are we to say of songs that croon, "Somehow, He needed me?" Or little ditties, that speak of God having "no hands but our hands, and no feet but our feet?" The great

God of the Bible wants us but he certainly does not need us!" And His Hand is not tied because ours is in our pocket.

D. The *Theology*. 4

[4] But when they arose early the next morning, behold, Dagon had fallen on his face to the ground before the ark of the LORD. And the head of Dagon and both the palms of his hands were cut off on the threshold; only the trunk of Dagon was left to him – the decapitation of this idol would be viewed as a military act, conquerors often cut the heads of their enemies off (1 Sam. 17:51; 31:9/ 2 Sam. 4:12). This show it was God who was the one, who not only defeated Israel in battle, but is the one troubling the Philistines as well. When God's people are defeated, it does not mean that God Himself is defeated!

By 1590 the Japanese warlord Hideyoski exercised control over all of Japan. On one occasion he commissioned a colossal statue of Buddha for a shrine in Kyoto. It took 50,000 men five years to build, and Hideyoski himself sometimes worked incognito alongside the laborers. But the work was scarcely completed when the earthquake of 1596 brought the roof of the shrine crashing down and wrecked the statue. In a rage Hideyoski shot an arrow at the fallen colossus. Shouting, "I put you here at great expense, and you can't even look after your own temple!"

It teaches us that idol, whether they be money; pleasures; or people; or whatever, cannot think (head) or act (hands) to save anyone. It also teaches that the Lord is a warrior (Ex.15:3/Isa.42:13/ Jer.20:11).

 E. The *Tenacity*. 5

Therefore neither the priests of Dagon nor all who enter Dagon's house tread on the threshold of Dagon in Ashdod to this day - obviously they did not learn a thing! They are afraid they might step on some residue of their god.

Trans: God is Supreme over all!

Pink, "the supremacy of the true and living God, might well be argued, from the infinite distance, which separates the mightiest creatures from the Creator. He is the Potter; they are but the clay in His hands, to be molded into vessels of honor, or to be dashed into pieces. Were all the inhabitants of heaven and earth to combine in open revolt against Him, it would cause Him no uneasiness. It would have less effect upon His eternal, unassailable throne then the spray of the Mediterranean's waves has upon the towering rock of Gibraltar!"

II. NEXT, THE *SEVERITY* OF GOD. 6-12

[6] *Now the* **hand of the LORD** *was heavy on the Ashdodites, and He ravaged them and*

*smote them with tumors, both Ashdod and its territories. ⁷ When the men of Ashdod saw that it was so, they said, "The ark of the God of Israel must not remain with us, for **His hand is severe** on us and on Dagon our god." ⁸ So they sent and gathered all the lords of the Philistines to them and said, "What shall we do with the ark of the God of Israel?" And they said, "Let the ark of the God of Israel be brought around to Gath." And they brought the ark of the God of Israel around.*
*⁹ After they had brought it around, the **hand of the LORD** was against the city with very great confusion; and He smote the men of the city, both young and old, so that tumors broke out on them. ¹⁰ So they sent the ark of God to Ekron. And as the ark of God came to Ekron the Ekronites cried out, saying, "They have brought the ark of the God of Israel around to us, to kill us and our people." ¹¹ They sent therefore and gathered all the lords of the Philistines and said, "Send away the ark of the God of Israel, and let it return to its own place, so that it will not kill us and our people." For there was a deadly confusion throughout the city; the **hand of God** was very heavy there. ¹² And the men who did not die were smitten with tumors and the cry of the city went up to heaven* - the key phrase is "the hand of God" vv. 6,7,9,11

First in Ashdod, then Gath, and onto Ekron – the judgment of God fell…God was like a hot-potato!

Cyril Barber speaks about these tumors:

"The first Hebrew word used is "opel" translated "tumor or boil." The most plausible explanation of the affliction, based on the mounting evidence of 5:6, 9 and 6:4-5, is that rodents began to decimate the area. Accompanying this devastation was an outbreak of the bubonic plague, swelling accompanied by a high fever. The lymph nodes of the infected area become enlarged to produce visible, round mounds, the size of a hens egg or a large walnut...The third Hebrew word which is found in 5:9 means "to be hidden, to break out." The swellings often discharge their contents through the skin, leaving a depression where the hard lump had been."

Trans: In a day where God's love has all but eclipsed God's wrath we do well to accept all of God's revelation about Himself. We should note both the goodness and the severity of God (Rom.11:22).
Parker noted, "The principle is that behind every display of divine goodness stands a threat of severity in judgment if that goodness is scorned."

III. THIRD WE HAVE THE *SOLITARY* GOD. 6:1-12

A. First they *Admitted* they were *Guilty*. 6:1-5a

¹ Now the ark of the LORD had been in the country of the Philistines seven months. ² And the Philistines called for the priests and the diviners, saying, "What shall we do with the ark of the LORD? Tell us how we shall send it to its place." ³ They said, "If you send away the ark of the God of Israel, do not send it empty; but you shall surely return to Him a guilt offering. Then you will be healed and it will be known to you why His hand is not removed from you." ⁴ Then they said, "What shall be the guilt offering which we shall return to Him?" And they said, "Five golden tumors and five golden mice according to the number of the lords of the Philistines, for one plague was on all of you and on your lords. ⁵ "So you shall make likenesses of your tumors and likenesses of your mice that ravage the land - Offering a trespass offering was an admission that they were guilty of sin. The golden tumors in rats were an expensive offering. The idea was that by putting the symbols of the plague on the ark and sending it off, the plague would go off with it.

Guilt does not equal salvation! 2 Cor. 7:10 Judas felt sorrow and guilt over his sin but he still went out and hung himself and went to hell...

B. Furthermore, they *Acknowledged* God's *Glory*. 5b-6

…and you shall give glory to the God of Israel; perhaps He will ease His hand from you, your gods, and your land. ⁶ "Why then do you harden your hearts as the Egyptians and Pharaoh hardened their hearts? When He had severely dealt with them, did they not allow the people to go, and they departed? - Yes even the lost can give glory to God. Dan. 2:46-47; 3:28-29 were all spoken *before* the king was saved. The truth is, a lot of people who speak well of the Lord Jesus Christ, are lost.

God alone has the right to be worshipped (Isa. 40:18-20; 41:5-7, 21-29; 44:9-20; 45:5,16; 46:1-2, 6-7; 48:5, 14).

One notes, "The Hebrew word *chabod* translated "honor" [or "glory"] in this passage is the same word found in Ichabod's name (4:21-22). The Philistines were directed to give "glory" to Israel's God. The irony of this is that the glory that Israel refused to ascribe to God (Psa. 29:2) by trying to use the ark for their own purposes would be offered to Him by the pagan Philistines."

C. Next, they *Adopted* to say *Goodbye* to the Lord. 6:7-12

⁷ "Now therefore, take and prepare a new cart and two milch cows on which there has never been a yoke; and hitch the cows to the cart and take their calves home, away from them. ⁸ "Take the ark of the LORD and place it on the cart; and put the articles of gold which you return to Him as a guilt offering in a box by its side. Then send it away that it may go. ⁹

"Watch, if it goes up by the way of its own territory to Beth-shemesh, then He has done us this great evil. But if not, then we will know that it was not His hand that struck us; it happened to us by chance." ¹⁰ Then the men did so, and took two milch cows and hitched them to the cart, and shut up their calves at home. ¹¹ They put the ark of the LORD on the cart, and the box with the golden mice and the likenesses of their tumors. ¹² And the cows took the straight way in the direction of Beth-shemesh; they went along the highway, lowing as they went, and did not turn aside to the right or to the left. And the lords of the Philistines followed them to the border of Beth-shemesh – these two cows had suckling calves and had never been yoked before to pull a cart.

This was clearly the hand of God. If you team up two cows that have never been yoked together, they are not going to pull a cart straight for several miles, especially if they have calves bawling out for them! These heifers kept going forward totally ignoring their maternal instincts.

What was the Philistine's problem? They were not willing to forsake Dagon and place their trust in God alone. 5:5,7; 6:5

God is a solitary God and will not join our other so-called gods. A few years ago a young man named Wesley came here and asked me what my religious beliefs were. I shared the gospel with him and gave him several books. He clearly respected my beliefs – but he also respected the beliefs of Buddha and many others. The problem is he wanted to *add* Jesus to his list of gods and that you cannot do! Ultimately he will either place total trust in the Lord Jesus Christ or he will die and spend eternity in hell.

A side note: Barnabas Shaw was a colleague of Robert Moffat in South Africa. He was influenced by this passage about the oxen and the ark of God and how God lead the cows right to the place He wanted them. Shaw was a missionary from England who journeyed to Capetown to preach the Gospel. He ran into an obstacle here as the governor forbade him to preach the Word of God. Shaw was in a predicament and wondered "What do I do now?" He was not exactly sure what God wanted him to do so he did what this story spoke about. He purchased a yoke of oxen and a cart and put all his goods on the cart. Shaw and his wife, taking their seat on the cart, gave the reins to the Lord and waited to see what would happen. The oxen rambled into the interior of Africa, lowing, and trudging ahead day after day, covering 200 miles in just under a month. They were like a boat drifting in the current of the ocean. One evening while camping in the jungle, Shaw heard noises near his camp. He investigated and found a tribe of Hottentots led by its chief, Little Namaqualand. These natives left their homes and village to travel to Capetown in search of a missionary that could teach them "The Great Word."

Had either group started a half-day sooner or later, veered off their path just a little, they would never have met each other. Missionary Barnabas Shaw established a fruitful, thriving, growing ministry among these people and spent eleven years preaching and teaching them the Great Word of God. All in all he ended up spending a total of forty years in advancing the Gospel in the country of South Africa.

IV. FOURTH, THE *SANCTITY* OF *GOD*.

A. The *Offering*. 6:13-18

13 Now the people of Beth-shemesh were reaping their wheat harvest in the valley, and they raised their eyes and saw the ark and were glad to see it. 14 The cart came into the field of Joshua the Beth-shemite and stood there where there was a large stone; and they split the wood of the cart and offered the cows as a burnt offering to the LORD.
15 The Levites took down the ark of the LORD and the box that was with it, in which were the articles of gold, and put them on the large stone; and the men of Beth-shemesh offered burnt offerings and sacrificed sacrifices that

day to the LORD. ¹⁶ When the five lords of the Philistines saw it, they returned to Ekron that day. ¹⁷ These are the golden tumors which the Philistines returned for a guilt offering to the LORD: one for Ashdod, one for Gaza, one for Ashkelon, one for Gath, one for Ekron; ¹⁸ and the golden mice, according to the number of all the cities of the Philistines belonging to the five lords, both of fortified cities and of country villages. The large stone on which they set the ark of the LORD is a witness to this day in the field of Joshua the Beth-shemite –this was actually a violation of God's Law.

- First, Beth-shemesh was a priestly city (Josh. 21:13-16). Therefore the people had been instructed on how to relate to the ark of God (Num. 4:4, 15).

- The people who sacrificed the cows as a burnt offering, should have known that the law demanded that it was to be a male animal (Lev. 1:3, 5; 22:18-19).

- Furthermore, looking into the ark was clearly disobedience to God's Word (Num. 4:5-6, 15). Since the ark was symbolic of God's holy presence, it was to be covered and carried only by certain people and only in a certain way and was not to be touched by anybody (2 Sam. 6:6-7).

B. The *Offense*. 19

19 He struck down some of the men of Beth-shemesh because they had looked into the ark of the LORD. He struck down of all the people, 50,070 men, and the people mourned because the LORD had struck the people with a great slaughter – according to the Masoretic text and the Septuagint 50,070 men died, the NIV and some other versions read 70 men, following a few Hebrew manuscripts.

Question: How come God did not kill the Philistines who were looking at the ark and caring it about from town to town? For one thing, this shows that the ark itself was not magical but symbolical.

Kaiser, "when the Philistines, who had no Revelation of God, sinned by touching the ark and using a new cart to transport it, God's anger did not burn against them. God is more merciful toward those less knowledgeable of His will then toward those who are more knowledgeable."

The more we know the more countable we are! For example, if you have a small boy just learning to talk and that boy lets out a cuss word, you tell him it's wrong but you realize he doesn't really know what he saying... Now when that same boy is a teenager and uses words like that, it's a totally different situation. The more we know, the more is expected from us and the more accountable we become, and of course, the greater blessings we are able to appropriate. That two year old cannot drive a car, but the teenage boy can.

The principle is simple – the more you know the more God expects from you. Like Moses who got angry at the rock and hit it twice, when God said he was only to speak to it. By that one act of disobedience he was not able to enter into the Promised Land. Why such a harsh response from God, because he knew better!

C. The *Off-limits* of God. 20

[20] The men of Beth-shemesh said, "Who is able to stand before the LORD, this holy God? And to whom shall He go up from us?" - In light of what happened to both the Philistines and the Israelites the only answer anybody could give would be – nobody!

D. Finally it is *Off* to Kirjath Jearim. 21

[21] So they sent messengers to the inhabitants of Kiriath-jearim, saying, "The Philistines have brought back the ark of the LORD; come down and take it up to you." – the ark will remain here until David takes it to Jerusalem (2 Sam. 6:2).

Trans: The Sanctity of God is designed to teach us that no matter how careful we are in our approaching God, we always end up violating His holiness! Then it's hopeless? No! Because God found a way, to make us as holy as He is, by placing us in Christ (Heb. 9:3-5, 11-14; 10:19-22).

Hal Lindsey, "On the basis of, Christ's propitiatory work, on the cross God's offended character has been satisfied and God is now free to impart a new dimension to all who receive His Son as Savior. He has clothed the person who believes in Him with His righteousness and He declares them judicially righteous…This righteousness is given to a person, free and complete the moment he places faith in Christ as Savior…It cannot be improved upon, added to, or ever revoked… Our acceptance with God is based on one key factor only: we are in His Son and His Son's righteousness is in us…We are placed positionally into Christ and that gives us a total identification with Jesus in the eyes of God. As he looks at The Son, He looks at me in the same way because He sees me in the Son and the Son in me."

In other words God has dealt with our unholiness by condemning Christ in our place and now Christ is our holiness and life! We don't have to worry about approaching God correctly by trying to keep hundreds of unkeepable laws. 2 Cor. 5:21

Con:

1. Who is able to stand before this holy Lord God? Nobody but the Lord Jesus Christ!

2. In the Old Testament things were only foreshadowed, in things like the animal sacrifices, the priest, the ark but today we have the substance.

3. Ravi tells about a man in India who lived out in a remote village – no electricity, no modern conveniences whatsoever. Once Ravi took the man to see a movie – it was the first time the man had ever seen such a thing. They arrived a little late and the movie had already started, this man stood at the back at first and was amazed at what he saw! A beam of light coming right out of the wall! He stared at the light for several minutes thinking he was watching the movie. Finally he turned to the side and saw a picture on the wall and shouted, "Eureka!" Ark pointed to Jesus!

Chapter Seven

SPIRITUAL RECOVERY

1 Sam. 7

Intro:

1. Frazier Glenn Miller, opened fire and killed three people in Kansas City. Miller, of Aurora, Mo., was a former Ku Klux Klan "grand dragon."

Robert Satloff, of the Washington Institute for Near East Policy, wrote a fascinating article about Miller in *The Washington Post*. Thirty-three years ago, Robert interviewed Miller. At the time, Miller was running a Ku Klux Klan paramilitary camp in rural North Carolina. During the interview, Miller said he could "sniff out" that Robert was Jewish, so Miller and his cohorts stuffed Robert into a steaming car, threatening him with guns before eventually letting him go. Looking back on that experience from 33 years ago, Robert concluded:

"Miller was a rabidly violent, racist anti-Semite when I met him 33 years ago, and apparently he never changed. He always had a gun. Sadly, this time he used it."

2. Miller is a sad and pathetic case, but I wonder if that could be said of us— that after 33 years we haven't changed much, and are just as carnal today as we were years ago. As we fast forward some twenty years, and the good news is that Israel had changed. God wants us to grow and progress spiritually; here we find some principles on how to make a spiritual recovery.

I..FIRST, *REALIZING* OUR *CARNALITY*. 7:1-2

A. The Arks *Location.*

¹ And the men of Kiriath-jearim came and took the ark of the LORD and brought it into the house of Abinadab on the hill, and consecrated Eleazar his son to keep the ark of the LORD. ² From the day that the ark remained at Kiriath-jearim, the time was long, for it was twenty years...and all the house of Israel lamented after the LORD - The Ark was brought to Kirjath Jearim instead of Shiloh because most believed that Shiloh had been destroyed by the Philistines. Prior to Israel's conquest of Canaan, the inhabitants of Kiriath-jearim were known as Gibeonites, after the name of a more important town in the region (Josh 9:3,17; see Gibeon). Kiriath-jearim was on the border between Benjamin and Judah, and was known also as Kiriath-baal, Baalah, Baale-judah and Kiriath-arim (Josh 15:9,60; 18:14,21-28; 2 Sam 6:2; Ezra 2:25). It is chiefly remembered because during the time of Saul and David the ark of the covenant rested there for twenty years.

   B. The People's *Lamentation.*

and all the house of Israel lamented after the LORD - the people had been defeated by the Philistines, they had buried many of their fellow Israelites, who were killed by God for their disobedience. Now as the years had passed their hearts finally began to soften.

Trans: They realized their sinful condition; we will get nowhere until we do. It is easy to have the attitude like the church of Laodicea, who said, "I am rich, and have become wealthy, and have need of nothing," and you do not know that you are wretched and miserable and poor and blind and naked." Revelation 3:17

It reminded me of the comic strip, where Snoopy is dancing around, smiling, having a great time. Lucy watching this comes up to him and says, "Anyone who would dance around like that in these troubled times is too stupid to know the difference!" Snoopy kisses her and says, "You're right! That's why this is my 'I'm too stupid to know the difference' dance."

There is nothing sadder than when we are living far from God and are too stupid to even know it. The first step is to get smart about our spiritual condition.

II. FURTHERMORE, *RETURNING* MUST BE *WHOLEHEARTEDLY*. 3a
3 Then Samuel spoke to all the house of Israel, saying, "If you return to the LORD with all your heart... - No one can return to the Lord halfheartedly.

9 "For the eyes of the LORD move to and fro throughout the earth that He may strongly support those whose heart is completely His. You have acted foolishly in this. Indeed, from now on you will surely have wars."
2 Chronicles 16:9

In February, 1879, British General Charles Gordon went to Cairo, Egypt to try to broker a peace between King John of Abyssinia and Egypt. Gordon had an interesting interview with the king, but was not able to do much, as the king wanted great concessions from Egypt. King John took the general prisoner and declared, "Do you know that I could kill you on the spot if I like?"

Gordon replied, "I am perfectly well aware of it, Your Majesty. Do so at once if it is your royal pleasure. I am ready."

After Gordon's death, John Bonar, a Scottish friend, wrote to Gordon's brother. "What at once, and always struck me was the way in which his oneness with God ruled all his actions, and his mode of seeing things. I never knew, who seemed so much to endure, as seeing Him who is invisible. Gordon, seemed "to live with God, and for God."

We need to have a heart like General Gordon had.

Trans: The problem is we want to return to the Lord while, at the same time, keeping our areas of rebellion. If we are going to do business with God, we have to confess and forsake all known sin. It is the law of access, we can own 100 miles of land but if we have just one lone acre in the middle of it the person who owns that acre has the right to put a road through our property to get to his.

When we give Satan just one stronghold he gets access straight to our hearts. God is a jealous God and when we serve him halfheartedly we make room for other gods (Deut. 6:5/Psa. 119:2/Prov.3:5/Jer. 29:13/Joel 2:12/etc.).

III. NEXT, *REMOVING* THE *IDOLATRY*. 3b-4

A. There must be a *Parting* with idols. 2 Cor. 6:14-7:1

remove the foreign gods and the Ashtaroth from among you and direct your hearts to the LORD – I have a building, I call it the shop because the man we bought the house from used it as his shop. It is actually a place to pray and it a good size building with a bathroom, sink, and wood stove. Every now and then it gets so filled with junk that I can hardly move around in it. So I clean house! I have to throw out stuff that is just getting in the way.
We also need to clean house spiritually! Get rid of the junk, things that are hindering our walk with God.

B. There needs to be a single-minded *Priority.*

and serve Him alone – it is not God plus!

[8] Jesus answered him, "It is written, 'YOU SHALL WORSHIP THE LORD YOUR GOD AND SERVE HIM ONLY.'" Luke 4:8

We must make a choice to serve either God or other gods – we cannot have it both ways!

[15] "If it is disagreeable in your sight to serve the LORD, choose for yourselves today whom you will serve: whether the gods which your fathers served which were beyond the River, or the gods of the Amorites in whose land you are living; but as for me and my house, we will serve the LORD." Joshua 24:15

The Civil War was a bloodbath; the problem was a lack of single-minded purpose. Both the North and the South had their own personal agenda and convictions and these were opposed to one another. After the Civil War a choice had to be made. On May 26, 1865, the last fighting of the Civil War took place when General Kirby Smith surrendered the Confederate forces west of the Mississippi. Three days later, President Andrew Johnson issued an Amnesty Proclamation. The object of the proclamation was "to suppress the existing rebellion, to induce all persons to return to their loyalty, and to restore the authority of the United States, issue proclamations offering amnesty and pardon to certain persons who had directly or by implication participated in the said rebellion."

The simple oath in the proclamation was: "I, do solemnly swear, (or affirm,) in presence of Almighty God, that I will henceforth faithfully support, protect, and defend the Constitution of the United States, and the union of the States thereunder; and that I will, in like manner, abide by, and faithfully support all laws and proclamations which have been made during the existing rebellion with reference to the emancipation of slaves. So help me God."

Sadly, there is often a War between God's will and ours, and we must choose to say no to our rebellious hearts and surrender to serve God alone.

C. Then we can claim the *Promise.*

and He will deliver you from the hand of the Philistines – as we saw over and over again in the book of Judges, disobedience brings bondage and obedience brings deliverance.

Trans: Ashtaroths were fertility gods, and Baal was also a god related to fertility in nature. These so-called gods encouraged immortality. Idolatry and immorality always go together.

Marcus Arethusius was a minister during the time of Constantine. They took him out and stripped him of all of his clothes and anointed his naked body with honey and then set them out in the sun to be stung to death by wasps. Why? Because the people were building an idol temple and he refused to have any part in it. They told him that if he would just give but a halfpenny to the project, he would be spared, but he refused to give even a halfpenny if that meant having anything to do with idolatry.

IV. FOURTH, THE *REGATHERING* OF GOD'S ASSEMBLY. 7:5-11

A. There was *Preaching*.

5 Then Samuel said… - Remember that Samuel was a prophet and therefore it was God who is speaking through him. Today we have the full and final word of God and we need to hear it preached often because it has transforming power. 2 Cor. 3:18

Dennis Prager asked his radio listeners this question, "If you were stranded on a lonely road in Los Angeles, in the dead of night, with your head under the hood of your car, and suddenly you heard the sound of footsteps and turned to see 10 big burly men walking toward you, would it or would it not make a difference to you if you knew they were coming out of a Bible study?" To ask such a question is to answer it – but why? Because of the transforming power of the word of God.

B. There was also *Praying*.

"Gather all Israel to Mizpah and I will pray to the LORD for you." – v. 9; 12:23 Samuel was a great prayer warrior (Psa. 99:6/Jer. 15:1).

Spurgeon, "Of course the preacher is above all others distinguished as a man of prayer. He prays as an ordinary Christian else he were a hypocrite. He prays more than ordinary Christians else he were disqualified for the office he has undertaken. If you as ministers are not very prayerful, you are to be pitied. If you become lax in the sacred devotion, not only will you need to be pitied, but your people also."

Bounds, "His preachers must be people who lean on Him, who look to Him, and who continually seek Him for wisdom, help, and power to effectively do the work of the ministry…A prayerless preacher is a misnomer. He has either missed his calling, or he has grievously failed God who called him into the ministry…The one weak spot in our churches, lies just here. Prayer is not regarded as being the primary factor in the church life and activity; other things, good in their places, are made primary. This should not be! First things, need to be put first, and the first thing, in the equipment of a minister is prayer."

"But we will devote ourselves to prayer and to the ministry of the word." Acts 6:4

C. *Pouring* out of the water before the Lord. 7:6

They gathered to Mizpah, and drew water and poured it out before the LORD – we are not sure what this means.

- Barber noted, "inasmuch as water, once poured on the ground, cannot be gathered up again, the people seemingly were indicating the irrevocability of their decision to follow the Lord and do His will. It was as if, they were dedicating themselves to Him with no thought of ever going back on their decision."

- Bergen, "was an action that they evidently were denying themselves liquids signifying that the Lord's favor was more important to them than life-sustaining water."

D. *Pointing* to the blood of the Lamb.

and fasted on that day and said there, "We have sinned against the LORD." And Samuel judged the sons of Israel at Mizpah - Israel knew that there was only one day designated for fasting. You can find examples of people fasting but God only gave one commandment for them to fast and that was on the Day of Atonement. Which ultimately finds its fulfillment in the Lord Jesus Christ.

Trans: I wonder how many churches have forgotten why they have come together in the first place. It is not for mere fellowship, or to be entertained but to hear God's Word Preached; it is to be a time of Prayer; it is also to remind ourselves that our commitment to the Lord Jesus Christ is Permanent; and to Point to the Person and Work of the Lord Jesus Christ.

VI. FIFTH, *RELYING* ON THE LORD IN *ADVERSITY*. 7:7-11

A. The *Foreseeable.* 7a

Now when the Philistines heard that the sons of Israel had gathered to Mizpah, the lords of the Philistines went up against Israel - we are never a blessing to God without bothering the devil.

B. The *Fear*. 7b

And when the sons of Israel heard it, they were afraid of the Philistines - since we still have an old sin nature we cannot totally eliminate fear, but we can allow it to drive us to God (Rev. 2:10).

Satan is a defeated enemy; if we keep our armor on he is just a lot of noise. Reminds me of something I read the other day. Residents of a German town were terrified when they discovered a mysterious crate marked "Wild Animals" and blasting out from it were lion's roars.

A spokesman for the police department in the southwestern German city said, "The crate was right in the town center and people thought there were real lions inside. A lot of people were really scared." They carefully opened the crate. There were no wild animals inside; instead they discovered a video machine playing a promotional video for Land Rover Vehicles intercut with shots of roaring lions.

C. The *Faith*. 8-11

1. Samuel *Prayed.* 8-10a

⁸ Then the sons of Israel said to Samuel, "Do not cease to cry to the LORD our God for us, that He may save us from the hand of the Philistines." ⁹ Samuel took a suckling lamb and offered it for a whole burnt offering to the LORD; and Samuel cried to the LORD for Israel and the LORD answered him - faith is trusting God and prayer is evidence of that faith – prideful people who trust in themselves are too sufficient to pray.

Notice they do not go and get the Ark, instead of trying to control God they are now praying for God is guidance and will.

2. Emmanuel *Performed*. 10b

Now Samuel was offering up the burnt offering, and the Philistines drew near to battle against Israel. **But the LORD thundered** *with a great thunder on that day against the Philistines and confused them, so that they were routed before Israel-* prayer releases the power of God. Power either to cure or to endure. Ja. 5:16-17

When we pray God performs – and even our prayers are often weak and filled with doubt.

The movie, *Flash of Genius,* was inspired by the true story of Dr. Robert Kearns (Greg Kinnear). After creating the intermittent windshield wiper—what he calls "the blinking eye"—Kearns pitches his idea to General Motors, Ford, and Chrysler. All three companies turn him down, only to steal his idea and add them to all their automobiles. Dr. Kearns decides to take on the Ford Motor Company in a legal battle that no one believes he can win. (He later challenged Chrysler, GM, and Mercedes, as well.) In one scene Robert needs to test his windshield wipers under real-life conditions so that Ford will give his invention serious consideration. However, there's no rain in the forecast—and there hasn't been for quite some time. Robert is seated at the dinner table with the rest of his family—his son Patrick is holding the newspaper, and he begins to read the weather forecast: "Thursday: clear. Friday: partly cloudy and colder. And a clearing on Saturday." Robert says, "Well, we need some rain." His daughter Kathy says, "Maybe instead of grace we should say a prayer," His son Tim, "Didn't we just say grace?" His wife Phyllis replies, "Yes, but a prayer is different." Robert says, "Let's do that, come on, let's say a little prayer." Everyone quiets down, and Robert begins to pray:

"Dear God—uh—thanks for all the sunshine you've been sending. We know in your infinite wisdom that you manage the elasticity of rain water different than tap. So, if you could see it in your grace to—you know—send us some rain so that we can test the 'blinking eye' in real life conditions, we'd appreciate it. Amen."

His daughter Maureen asks, "Do you think he heard you, Daddy?" Robert replies, "With my luck, He's a GM man,"

The next scene begins with the sound of thunder, and the entire family is running to the car as the rain pours down.

The key is not our faith or our prayers but the object of our faith and prayers!

3. Israel *Pursued*. 11b

The men of Israel went out of Mizpah and pursued the Philistines, and struck them down as far as below Beth-car - notice that Israel did not just sit there and do nothing, faith always produces works. Ja.2:

Wiesbe, "Because of this victory, the Jews recovered cities they had lost in battle and even gained the Amorites as allies. Whenever God's people depend on their own plans and resources, their efforts fail and bring disgrace to God's name; but when God's people trust the Lord and pray, He meets the need and receives the glory."

Trans: All of this reminds me of Ex. 17:8-16.

Stanley noted, "The battle wasn't won because of the Army strength or because of Joshua's military genius. The battle was won on the hilltop… It was the action on the hilltop that determined the outcome of the action in the Valley... Life's battles are won or lost in the place of prayer, not on the battlefield of everyday life. The real spiritual success or failure of the church does not depend on the talent of the preacher, the size of the congregation, or the strength of the organization. Success from God's point of view will only be obtained through prayer. God's business, for the most part, is to be taken care of on our knees."

VI. FINALLY, *REMEMBERING* WHO GAVE THE *VICTORY*. 7:12-17

A. An *Ebenezer.* 12-14

12 Then Samuel took a stone and set it between Mizpah and Shen, and named it Ebenezer, saying, "Thus far the LORD has helped us." 13 So the Philistines were subdued and they did not come anymore within the border of Israel. And the hand of the LORD was against the Philistines all the days of Samuel. 14 The cities which the Philistines had taken from Israel were restored to Israel, from Ekron even to Gath; and Israel delivered their territory from the hand of the Philistines. So there was peace between Israel and the Amorites – this stone was a monument. We have many monuments in America, granite monuments in Washington D.C., to Washington, Jefferson, and Lincoln. There are many monuments to various wars like the Vietnam War. Bob Dole raised funds for a

World War II monument. In the New York Harbor, the Statue of Liberty is a monument related to liberty and our willingness to welcome those who come here seeking freedom.

The name Ebenezer is an acknowledgment that it was God who brought us this far. This was not a monument to man but to God. Ebenezer is a compound word meaning lit. "stone of help." If you are ever walking through the woods and see a turtle on top of a tall stump, you can be sure that somebody placed it there.

I love the song, Come Thou Fount of Every Blessing.

"Come Thou fount of every blessing; Tune my heart to sing Thy grace;
Streams of mercy, never ceasing; Call for songs of loudest praise;
Teach me some melodious sonnet, sung by flaming tongues above;
Praise His name – I'm fixed upon it – Name of God's redeeming love;

Here I raise mine Ebenezer, Hither by Thy help I come;
And I hope by Thy good pleasure, safely to arrive at home.

Jesus sought me when a stranger, wandering from the fold of God;
He, to rescue me from danger, Interposed His precious blood;

Oh to grace how great a debtor, daily I'm constrained to be!
Let Thy goodness, like a fetter,
Bind my wandering heart to Thee;

Prone to wander Lord I feel it, prone to leave the God I love; Here's my heart, Lord, take and seal it; seal it for Thy courts above."

B. An *Altar*. 15-17

15 Now Samuel judged Israel all the days of his life. 16 He used to go annually on circuit to Bethel and Gilgal and Mizpah, and he judged Israel in all these places. 17 Then his return was to Ramah, for his house was there, and there he judged Israel; and he built there an altar to the LORD -

Trans: These are two visible reminders that it was God who had given them the victory. Let us never forget that every single victory we have ever had or will ever have is due to our union with Jesus Christ. 1 Cor. 15:57

Con:

1. Do you need Spiritual Recovery? Have we really changed much in the past 10 years? If not – something is desperately wrong.

2. It begins when we Realize our Carnality; and then Return Wholeheartedly; willing to Remove all Idolatry; it is also Related to being part of a Assembly that believes in Preaching, Prayer, and Points to the Lord Jesus Christ;

and all of this we must Remember is exclusively for God's Glory.

3. William Cowper wrote these words:

"Return, O holy Dove, return; Sweet Messenger of rest!

I hate the sins that made thee mourn; And drove you from my breast.

The dearest idol I have known, Whatever that idol be;

Help me to tear from my throne, And worship only Thee, and Thee alone."

Chapter Eight

HOW TO HANDLE THE STING OF REJECTION

1 Sam. 8

Intro:

1. Robert McGee, "Virtually all of us fear rejection…Our fear of rejection will control us, to the degree, by which we base our self-worth on the opinions of others, rather than on our relationship with God. Our dependence on others, for value brings bondage, while abiding in the truths of Christ's love and acceptance brings freedom and joy…Therefore, the only way we can overcome the fear of rejection, is

to value the constant approval of God over the conditional approval of people."

2. Rejection is an unpleasant fact, and we need to learn how to deal with it God's way.

I. FIRST, THE *REJECTION* OF SAMUEL. 8:1-5

A. First, by his own *Children*. 8:1-3

1. They rejected his *Example*. 1-3a

¹ And it came about when Samuel was old that he appointed his sons judges over Israel. ² Now the name of his firstborn was Joel, and the name of his second, Abijah; they were judging in Beersheba. ³ His sons, however, did not walk in his ways… – this is different than what happened with Eli's sons.

- There is nothing in Scripture that indicates Samuel was negligent with his sons.

- While Eli's sons were outwardly sinning in his presence, Samuel's sons were quietly taking bribes some 57 miles away. That's how far it is from Ramah to Beersheba.

Principle: *Godly parents do not always have godly children.*

Samuel was godly but his son Joel was ungodly, and keep in mind Samuel was known for being a great prayer warrior! And yet Joel's son was godly! These are those who served with their sons: From the sons of the Kohathites *were* **Heman** the singer, the son of Joel, the son of Samuel, 1 Chronicles 6:33 With them *were* **Heman** and Jeduthun, and the rest who were chosen, who were designated by name, to give thanks to the LORD, because His lovingkindness is everlasting. 1 Chronicles 16:41

Ahaz was ungodly but his son Hezekiah was godly (2 Kings 18:1-3), however Hezekiah's son Manasseh was ungodly (2 Kings 21:1-2).

We are not responsible for our children, unless like Eli, we fail to discipline them.

"Fathers shall not be put to death for *their* sons, nor shall sons be put to death for *their* fathers; everyone shall be put to death for his own sin. Deuteronomy 24:16

The bottom line we better find our purpose for living in the Lord not our children. *Matt Woodley* noted, "Does raising children make you happy? Well, that's a complicated question. Of course we love our kids, but that doesn't mean that they make our lives "happier." According to recent research, having children has either a negative or a neutral impact on our happiness. In the early stages of parenting, the joys are offset by the strains of child-raising: lack of sleep, concerns about your child's well-being, and financial strains."

It also tells us that a godly example can only go so far, Samuel presented his children with a godly example but it did not rub off on them! What we need to give our children is the gospel of Jesus Christ; instead of pointing them to us we need to remember that Jesus Christ is alive! He is real and has risen from the dead – not just an example but a Presence that makes the example possible.

In his book *Has Christianity Failed You?* Ravi Zacharias points to one of the greatest proofs for the truth of Christ and the reality of His resurrection: the changed lives of Christians. He writes:

"During the course of nearly 40 years, I have traveled to virtually every continent and seen or heard some of the most amazing testimonies of God's intervention in the most extreme circumstances. I have seen hardened criminals touched by the message of Jesus Christ and their hearts turned toward good in a way that no amount of rehabilitation could have accomplished. I have seen ardent followers of radical belief systems turned from being violent, brutal terrorists to becoming mild, tenderhearted followers of Jesus Christ. I have seen nations where the gospel, banned and silenced by governments, has nevertheless conquered the ethos and mind-set of an entire culture."

Then in his own words Zacharias lists examples of Christ's power to transform lives:

"In the middle of the twentieth century, after destroying all of the Christian seminary libraries in the country, Chairman Mao declared that ... Christianity had been permanently removed from China, never to make a return. On Easter Sunday in 2009, the leading English language newspaper in Hong Kong published a picture of Tiananmen Square on page 1, with Jesus replacing Chairman Mao's picture on the gigantic banner, and the words "Christ is Risen" below it."

2. They rejected God's *Exhortation*.

but turned aside after dishonest gain and took bribes and perverted justice – God's Word was rejected (Deut. 16:18-19).

Trans: Samuel was a godly man who gave an Example to his children and followed God's Exhortations had children who did not walk with the Lord. All we can do is walk with the Lord, we simply cannot understand the effect it has on others.

Jonathan Edwards was a great man of God, while Max Juke was a confirmed unbeliever. A study that followed their descendants found that Edwards descendants were "college presidents, lawyers, judges, physicians, authors, and more than 100 of them pastors, missionaries and theology professors – this shows that godly parents do make a positive impact; On the other hand Juke's descendants were "murderers, rapists, prostitutes, thieves, and the like." But as we have noted things are not so simple or consistent. Jonathan Edwards for example had a daughter who was a hellion – and obnoxiously proud of it! Once a boy asked for her hand in marriage and Edwards turned him down. The boy protested, "But we're in love! And is she not a Christian?" To which Edwards said, "Yes, but the grace of God can live with some people that no one else can!"

Like it or not God's plans and ways remain a mystery, what we can say is this:

- Don't say a godly example doesn't matter – it does.
- Don't say a godly example guarantees you will have godly children – it does not.
- It is not our example but the Lord Jesus Christ who saved us and enables us to have a good.

B. Furthermore, rejected by his own *Congregation*. 8:4-5

1. Their *Appeal* and *Reasoning*. 4-5a

a. You're *Senile!*

⁴ Then all the elders of Israel gathered together and came to Samuel at Ramah; ⁵ and they said to him, "Behold, you have grown old… - he was probably around 65 years old, nothing indicates that he could not continue to judge

Israel, and besides the judges retired when they died!

The New York Times shares a series of portraits and an accompanying essay on men and women who, though of advancing age, remain at the top of their game in their life work. From Roy Haynes (89), jazz drummer and bandleader; to Ruth Bader Ginsburg (81), Supreme Court Justice; to other filmmakers, naturalists, and more." Lewis H. Lapham writes:

"I'm asked why their love's labor is not lost but still to be found, why do they persist, the old masters? To what end the unceasing effort to discover or create something new? Why not rest on the laurels and the oars?" As noted, "It's a potent question, flying in the face of the ideals of retirement and inactivity as we age. What if we viewed the closing years of our lives not as a dim twilight, but a blazing, brilliant sunset? I suspect that we would age happier, and more fulfilled—and that God would be pleased with our stewardship of our time on the earth."

  b. Your *Son's* have *Sinned*.

and your sons do not walk in your ways – the truth is that bunch could identify more with Samuel's sons then with Samuel! Not only that but his sons did not disqualify him from the ministry (Ezk. 18:20).

2. The *Real Reason*.

Now appoint a king for us to judge us like all the nations – the sin was not in wanting a king (Gen. 49:10/Deut.17:14-17).

The sin was related to their *motive* for wanting a king. The reason *why* they wanted a king was to be like other nations. Israel was not like other nations, she was supposed to be set apart from them, different from them (Ex.11:7/Lev.19:1-2; 20:26/Rom.12:2/2 Cor. 6:14-18/1 Pet. 2:9).

We have convinced ourselves that we must act, live, and do like the world. It is told that a man came to Tertullian about this issue of separation and taking a stand. He told him his problem and then he said, "But after all I must live." Tertullian's reply was, "Must you?" The answer is a resounding – No! We do not have to live, but we do have to obey God.

Too many have a Steve Harvey mentality, we think we can talk dirty, cuss, get divorced when things don't suit us, act like the world and still smile and say, "Hey, I'm a Christian." Maybe, but not a Christian who takes the Word of God seriously!

"He [Steve Harvey] specifically discussed the "90 day rule." This rule tells women to put a man on probation before giving away any "benefits." Harvey went on to state that he knows that the Bible says a person should wait until s/he gets married to have sex and he agrees with that whole-heartedly. But he states that since people are not going to wait until marriage to have sex, they should at least wait for 90 days. Paula White wholeheartedly agreed with him and didn't correct him at all! The crowd laughed in agreement. He basically tells others what the Word of God says and agrees with it, "Abstain from sex before marriage!" Then slyly adds, "Hardly any Christians keep the Word of God anyway. So since we all know you're not going to abstain, its okay to do it…just wait 90 days until you do." He speaks as if the Word has loopholes in it…So will you listen to the Word of God or Steve Harvey?"

Trans: Well Samuel is having a bad day both his children and his congregation have rejected him. I came across this:

"It's a bad day for a pastor when he accidently calls the groom by the bride's former boyfriend's name; when he forgets to turn off his cordless microphone while using the rest room; when the church begins exploring the possibility of a missionary trip for you – to an Isis training camp; when the organist is asked to play – while you preach; when the church votes to change you day off – to Sunday; when you preach the same sermon five Sundays in a row – and no one notices it.

II. FURTHERMORE, THE *REACTION* OF SAMUEL. 8:6-18

A. He *Prayed.* 6

⁶ But the thing was displeasing in the sight of Samuel when they said, "Give us a king to judge us." And Samuel prayed to the LORD – when rejected by man go directly to God. Don't argue, don't try and change them – just go to God.

Campbell Morgan was one of 150 young men who sought entrance to the Wesleyan ministry in 1888. He passed the doctrinal examinations, but then faced the trial sermon.

In an auditorium that could seat more than 1,000 sat three ministers and 75 others who came to listen. When Morgan stepped into the pulpit, the vast room and the searching, critical eyes caught and unnerved him. Two weeks later Morgan's name appeared among the 105 REJECTED for the ministry that year. Jill Morgan, his daughter-in-law, wrote in her book, *A MAN OF THE WORD*, "He wired to his father the one word, 'Rejected,' and sat down to write in his diary: 'Very dark everything seems. Still, He knows best.' Quickly came the reply from his father, "Rejected on earth. Accepted in heaven. Dad.'"

In later years, Morgan said: "God said to me, in the weeks of loneliness and darkness that followed, 'I want you to cease making plans for yourself, and let Me plan your life.'"

First thing we need to do when rejected is pray (1 Pet. 5:7). Tom Monaghan in his book *Pizza*

Tiger shares an incident that occurred when he was flying his Cessna 172.

"I flew over to Pontiac one day that summer to see Eldon Huff. The ceiling was very low when I started back, and once again clouds closed in on me. In trying to ease myself below them, I lost control of the plane. It stalled, and I found myself in a spin. I pulled back on the control yoke with all my might, but I couldn't budge it. Plowed fields were whirling up toward me, and I realized there was nothing left to do but pray. I released the controls, closed my eyes, and folded my hands under my chin: "Father in Heaven, please help me" I began, and I felt a miraculous change take place. The spinning stopped and suddenly the plane was flying level again."

Great advice, when we're in a tail spin, release the controls, close our eyes, and pray!

B. Next, he was told not to take it *Personally*. 7-8

[7] The LORD said to Samuel, "Listen to the voice of the people in regard to all that they say to you, for they have not rejected you, but they have rejected Me from being king over them. [8] "Like all the deeds which they have done since the day that I brought them up from Egypt even to this day—in that they have forsaken Me and served other gods so they are doing to you also – If we are walking with God, then those who reject us are in reality not

rejecting us but God. After all it is not our words we are sharing but God's Word!

Moses understood this principle: Ex. 16:2, 8.

but if it is of God, you will not be able to overthrow them; or else you may even be found fighting against God." Acts 5:39

and he fell to the ground and heard a voice saying to him, "Saul, Saul, why are you persecuting **Me**?" Acts 9:4

Don't take it personally, it is ultimately against the Lord and He can take it – but realize we are not really the focus but the critic is the one with the problem.

In his book *Confessions of a Pastor*, Craig Groeschel offers some advice on how to handle critics:

"It's a fact that "hurt people hurt people." They usually dislike themselves and criticize others in a misguided effort to validate themselves. If one of these injured souls lobs a criticism grenade in your direction, defuse it with understanding. Part of considering the source is seeking awareness of what that person may be going through…One time I was praying during worship, a few moments before preaching. Eyes closed, focusing on God, I felt someone slip a note into my hand. I never saw who it was, but the note was marked

"Personal." I thought to myself, *Someone probably wrote a nice note to encourage me before I preach.* A warm, loving feeling settled over me as I unfolded the paper. A moment later, I lost that loving feeling. Evidently, the note was from a woman who had tried to see me on Friday, my day off. She took offense at my absence and blasted me with hateful accusations. This happened literally seconds before I was to stand up to preach. In that moment, I had a choice. I could internalize the offense and become demoralized and discouraged. Or I could ask myself, *I wonder what she's experiencing that caused her to lash out?* I chose compassion over depression. My heart hurt for her. I knew that such a disproportionate reaction must indicate deep pain, so I didn't take her note personally. Consider the source. And consider the possibility that the jab may have come from an injured heart. Dismiss it and move on. If you don't, you may become the very thing you despise."

C. Last he was given a message to *Proclaim*. 9-18

[9] "Now then, listen to their voice; however, you shall solemnly warn them and tell them of the procedure of the king who will reign over them." [10] So Samuel spoke all the words of the LORD to the people who had asked of him a king. [11] He said, "This will be the procedure of the king who will reign over you: he will take your sons and place them for himself in his

chariots and among his horsemen and they will run before his chariots. ¹² "He will appoint for himself commanders of thousands and of fifties, and some to do his plowing and to reap his harvest and to make his weapons of war and equipment for his chariots. ¹³ "He will also take your daughters for perfumers and cooks and bakers.
¹⁴ "He will take the best of your fields and your vineyards and your olive groves and give them to his servants.
¹⁵ "He will take a tenth of your seed and of your vineyards and give to his officers and to his servants. ¹⁶ "He will also take your male servants and your female servants and your best young men and your donkeys and use them for his work. ¹⁷ "He will take a tenth of your flocks, and you yourselves will become his servants. ¹⁸ "Then you will cry out in that day because of your king whom you have chosen for yourselves, but the LORD will not answer you in that day." ¹⁹ Nevertheless, the people refused to listen to the voice of Samuel, and they said, "No, but there shall be a king over us, ²⁰ that we also may be like all the nations, that our king may judge us and go out before us and fight our battles." ²¹ Now after Samuel had heard all the words of the people, he repeated them in the LORD'S hearing. ²² The LORD said to Samuel, "Listen to their voice and appoint them a king." So Samuel said to the men of Israel, "Go every man to his city." – he just continued to do what he had been called to do – deliver God's Word!

Part of that message is giving a warning:

- There will be a military draft. 11-12
- There will be forced labor. 13
- Their land will be confiscated. 14
- They will pay taxes. 15
- They will experience loss of freedoms. 16-17
- They will experience loss of spiritual well-being. 18

The key word is "He will take…"

Blake, "Samuel now shows them the "manner of the king" and the relation, in which he and they, will stand to one another. He is not a king that gives, but a king that takes. What a contrast between this exacting king and the true King, the King that in the fullness of time, is to come bringing salvation. He will be a giving King. As Prophet He gives Himself to teach; as Priest to atone and intercede, as King to rule and to defend. How different the attributes of this king from the one Samuel spoke of! The one exacting all that is ours; the other giving all that is His."

It was God's will that Israel have a king but they went about it the wrong way. Then why did God give them the king they wanted? As a form of judgment. One way God judges us is to give us what we want!

- Israel wanted meat, they complained about the manna that He provided. As a judgment God gave them meat until it made them sick!

- Book of Romans tells us that a homosexual is a result of rejecting God. They wanted to be sexually perverted so as a judgment God gave them over to their own vile natures.

- You go fly a kite, and it keeps pulling away from you, let go of the string and let the kite do what it wants to do and it will come crashing down.

- A boat tied up to the dock, keeps pulling to get free, untie it and it will soon capsize.

"Ephraim is joined to idols; Let him alone." Hosea 4:17

How many say, "I don't want to go to church, I don't want to obey God in my giving, I don't want to be holy..." God says, "Ok, have it your way!" Their heart became hardened and they soon become miserable. We are like fish going after a plastic lure – they get want they wanted but afterwards they realize it's not want they needed.

John Ortberg, shared this:

"Recently my wife and I went fly-fishing for the first time. Our guides told us that "to catch a fish you have to think like a fish." They said that to a fish life is about the maximum gratification of appetite at the minimum expenditure of energy. To a fish, life is "see a fly, want a fly, eat a fly." A rainbow trout never really reflects on where his life is headed. A girl carp rarely says to a boy carp, I don't feel you're as committed to our relationship as I am. I wonder, do you love me for me or just for my body? The fish are just a collection of appetites. A fish is a stomach, a mouth, and a pair of eyes.

While we were on the water, I was struck by how dumb the fish are. *Hey, swallow this. It's not the real thing; it's just a lure. You'll think it will feed you, but it won't. It'll trap you. If you were to look closely, fish, you would see the hook. You'd know once you were hooked that it's just a matter of time before the enemy reels you in.* You'd think fish would wise up and notice the hook or see the line. You'd think fish would look around at all their fish friends who go for a lure and fly off into space and never return. But they don't. It is ironic. We say fish swim together in a school, but they never learn."

When will we learn that what we need is God's will, and what we want outside of God's will is not only a waste of our time but dangerous. But if we persist, often God will let us have what we want, it is a form of judgment.

III. FINALLY, THE *RESIGNATION* OF SAMUEL. 19-22

A. The people refused to *Obey.* 19-20

19 Nevertheless, the people refused to listen to the voice of Samuel, and they said, "No, but there shall be a king over us, 20 that we also may be like all the nations, that our king may judge us and go out before us and fight our battles."

B. Samuel continued to *Pray.* 21

21 Now after Samuel had heard all the words of the people, he repeated them in the LORD'S hearing

C. Samuel accepted God's *Way.* 22

22 The LORD said to Samuel, "Listen to their voice and appoint them a king." So Samuel said to the men of Israel, "Go every man to his city." – God's way was to teach them a lesson by giving them their way.

Trans: I have learned some in the Congregation will choose Work over Worship; Staying home over coming to God's House; Sin over being Spirit-filled; Buy things, over bringing their tithes and offering to God; and my job is not to try and force them but to keep praying, preparing sermons, and preaching God's Word.

Con:

1. Rejection is a part of life, if we respond to it like Samuel did it will draw us closer to God – the God who accepts us in the midst of our rejection.

2. I came across this true story. Shortly after the Korean War, a Korean woman had an affair with an American soldier, and she got pregnant. He went back to the United States, and she never saw him again. She gave birth to a little girl, and this little girl looked different than the other Korean children. She had light-colored, curly hair. In that culture, children of mixed race were ostracized by the community. In fact, many women would kill their children because they didn't want them to face such rejection. This woman didn't do that, she did something worse - she abandoned her little girl to the streets. This little girl was ruthlessly taunted by people. They called her the ugliest word in the Korean language, *tooki,* alien devil. After living on the streets for 2 years she finally made her way to an orphanage.

One day, word came that a couple from America was going to adopt a little boy. So this little girl spent the day cleaning up the little boys giving them baths and combing their hair and wondering which one would be adopted by the American couple.

The next day the couple came, and this is what the girl recalled:

"It was like Goliath had come back to life. I saw the man with his huge hands lift up each and every baby. I knew he loved every one of them as if they were his own. I saw tears running down his face, and I knew if they could, they would have taken the whole lot home with them. He saw me out of the corner of his eye. Now let me tell you. I was nine years old, but I didn't even weigh 30 pounds. I was a scrawny thing. I had worms in my body. I had lice in my hair. I had boils all over me. I was full of scars. I was not a pretty sight. But the man came over to me, and he began rattling away something in English, and I looked up at him. Then he took this huge hand and laid it on my face. What was he saying? He was saying, 'I want this child. This is the child for me.'"

That's the way God feels about you! You may be rejected on earth but never forget that you are always accepted in heaven.

Chapter Nine

HOW TO LET GOD'S WILL FIND US – PART ONE.

1 Sam. 9-10

Intro:

1. The story is told of a Lion that was hiding in the bushes, listening to two hunters arguing over who was the king of the jungle. They concluded that the lion was, and of course that greatly pleased the lion. The lion came upon a Tiger and asked him, "Tiger, who is the king of the jungle?" The tiger replied, "You are!" Later he met a panther, a rhinoceros, and various animals asking them the same question, getting the same answer. Then towards the end of the day, he met a huge elephant and asked him who the king of the jungle was. The elephant took his mighty trunk and wrapped it around the lion and slammed him to the ground several times. Then he took his big foot and kicked him several feet into the air, then with his massive head, head butted him into a tree." The lion dazed and bleeding shook his head and said, "Gee whiz, just because you don't know the answer, no need to get sore!"

2. I feel like that lion every time I have to find the answer to the question, what is God's will for my life. Sort of dazed and beat-up.

I. FOR STARTERS, LOOK TO THE *PROVIDENCE* OF God. 9:1-5, 11-14

A. The *Logic.*

Since God is sovereignly behind every circumstance of life, we can believe that His invisible hand is making events happen.

1. The *Premise:*

    - God works *Sovereignly.*

Which He will bring about at the proper time—He who is the blessed and **only** Sovereign, the King of kings and Lord of lords, 1 Timothy 6:15 Almost every Christian agrees this is true, when good things happen, but what about bad, evil things?

37 Who is there who speaks and it comes to pass, Unless the Lord has commanded *it?* 38 *Is it* not from the mouth of the Most High That both good and ill go forth? Lamentations 3:37-38

The word "ill" is *ra'ah* it means "calamity, evil, disaster," and the like.

Is it not from the mouth of the Most High that both calamities and good things come? Lamentations 3:38 (NIV)

38 Is it not from the mouth of the Most High that good and bad come? Lamentations 3:38 (ESV)

38 Is it not out of the mouth of the Most High that evil and good both proceed [adversity and prosperity, physical evil or misfortune and physical good or happiness]? Lamentations 3:38 (AMP)

Pilate thought he had the power to crucify the Lord Jesus, which was the murder of a sinless person. However, Jesus sees it from God's hand.

[10] So Pilate *said to Him, "You do not speak to me? Do You not know that I have authority to release You, and I have authority to crucify You?" [11] Jesus answered, "You would have no authority over Me, unless it had been given you from above…" John 19:10-11

God is working it all out! As one noted:

"Our lives are also cluttered with a lot of "if onlys," "If only I had done this," or "If only that had not happened." But again, God has no "if onlys." God never makes a mistake; God has no regrets. "As for God, His way is perfect" (Psa. 18:30). We can trust God. He is trustworthy."

- God works *Wisely.*

Oh, the depth of the riches both of the wisdom and knowledge of God! How unsearchable are His judgments and unfathomable His ways! Romans 11:33

Of course, the problem is we cannot understand God's eternal perspective.

[8] "For My thoughts are not your thoughts, Nor are your ways My ways," declares the LORD. [9] "For *as* the heavens are higher than the earth, So are My ways higher than your ways And My thoughts than your thoughts. Isaiah 55:8-9

Philip Hughes, "Under God, however, all things are without exception fully controlled – despite all appearances to the contrary."

Bridges, "Again it is difficult for us to appreciate the reality of God sovereignly doing as He pleases in our lives, because we do not *see* God doing anything. Instead we see ourselves or other people acting and events occurring, and we evaluate those actions and events according to our own preferences and plans. We see ourselves influencing or perhaps even controlling or being controlled by the actions of other people, but we do not see God at work. But over all the actions and events of our lives, God is in control doing as He pleases – not apart from those events, or in spite of them, but *through* them."

Joseph could say, "Now, therefore, it was not you who sent me here, but God…" Genesis 45:8

We may not see it with our physical eyes but we can with our eyes of faith! 2 Cor. 5:7

- God works *Lovingly.*

It is for our good, benefit, and advantage.

'For I know the plans that I have for you,' declares the LORD, 'plans for welfare and not for calamity to give you a future and a hope. Jeremiah 29:11

King Hezekiah said, "Lo, for *my own* welfare I had great bitterness..." Isaiah 38:17

Even if He causes suffering, He will show compassion according to His abundant, faithful love. Lamentations 3:32 (HCSB)

If God cares for an insignificant sparrow, how much more over His own children!

[29] "Are not two sparrows sold for a cent? And *yet* not one of them will fall to the ground apart from your Father. [30] "But the very hairs of your head are all numbered. [31] "So do not fear; you are more valuable than many sparrows. Matthew 10:29-31

[38] For I am convinced that neither death, nor life, nor angels, nor principalities, nor things present, nor things to come, nor powers, [39] nor height, nor depth, nor any other created thing, will be able to separate us from the love of God, which is in Christ Jesus our Lord. Romans 8:38-39

[10] "For the mountains may be removed and the hills may shake, But My lovingkindness will not be removed from you, And My covenant of peace will not be shaken," Says the LORD who has compassion on you. Isaiah 54:10

Trans: The Premise is that a wise and loving God is in control of all things in our lives for His glory and our good.

2. The *Providence*.

"God's providence is His constant care for and His absolute ruler over *all* His creation for His own glory and the good of His people." [Bridges]

He sovereignly rules over all things: 1 Chron. 29:12/Mt. 10:29/Dan.4:17,35/Psa.33:10-11).

Why do we fight this truth? It is the only real comfort we can build our lives upon!

The mind of man plans his way, But the LORD directs his steps. Proverbs 16:9

[21] Many plans are in a man's heart, But the counsel of the LORD will stand. Proverbs 19:21

[30] There is no wisdom and no understanding and no counsel against the LORD. Proverbs 21:30

[37] Who is there who speaks and it comes to pass, unless the Lord has commanded *it?* Lamentations 3:37

Who really decides whether that business venture will succeed?

[13] Come now, you who say, "Today or tomorrow we will go to such and such a city, and spend a year there and engage in business and make a profit." [14] Yet you do not know what your life will be like tomorrow. You are *just* a vapor that appears for a little while and then vanishes away. [15] Instead, *you ought* to

say, "If the Lord wills, we will live and also do this or that." [16] But as it is, you boast in your arrogance; all such boasting is evil. James 4:13-16

Who really opens and shuts doors?

[7] "And to the angel of the church in Philadelphia write: He who is holy, who is true, who has the key of David, who opens and no one will shut, and who shuts and no one opens, says this: [8] 'I know your deeds. Behold, I have put before you an open door which no one can shut, because you have a little power, and have kept My word, and have not denied My name. Revelation 3:7-8

The Logic is simple – God is working all things out according to His plan and therefore how could it be possible for the will of God not to find us!

B. The *Loss* is really gain! 9:1-5

1. His *Father*. 1

a. His *Tribe.*

Now there was a man of Benjamin… - Saul was of the tribe of Benjamin. The apostle was of this tribe (Rom. 11:1/Phil. 3:5). The Benjamites descended from Rachel, Jacob's beloved wife. The name Benjamin means *"son of my right hand."* He is a type of Christ who is at the right hand of God. The inheritance of

Benjamin included Jerusalem, Bethel, Mizpeh, and Ramah which was Saul's home.

b. His name *Tag*.

whose name was Kish the son of Abiel, the son of Zeror, the son of Becorath, the son of Aphiah, the son of a Benjamite – Kish was his name.

c. His *Treasure*.

a mighty man of valor – this speaks of being powerful in wealth, thus had influence and power.

There was a man of Benjamin whose name was Kish, the son of Abiel, son of Zeror, son of Becorath, son of Aphiah, a Benjaminite, a man of wealth. 1 Samuel 9:1 (ESV)

One reason for this might have been related to the fact that the tribe had been greatly reduced (Jud. 20:46-47) and thus every man would have more land to share than those of the other tribes.

2. His *Features*. 2

a. He was *Handsome*.

He had a son whose name was Saul, a choice and handsome man, and there was not a more handsome person than he among the sons of Israel

b. He was of great *Height*.

from his shoulders and up he was taller than any of the people

Trans: People are impressed with men who are tall and handsome! Even Samuel was impressed with Saul:

²³ So they ran and took him from there, and when he stood among the people, he was taller than any of the people from his shoulders upward. ²⁴ Samuel said to all the people, "Do you see him whom the LORD has chosen? Surely there is no one like him among all the people." So all the people shouted and said, "*Long* live the king!" 1 Samuel 10:23-24

Samuel still has the bigger is better mentality when he was looking for Saul's replacement. 1 Sam. 16:1-7

Trans: Adrian Rogers, "Now what does all of this say in a nutshell? This young man, with a godly dad, was a man among men. He was tall, head and shoulders above other people. He was handsome, goodly. As a matter of fact, today, Hollywood would love to have him. They'd had made a movie star out of him. He had health. He had height. He had handsomeness. He had it all. And you would think that with all of that going for him that he, ha, ha, he, he might prone, he might be prone to swagger a little bit, to be arrogant. But not so. Oh, what a humble man he was. Look, if you will, in, in 9:21.

3. His *Fortune* – three lost donkeys!

³ Now the donkeys of Kish, Saul's father, were lost. So Kish said to his son Saul, "Take now with you one of the servants, and arise, go search for the donkeys." ⁴ He passed through the hill country of Ephraim and passed through the land of Shalishah, but they did not find them. Then they passed through the land of Shaalim, but they were not there. Then he passed through the land of the Benjamites, but they did not find them. ⁵ When they came to the land of Zuph, Saul said to his servant who was with him, "Come, and let us return, or else my father will cease to be concerned about the donkeys and will become anxious for us." – this seems like a misfortune, but it is God's hand moving Saul to have an ordained meeting with Samuel.

C. His *Location*. 11-14

¹¹ As they went up the slope to the city, they found young women going out to draw water and said to them, "Is the seer here?" ¹² They answered them and said, "He is; see, he is ahead of you. Hurry now, for he has come into the city today, for the people have a sacrifice on the high place today. ¹³ "As soon as you enter the city you will find him before he goes up to the high place to eat, for the people will not eat until he comes, because he must bless the sacrifice; afterward those who are invited will eat. Now therefore, go up for you will find him at once." ¹⁴ So they went up to the city. As they came into the city, behold, Samuel was coming out toward them to go up to the high place – notice he doesn't find God's will – God's will finds him and brings him to the exact place He wants him to be! His loss would prove to be a great gain!

- Do his donkeys just happen to go astray?
- Is it just good luck that Saul is sent to look for them and not one of his brothers?
- Does he just happen to come to the very place where Samuel lives?
- Does Samuel just happen to be home? Keep in mind if he had come a day earlier Samuel would not have been there.
- Does he just happen to meet a woman who had just seen Samuel?
- Upon entering the city did he just happen to run into Samuel?

We need to realize that God does not just work in some miraculous way but through the mundane happenings of life like donkeys going astray!

Alexander Carson, "For the wisdom of man cannot see how the providence of God can arrange human actions to fulfill His purpose without any miracle."

Take the book of Esther, the name of God is not mentioned even one time in that book – and yet we see God behind it all. Haman plans to destroy every Jew but listen to this:

¹ During that night the king could not sleep so he gave an order to bring the book of records, the chronicles, and they were read before the king. ² It was found written what Mordecai had reported concerning Bigthana and Teresh, two of the king's eunuchs who were doorkeepers, that they had sought to lay hands on King Ahasuerus. ³ The king said, "What honor or dignity has been bestowed on Mordecai for this?" Then the king's servants who attended him said, "Nothing has been done for him." ⁴ So the king said, "Who is in the court?" Now Haman had just entered the outer court of the king's palace in order to speak to the king about hanging Mordecai on the gallows which he had prepared for him. ⁵ The king's servants said to him, "Behold, Haman is standing in the court." And the king said, "Let him come in." ⁶ So Haman came in and the king said to him, "What is to be done for the man whom the king desires to honor?" And Haman said to himself, "Whom would the king desire to honor more than me?" ⁷ Then Haman said to the king, "For the man whom the king desires to honor, ⁸ let them bring a royal robe which the king has worn, and the horse on which the king has ridden, and on whose head a royal crown has been placed; ⁹ and let the robe and the horse be handed over to one of the king's

most noble princes and let them array the man whom the king desires to honor and lead him on horseback through the city square, and proclaim before him, 'Thus it shall be done to the man whom the king desires to honor.'" [10] Then the king said to Haman, "Take quickly the robes and the horse as you have said, and do so for Mordecai the Jew, who is sitting at the king's gate; do not fall short in anything of all that you have said." Esther 6:1-10

- Why was it that on the very night King Xerxes could not sleep?

- Why would he order the dry book of chronicles brought to him? Why not some music? Some thriller novel?

- Why did he read at that exact place?

- Why was not Mordecai rewarded at the time?

- Why did he feel compelled to immediately have Mordecai rewarded?

- Why did Haman come to him at that exact moment?

Bridges, "God was sovereignly orchestrating the events of that night to save His people. The question naturally arises, "Does God always orchestrate the events of my life for my good?" If we grant that the unusual outworking of events in Esther was due to the sovereign hand of God, are we justified in concluding that God *always* orchestrates the events of our lives to fulfill His purpose? According to Romans 8:28 the answer is a solid yes...It is this assurance that God works *all* events of our lives that gives sense to Paul's exhortation elsewhere to "give thanks in *all* circumstances" (1 Thess. 5:18). How could we possibly give thanks to God for all the circumstances of our lives if He were not at work in them for our good?"

The Bible is clear; we either believe it or we do not!

"I know that You can do all things, And that no purpose of Yours can be thwarted. Job 42:2

But our God is in the heavens; He does whatever He pleases. Psalm 115:3

The LORD will accomplish what concerns me; Your lovingkindness, O LORD, is everlasting; Do not forsake the works of Your hands. Psalm 138:8 (NASB)

"For the LORD of hosts has planned, and who can frustrate *it?* And as for His stretched-out hand, who can turn it back?" Isaiah 14:27

"Even from eternity I am He, And there is none who can deliver out of My hand; I act and who can reverse it?" Isaiah 43:13

Declaring the end from the beginning, And from ancient times things which have not been done, Saying, 'My purpose will be established, And I will accomplish all My good pleasure'; Isaiah 46:10 (NASB)

What about Ruth? Notice Ruth 2:1-10:

¹ Now Naomi had a kinsman of her husband, a man of great wealth, of the family of Elimelech, whose name was Boaz. ² And Ruth the Moabitess said to Naomi, "Please let me go to the field and glean among the ears of grain after one in whose sight I may find favor." And she said to her, "Go, my daughter." ³ So she departed and went and gleaned in the field after the reapers; and she happened to come to the portion of the field belonging to Boaz, who was of the family of Elimelech. ⁴ Now behold, Boaz came from Bethlehem and said to the reapers, "May the LORD be with you." And they said to him, "May the LORD bless you." ⁵ Then Boaz said to his servant who was in charge of the reapers, "Whose young woman is this?" ⁶ The servant in charge of the reapers replied, "She is the young Moabite woman who returned with Naomi from the land of Moab. ⁷ "And she said, 'Please let me glean and gather after the reapers among the sheaves.' Thus she came and has remained from the morning until now; she has been sitting in the house for a little while." ⁸ Then Boaz said to Ruth, "Listen carefully, my daughter. Do not go to glean in another field; furthermore, do not go on from this one, but stay here with my maids.

⁹ "Let your eyes be on the field which they reap, and go after them. Indeed, I have commanded the servants not to touch you. When you are thirsty, go to the water jars and drink from what the servants draw." ¹⁰ Then she fell on her face, bowing to the ground and said to him, "Why have I found favor in your sight that you should take notice of me, since I am a foreigner?" Ruth 2:1-10

- How did she end up in just the right field?
- How is it the Boaz arrived just at that time?
- Why would he notice just one poor worker?
- Who turned Boaz's heart to favor Ruth?

These may seem like normal events but God worked through these normal events to accomplish His will in Ruth life.

Things don't just happed!

- John Bunyan was drafted as a soldier during the Civil War in England. He was about to begin sentry duty when another soldier asked him if he would trade duties with him. He did and that night the man who took his place was shot in the head! God had John Bunyan exactly where he wanted him – alive and well so that he could later write Pilgrim's Progress.

- Christopher Columbus was discouraged after trying to get financial backing for his adventures. While coming back from Italy he met a monk and asked him for a drink of water. They then traveled together for a while striking up a friendship. The result was that monk went on to convince Queen Isabella to give Christopher financial backing.

- Abraham Lincoln was rummaging through a barrel when he found a copy of Lord Blackstone's commentaries on law. This seemingly accidental finding resulted in Lincoln become interested in politics."

- This is a true story that was in Reader's Digest way back in 1949.

"On January 10, 1948, just over two years after the conclusion of WWII, Marcel Sternberger got on a train in the Brooklyn subway he had never been on before. He normally took a different line, but he had changed his schedule in order to visit a sick friend that morning and was now boarding a noon train to get to work. The train was full.

But just as he stepped in, one man jumped up and ran off, realizing he was about to miss his station. Sternberger quickly took the seat and sat down. Next to him was a man reading a Hungarian newspaper…He looked over the man's shoulder and said in Hungarian, "I hope you don't mind if I glance at your paper." The man was surprised to be addressed in his native language, and during the half-hour ride to town, they became acquainted.

Sternberger's companion voluntarily shared his tragic story. His name was Paskin, and he had been a law student when the war started. He was eventually put into a labor battalion and sent to the Ukraine. Later he was captured by the Russians and put to work burying the German dead. After the war he covered hundreds of miles on foot, returned to his home in Debrecen, Hungary and discovered his entire family gone. Strangers were living in the apartment once occupied by his father, mother, brothers, and sisters. When he reached the apartment he and his wife had shared, it also was occupied by strangers. Finally, he located old friends in Debrecen who had survived the war. They sadly informed him his entire family was dead. The Nazis had taken them and his wife to Auschwitz, where they were all presumably killed in the gas chambers. Stunned by the news, the man fled Hungary, which had become a funeral land for him. He headed west toward Paris and immigrated to the United States in October, 1947. As Sternberger listened, the story seemed somehow familiar. Suddenly he remembered why. He had recently met a young woman at the home of friends who had also been from Debrecen. She had been taken to Auschwitz but was then transferred to work in a German munitions factory. All her relatives had been killed in the gas chambers. After she had been liberated by the Americans, she was brought to New York in the first boatload of Displaced Persons in 1946. Sternberger had been so moved by her story he had written down her address and phone number, hoping to invite her to meet his family in order to help with her terrible loneliness and grief. Sternberger thought it impossible that there could be a connection between these two people, but when he reached his station, he stayed on the train with his new friend. He asked as casually as possible, "Is your first name Bela?" The man went pale as he said, "Yes! How did you know?" Sternberger fumbled for his address book, as he asked, "Was your wife's name Marya?" Looking as though he might faint, Paskin said, "Yes! Yes!" Sternberger suggested they get off at the next station without explaining why. He took Paskin to a nearby phone booth. While Paskin stood there like a man in a trance, Sternberger dialed the number, and after a long delay, he had Marya Paskin on the line. Sternberger reminded her of their recent meeting and she remembered him. Without explaining why, Sterberger asked Marya where she lived in Debrecen before the war, and she told him the address. He then turned to Bela and said, "Did you and your wife live on such-and-such a street?" "Yes!" Bela exclaimed, as he turned white as a sheet and trembled. Sternberger urged him to stay calm but then explained that something miraculous was about to happen to him. Then he handed Bela the phone saying, "Here, take this telephone and talk to you wife! When Bela realized he was really speaking with his Marya, he broke into uncontrollable crying. Sternberger sent him by taxi to the address to be reunited with his wife."

Reader's Digest ends the article:

"Skeptical persons would no doubt attribute the events of that memorable afternoon to mere chance. But was it chance that made Sternberger suddenly decide to visit his sick friend, and hence take a subway line that he had never been on before? Was it chance that caused the man sitting by the door of the car to rush out just as Sternberger came in? Was it chance that caused Bela Paskin to be sitting beside Sternberger, reading a Hungarian newspaper? Was it chance – or did God ride the Brooklyn subway that afternoon?"

The truth is God rides the Brooklyn subway every second of everyday – and everywhere else also!

Also we have obtained an inheritance, having been predestined according to His purpose who works all things after the counsel of His will, Ephesians 1:11

F. B. Meyer, "All these things, if carefully observed, yield their testimony and assurance that God is in all events permitting, directing, controlling, and causing all things to work out for His perfect plan."

Trans: So we first begin by realize that we don't really have to find God's will – it will find us. It is called God's Providence. It says that no matter what, it is all going to end well! In the fall of 1991, a car driven by a drunk driver jumped its lane and smashed headfirst into a mini-van driven by Jerry Sittser. Sittser and three of his children survived, but Sittser's wife, four-year-old child, and mother died in the crash. Over the years Sittser has offered some profound reflections about loss, grief, and suffering. In his book *A Grace Revealed*, Sittser shares the following story about how his son David responded to the tragic accident. My son David is—and always has been—quiet and reflective. After the accident, he was the least likely to talk about it; but when he chose to, he usually had something significant to say or ask. One particular conversation has stayed fresh in my memory. David was eight at the time; we were driving to a soccer match some distance from our home. Typical for these occasions, David was quiet. He suddenly asked, "Do you think Mom sees us right now?" I paused to ponder. "I don't know, David. I think maybe she does see us. Why do you ask?" He said, "I don't see how she could, Dad. I thought Heaven was full of happiness. How could she bear to see us so sad?" I finally replied, "I think she does see us, but she sees the whole story, including how it all turns out, which is beautiful to her. It's going to be a good story, David." That is the beauty of believing in God's providential hand...

Chapter Ten

HOW TO LET GOD'S WILL FIND US – PART TWO

1 Sam. 9-10

Intro:

1. The world was grieved by the recent death of young American hostage Kayla Mueller by the ISIS terrorist. News of her death made headlines globally, with expressions of sympathy for her family. She wrote these words to her family from her imprisonment:

"I remember mom always telling me that all in all in the end the only one you really have is God. I have come to a place in experience where, in every sense of the word, I have surrendered myself to our creator because literally there was no else. ... and by God and by your prayers I have felt tenderly cradled in freefall. I have been shown in darkness, light and have learned that even in prison, one can be free. I am grateful."

2. God's will found Kayla, she didn't have to wonder what God's will was for her, it found her. For her, it was God's will that she be imprisoned, and then martyred, and then enter glory!

I. LAST WEEK, WE LOOKED AT THE *PROVIDENCE* OF GOD. 9:1-5, 11-14

The providence of God is related to the circumstances that God has placed us in, like Kayla we did not plan them, we may not have wanted them, but as they say – it is what it is.

II. SECOND, LOOK TO THE *PRECEPTS* OF GOD. 9:6-10

A. The *Seer.* 7, 9

⁷He said to him, "Behold now, there is a man of God in this city, and the man is held in honor; all that he says surely comes true. Now let us go there, perhaps he can tell us about our journey on which we have set out."… ⁹ (Formerly in Israel, when a man went to inquire of God, he used to say, "Come, and let us go to the seer"; for he who is called a prophet now was formerly called a seer.)

- Man of God.

Man of God is a technical phrase used only of Timothy in the New Testament. In the Old

Testament it is frequently used as a title for one who proclaimed the Word of God.

- Prophet.

In the Old Testament, it was one who got direct revelation from God. Their words were often written down and are now part of Scripture, but not all they said was written down.

- Seer.

A name sometimes applied to the prophets because of the visions granted to them.

The point is, that Samuel was in a sense, their Bible. Today we have the full and final Word of God which reveals to us God's will for our lives. 2 Tim. 3:16-17

Your word is a lamp to my feet and a light to my path.
Psalm 119:105

The unfolding of Your words gives light; It gives understanding to the simple. Psalm 119:130

It is amazing that we have people today who will put their full confidence in gadgets but find little interest in following God's infallible Word!

Reports continue to pour in of motorists who got into trouble because they blindly followed instructions from navigational systems.

- A German driver drove into a river on a foggy day;

- A British woman dodged oncoming traffic on a one-way highway for 12 miles, telling police she was only following the sat nav orders.

- An American music group missed a sold-out concert after someone entered the wrong destination, sending them 170 miles in the wrong direction.

Joachim Sieder, spokesman for Blaupunkt, said:

"It is absurd to blame the gadgets for human error and noted motorists are clearly warned the devices are there to help, not to make decisions. If a traffic light is red, it's obvious you have to stop even if the sat nav says 'drive straight on.' People who drive into rivers and then blame their sat nav are just too humiliated to accept blame themselves."

Maximilian Maurer, spokesman for a German motor club added, "You'd think they have their own eyes and brains engaged to make decisions and not rely on the sat nav. I used to think sat navs were 'idiot-proof', but perhaps not."

Truth is if we would obey the Word of God like that, we would have no trouble letting God's will find us!

B. The *Shekel*. 7-10

⁷ Then Saul said to his servant, "But behold, if we go, what shall we bring the man? For the bread is gone from our sack and there is no present to bring to the man of God. What do we have?" ⁸ The servant answered Saul again and said, "Behold, I have in my hand a fourth of a shekel of silver; I will give it to the man of God and he will tell us our way." ⁹ (Formerly in Israel, when a man went to inquire of God, he used to say, "Come, and let us go to the seer"; for he who is called a prophet now was formerly called a seer.) ¹⁰ Then Saul said to his servant, "Well said; come, let us go." So they went to the city where the man of God was – paying someone who is giving us God's Word is a Biblical principle.

See 1 Ki. 14:2-3/2 Cor. 9:11, 13-14.

¹⁷ Pastors who do their work well should be paid well and should be highly appreciated, especially those who work hard at both preaching and teaching. ¹⁸ For the Scriptures say, "Never tie up the mouth of an ox when it is treading out the grain—let him eat as he goes along!" And in another place, "Those who work deserve their pay!" 1 Timothy 5:17-18 (TLB)

Reminds me of a pastor that went to a new church, the chairman of the deacon board said to him, "Now, Pastor, we only pay our pastors $50 dollars a week around here." The pastor said, "Why, that's an insult!" The deacon agreed and then replied, "Yes, but we only pay every other week – that way you aren't insulted as often!"

III. THIRD, GOD'S WILL FINDS US AS WE PRAY. 15-17

15 Now a day before Saul's coming, the LORD had revealed this to Samuel saying, 16 "About this time tomorrow I will send you a man from the land of Benjamin, and you shall anoint him to be prince over My people Israel; and he will deliver My people from the hand of the Philistines. For I have regarded My people, because their cry has come to Me." 17 When Samuel saw Saul, the LORD said to him, "Behold, the man of whom I spoke to you! This one shall rule over My people." – that phrase, "the Lord had revealed this to Samuel, is speaking of God communicating to Samuel in prayer.

Jon Courson notes, "Samuel was a man who understood what it meant to pray without ceasing. As a result, the Lord whispered in his ear, telling him the man who would be king was on his way."

When we spend time in prayer, God speaks to our spirit in that still small voice.

The Spirit Himself testifies with our spirit that we are children of God, Romans 8:16

This also brings up an important point in the relationship of prayer to God's providence.

We cannot say, "Since God is in control, I will simply not be concerned about anything." The Bible is clear that providence of God does not eliminate the need to pray!

Be anxious for nothing, but in everything by prayer and supplication with thanksgiving let your requests be made known to God.
Philippians 4:6

I will cry to God Most High [that's prayer], To God who accomplishes *all things* [that's providence] for me.
Psalm 57:2

The disciples were under great persecution, they believed in God's Sovereign hand – yet it motivated them to pray, notice the blending of prayer and providence (Ac. 4:24-29).

It was their belief in the Sovereignty of God that encouraged them to pray – only a sovereign God would be able to answer their prayers!

Paul believed in both God's providence and prayer (Philemon 1:22).

We don't know how it all works out or how it works together but we need to keep both our responsibility and God's sovereignty in our minds. God's providence was revealed to Paul during a shipwreck:

²² "*Yet* now I urge you to keep up your courage, for there will be no loss of life among you, but *only* of the ship. ²³ "For this very night an angel of the God to whom I belong and whom I serve stood before me, ²⁴ saying, 'Do not be afraid, Paul; you must stand before Caesar; and behold, God has granted you all those who are sailing with you.' ²⁵ "Therefore, keep up your courage, men, for I believe God that it will turn out exactly as I have been told. ²⁶ "But we must run aground on a certain island." Acts 27:22-26

Yet they were still responsible to do their part:

Paul said to the centurion and to the soldiers, "Unless these men remain in the ship, you yourselves cannot be saved."
Acts 27:31

Providence never eliminates our responsibility to act wisely nor our need for prayer. God has promised to watch over us – yet we are still told to pray for our safety and lock our doors at night!

It was God in His providence that allowed the Jews to return back to Jerusalem; he also believed that God would fight for them:

"…Our God will fight for us." Nehemiah 4:20

And yet Nehemiah both prayed and posted a guard!

⁸ All of them conspired together to come *and* fight against Jerusalem and to cause a disturbance in it. ⁹ But we prayed to our God, and because of them we set up a guard against them day and night. Nehemiah 4:8-9

Thomas Lye, "Trust…[uses] such means as God prescribes for the bringing about his appointed end…God's means are to be used, as well as God's blessing to be expected."

My point is providence does not eliminate our need for prayer. And this passage indicates that prayer is not just our talking to God but His talking to us. Caution: We are not talking about hearing voices!

Fenelon, "Be silent and listen to God. Let your heart be in such a state of preparation that His Spirit may impress upon you such virtues as will please Him."

Kierkegaard, "Prayer is not to hear oneself speak, but to arrive at silence and continue being silent; to wait till one hears God speak."

Amy Carmichael, "Do not be afraid of silence in your prayer time. It may be that you are meant to listen, not to speak. So wait before the Lord. Wait in stillness. Wait as David waited when he "sat before the Lord."

Martin Luther, "I do not know it and do not understand it, but sounding from above and ringing in my ears I hear what is beyond the thought of man."

Nouwell, "The Desert fathers did not think of solitude as being alone, but as being alone with God. They did not think of silence as not speaking, but as listening to God. Solitude and silence are the context within which prayer is practiced."

Tozer, "Lord teach me to listen…Give me the spirit of the boy Samuel when he said, "Speak for Thy servant hears." Let me hear You speaking in my heart. Let me get used to the sound of Your voice."

Adie Johnson, who serves on the staff of a small church in Colorado as Pastor of Spiritual Formation, shares a few thoughts about the power of group solitude:

"I have found that one of the most powerful tools God has used to sculpt me in my spiritual life has been solitude, extended times set aside to be just with God. It was nearly 15 years ago that an older woman at the church I attended invited me to join her and others going to a park to spend a half day in prayer. I remember thinking I was pretty sure I couldn't pray for that long, but still, something about it drew me…That clear, fall morning beside the Chesapeake Bay would change the direction of my journey with Jesus irrevocably. With very simple instructions, my friend sent us off with a Bible, a journal, and what felt like all the time in the world. Once I figured out that I didn't need to speak to God nonstop for the next three hours, I settled into a listening mode that was new and surprisingly comfortable. Unbeknownst to me, God began that day to answer a prayer I had uttered to him a few months earlier: "Lord, help me to hear and recognize your voice. I just want to know it's you."

In those three hours, God, in his lovingly tender way, began to teach me just that—how to listen to him. Like Elijah in 1 Kings 19, I discovered that God sounds much more like a soft whisper blowing through my heart than a raging wind tearing apart the mountains. It was an unimaginably rich experience for me, and it has only grown richer and deeper since then."

Con:

1. God's will, will find us not only in Providence but when we get serious about His Precepts and Prayer.

2. That is key – Behold God through His Word and Be still and know that He is God.

3. All of this reminded me of a true story I read about some years ago. A preacher was in prayer and meditation on God's Word. He just had a deep desire to go to a nearby logging camp. So he went but was sorely disappointed to find nobody there! He went into a building, it was the dining hall, but again no one was there.

He almost left but then prayed, "Lord, this is where I believe you led me." He then opened his Bible and began preaching the Bible out loud. He felt like a fool and when he was done he went back home.

It was years later, after preaching a revival, a man came up to him after the service and shared with him that he was hiding years ago in the logging camp dining hall – while the preacher preached the gospel. He listened and was saved!

Chapter Eleven

HOW TO LET GOD'S WILL FIND US – PART THREE

1 Sam. 9-10

Intro:

1. A basketball coach could call a time-out for any number of reasons at any different point in a ball game, or so I am told:

- He might see a flaw in the opponent's defense, for example, that he thinks his team could exploit with a hastily designed play.
- He might want to stop a flurry of momentum.

- He might want to stop a hot hand by one of the opposing players.

- He might use it to try icing a free-throw shooter.

- He might use it to stop the clock near the end of the half or regulation.

- He might use it to force an instant-replay review of a questionable call by the officials.

That's six different options right there. And they're all determined not by fixed rules but by the flow of the game; the nature of the opponent; the time left on the shot clock or the game clock—any of these factors and many others could dictate his purpose in asking for a stoppage in play. Plus it's all dictated by the coach's unique, personal knowledge of his players, his awareness of what each of them can do, what makes them perform best, what puts them in the best position to win the game. [Andreas Kostenberger, Darrell Bock, and Josh Chatraw, Truth Matters: Confident Faith in a Confusing World(B&H Publishing, 2014); Submitted by Van Morris, Mt. Washington, Kentucky]

2. God knows what is best for our lives, even though from our limited perspective we cannot always make sense out of it.

I. FIRST, WE LOOKED AT GOD'S *PROVIDENCE* 9:1-5, 11-14

II. THEN, WE LOOKED AT HIS *PRECEPTS.* 9:6-10

God's will, will never contradict God's Word. Somebody told Billy Graham that they had to work every Sunday and tried to justify it by using the fact that Jesus said that if your sheep falls into a ditch on the Sabbath it was right to pull him out. Billy said, "That's right. But if it falls into the ditch every Sabbath either sell the sheep or fill in the ditch!"

Of course, we are not under the Sabbath, but we are to actively observe the Lord's Day. Heb. 10:24-25

III. ALSO, WE LOOKED AT THE NEED FOR *PRAYER.* 9:15-17

Providence is no excuse for not praying as we looked at last week. Phil. 4:6-7

IV. FOURTH, LOOK TO GOD'S *PROMISES.* 9:18-27

A. The *Request.* 18

Then Saul approached Samuel in the gate and said, "Please tell me where the seer's house is." – a good place to start is with the asking!

God's Word is full of promises but we need to claim them and meet any conditions there might be. Jn. 16:24/Jam. 4:2

On June 6, 1981 Doug Whitt and his bride Sylvia were married. After the marriage ceremony, they began their honeymoon and went to the hotel. Doug had spared no expense for Sylvia—he bought that night the honeymoon suite. They went to the door of the honeymoon suite and opened the door, and quite frankly, the room was a bit small. In fact it was really small! It wasn't very well decorated either. There was a couch with a pull out bed in it, and kind of a side table with some flowers on it, and that was it. In the morning, Doug said, "You know, I paid a lot for this suite; I don't think I got my money's worth." So he went down to complain to the manager. The manager said, "What's the problem?" Doug said, "I really don't think your honeymoon suite delivered what it promised." The manager said, "Why do you say that?" He said, "All there was, was a tiny room to begin with, and there was just a couch and a table." The manager asked, "Did you open the door?" Doug said, "What door?" "The one on the wall." "I thought that was a closet." So they went back up and opened the door from this entryway little room, and there was this huge honeymoon suite! There was a heart-shaped bed and chocolates and flowers everywhere, and it was just perfect. They had robbed themselves because they didn't go far enough.

Prayerless Christians don't go far enough! We will never claim the promises and enjoy intimacy with God without spending time in the Word and in prayer.

B. The *Requirement.* 19-24

1. First, the need for *Forbearance.* 19, 22-24

Samuel answered Saul and said, "I am the seer. Go up before me to the high place, for you shall eat with me today; and in the morning I will let you go, and will tell you all that is on your mind... ²² Then Samuel took Saul and his servant and brought them into the hall and gave them a place at the head of those who were invited, who were about thirty men. ²³ Samuel said to the cook, "Bring the portion that I gave you, concerning which I said to you, 'Set it aside.'" ²⁴ Then the cook took up the leg with what was on it and set it before Saul. And Samuel said, "Here is what has been reserved! Set it before you and eat, because it has been kept for you until the appointed time, since I said I have invited the people." So Saul ate with Samuel that day – notice he doesn't immediately tell him what he wants to know. He has to wait on God's timetable. Everything we know about Saul at this stage indicates that he was shy, look at 10:20-22.

²⁰ Thus Samuel brought all the tribes of Israel near, and the tribe of Benjamin was taken by lot. ²¹ Then he brought the tribe of Benjamin near by its families, and the Matrite family was taken. And Saul the son of Kish was taken; but when they looked for him, he could not be found. ²² Therefore they inquired further of the LORD, "Has the man come here yet?" So the LORD said, "Behold, he is hiding himself by the baggage."

He is going to have to put up with being in the limelight. And that will make him uncomfortable.

Trans: We need to learn to patiently wait on the Lord, willing to put up with delays and disappointments.

Because of erosion, the historic Cape Hatteras Lighthouse was in peril of washing into the Atlantic Ocean. So Congress appropriated $12 million for the National Park service to move it 2900 feet to safety.

With a combination of care, expertise, patience and raw power, The Expert House Movers of Sharptown, Maryland moved the 208 foot tall, 9.7 million pound structure to its current home. The option of moving the lighthouse was first proposed in April of 1982, but the light wasn't lit at its new location until November 13, 1999. 17 years of study and 23 days of moving later.

God often moves in our lives like that – slowly!

2. Furthermore, the need for *Faith*.

a. That the *Donkeys* were found. 20a

"As for your donkeys which were lost three days ago, do not set your mind on them, for they have been found… - when we believe God's promises our worries are over. Saul no longer had to be concerned about the lost donkeys.

Reminds me of Hannah's reaction to God's promise:

Remember the background, "[4] When the day came that Elkanah sacrificed, he would give portions to Peninnah his wife and to all her sons and her daughters; [5] but to Hannah he would give a double portion, for he loved Hannah, but the LORD had closed her womb. [6] Her rival, however, would provoke her bitterly to irritate her, because the LORD had closed her womb. [7] It happened year after year, as often as she went up to the house of the LORD, she would provoke her; so she wept and would not eat. 1 Samuel 1:4-7

Then she got a promise - [17] Then Eli answered and said, "Go in peace; and may the God of Israel grant your petition that you have asked of Him." 1 Samuel 1:17

Her immediate reaction was one of faith - [18] She said, "Let your maidservant find favor in your sight." So the woman went her way and ate, and her face was no longer *sad.* 1 Samuel 1:18

Rom. 4:20-21...

Syntel was established in 1980 as a provider of software services with revenues of just $30,000 in its first year, Syntel has grown into a 911.4 million corporation. But the thing I like is its motto – *Consider it done!* Faith Considers it done!

b. That he was *Desirable* in Israel. 20b-21

...And for whom is all that is desirable in Israel? Is it not for you and for all your father's household?" ²¹ *Saul replied, "Am I not a Benjamite, of the smallest of the tribes of Israel, and my family the least of all the families of the tribe of Benjamin? Why then do you speak to me in this way?"* – Israel desired a king, and Saul was to be the fulfillment of that desire. It took faith to believe that! After all he is nobody special humanly speaking.

It takes a lot of faith to believe that we are one day going to be somebody the whole universe is going to marvel at – glorified saints (Phil. 3:20-21/1 Jn.3:2/1 Cor. 15:42-43).

Faith believes everything that God has promised us in the future – right now!

A woman named Clara said, "It was one of the worst days of my life: the washing machine broke down, the telephone kept ringing, my head ached, and the mail carrier brought a bill I had no money to pay. Almost to the breaking point, I lifted my one-year old into his highchair, leaned my head against the tray, and began to cry. Without a word, my son took his pacifier out of his mouth and stuck it in mine."

Faith is like a pacifier! When you have those days where everything goes wrong and frustrations abound just stick a promise of God in your mouth!

C. The *Result* - promise is fulfilled. 9:22-10:1

1. He was *Elevated.* 22-24

[22] Then Samuel took Saul and his servant into the great hall and placed them at the head of the table, honoring them above the thirty special guests. [23] Samuel then instructed the chef to bring Saul the choicest cut of meat, the piece that had been set aside for the guest of honor. [24] So the chef brought it in and placed it before Saul. "Go ahead and eat it," Samuel said, "for I was saving it for you, even before I invited these others!" So Saul ate with Samuel. 1 Samuel 9:22-24 (TLB)

2. He was *Detained.* 25-27

[25] Afterward they went down from the shrine into the city. A bed was prepared for Saul on the breeze-cooled roof of Samuel's house. [26] They woke at the break of day. Samuel called to Saul on the roof, "Get up and I'll send you off." Saul got up and the two of them went out in the street. [27] As they approached the outskirts of town, Samuel said to Saul, "Tell your servant to go on ahead of us. You stay with me for a bit. I have a word of God to give you." 1 Samuel 9:25-27 (MSG)

3. He was *Anointed.* 10:1

Then Samuel took the flask of oil, poured it on his head, kissed him and said, "Has not the LORD anointed you a ruler over His inheritance? - The familiar Hebrew term messiah is derived from the same verb mashach ("anoint") used here. From this point on the king became known as "the Lord's anointed" or "the Lord's messiah" (1 Sam. 24:6,10; 26:9,11,16,23). David would also be known as the Lord's anointed (2 Sam. 19:21). Ultimately, Jesus, the Messiah, came from David's lineage.

Trans: God's will is found in God's promises.

And we can truth those promises because of the one making them – Num. 23:19.

My estate consists principally of my books. I have a house which is really the banks; most of my stuff is old, used junk. But suppose when I die my family is gathered at the reading of my will, and they hear:

"I leave to my son Jeremy a yacht in the Gulf of Mexico; I leave to my daughter Missi an estate of one thousand acres in Florida; I leave to my grandson Hunter all the mineral rights that I hold in Nevada." To my grandson Dylan I leave my millions in my Swiss bank account. To my granddaughter Maddie, I leave my collection of antique Barbie dolls, worth 2.3 million."

What would they think? Dad must have lost it at the end – mentally disillusioned! And they would be right! Those promises would be meaningless because I own none of those things. But when Donald Trump dies and his will reads like that, his family will rejoice – why? He has the resources to back it up. In the same way, faith doesn't merely rest on the promises but on the God who has given them.

V. FIFTH, LOOK TO HIS *PEACE.* 10:2-

A. The *Confusion.*

I have no doubt all of this was difficult for Saul to take in and I am sure at first I am sure that he had no peace about what was happening.

B. The *Confirmation.*

1. At Rachel's *Tomb.* 2

"When you go from me today, then you will find two men close to Rachel's tomb in the territory of Benjamin at Zelzah; and they will say to you, 'The donkeys which you went to look for have been found. Now behold, your father has ceased to be concerned about the donkeys and is anxious for you, saying, "What shall I do about my son?"' – He was right about the donkeys.

2. At the *Terebinth tree of Tabor.* 3-4

[3] "Then you will go on further from there, and you will come as far as the oak of Tabor, and there three men going up to God at Bethel will meet you, one carrying three young goats, another carrying three loaves of bread, and

another carrying a jug of wine; ⁴ and they will greet you and give you two loaves of bread, which you will accept from their hand – again this will happen as predicted.

3..At the *Top* of the hill of God. 5

"Afterward you will come to the hill of God where the Philistine garrison is; and it shall be as soon as you have come there to the city, that you will meet a group of prophets coming down from the high place with harp, tambourine, flute, and a lyre before them, and they will be prophesying – again this will happen just as predicted.

Trans: All of this is designed to give Saul peace about what Samuel had said. It is confirmation that this is God's will. Dr. Hugh Ross, "The probability of the events mentioned happening in the sequence and as Samuel predicted would be 1 in 8 million!

God will confirm His will with peace. Col. 3:15

Barclay notes, "Paul uses a vivid picture. "Let the peace of God be the decider of all things within your heart." Literally what he says is, "Let the peace of God be the umpire in your heart." He uses a verb from the athletic arena; it is the word that is used of the umpire who settled things in any matter of dispute. If the peace of Jesus Christ is the umpire in any man's heart, then, when feelings clash and we are pulled in two directions at the same time, the decision of Christ will keep us in the way...The way to right action is to appoint Jesus Christ as the arbiter between the conflicting emotions in our hearts; and if we accept his decisions, we cannot go wrong."

If we cannot find peace in what we are doing we better stop doing it! God's peace is like getting a green light to go ahead – of course this assumes that we are in fellowship with God. The flesh can urge us to do things that are wrong and violate Scripture. If you have peace about getting a divorce or taking a job as a beer taster or using your tithe to pay off bills you are being deceived!

Years ago, there was a Major League Baseball manager by the name of Leo "the Lip" Durocher. He picked up his nickname because he was always arguing with the umpires decisions. On more than one occasion, the umpire would grow weary of this onslaught and put Leo the Lip in his place—off the field and in the shower. His involvement in the game that day was finished. We are foolish to become "Leo the Lip" by constantly arguing with God's peace.

Con:

1. I know almost nothing about basketball, and when I am trying to find God's specific will in a situation, most of the time I know even less! Yet that's alright because I have a coach who steps in to keep me on track.

2. Peyton Manning has the best quarterback statistics in the history of the NFL. His younger brother Eli is also an elite NFL quarterback. Both brothers have spent the past few off-seasons going back to their old coach-Coach David Cutcliffe, called Coach Cut. He takes them back to their most basic quarterback fundamentals. Coach Cut was Peyton's quarterback coach at the University of Tennessee. They have stayed tight. Peyton said, "He's always been my coach."

Peyton Manning was released by the Indianapolis Colts in 2012, with a serious neck injury, and most thought his career was over. Enter coach Cut. After watching a tape of Peyton's throwing sessions, Coach Cut told him, "Your mechanics are all wrong, you're going to blow out your arm." Cut then spent the next two years taking the quarterback back to the basics. [Adapted from Howie Espenshied, "'Coach Cut' and the Deconstruction of Peyton and Eli," Mbird blog (9-26-14)]

We likewise have a coach in life – an all-powerful, all wise, all loving God who is always there taking us back to the basics – Jesus Christ!

Chapter Twelve

HOW TO BE FOUND BY GOD'S WILL – PART FOUR

1 Sam. 9-10

Intro:

1. I read about a Chinese man who has a small ministry making pop-up cards and giving them to people who need encouragement. People are eager to have him teach them how to make one. But making these cards is an art. This man, Chatani has written a book on how to make pop-up cards. His book makes the procedure look so simple; though, in fact, it is a very complicated task. A frequent criticism of his book is that there is not enough instruction to ensure success. One noted:

"The logic behind his book is to give just enough instruction so that first, the new card-maker will not despair and quit trying to make his first card perfect, and second, that he will learn more through exploring and making mistakes."

2. Sometimes the Bible is like that, we wish it would simply say, "Take this job" or "Buy that particular house." Etc. But God rarely spell out what He wants us to do but He gives us principles for guidance, leaving room for us to learn to walk by faith.

Trans: We have already looked at the principle of God's Providence, Precepts, Prayer, Promises, and Peace. 1 Sam. 10:6-26.

VI. SIXTH, LOOK TO GODS *PRESENCE.* 10:6-16

A. He alone can *Change* us. 6-13

1. The *Source.*

a. The Spirit. 6a

"Then the Spirit of the LORD... - *ruach* [rue-ah]. The basic idea of *rûach* is air in motion—"breath" or "wind."

- It is the major word for wind in the OT.
- It came to be used of enabling or empowering for action.
- It is also used to refer to invisible, powerful, supernatural beings—God, angels and evil spirits.
- Finally, it often refers to the inner person of humans, especially their deepest emotions, motivations and dispositions, the source of willpower.

Here it is the Spirit of Yahweh speaking of the Holy Spirit. The Holy Spirit is the key to everything in our lives! He is within every believer today and can lead us into God's will. The Holy Spirit is compared to the wind (Jn. 3:8). That's a good picture of the Spirit's leading:

- If you're in a sail boat and the wind is not blowing you just sit there – sometimes the Spirit of God is silent and we just need to patiently wait on Him;

- other times the wind is blowing hard in a certain direction – if the Holy Spirit is putting strong desires in us to do something we need to go along with Him;
- Many times the wind is just a breeze – we just keep on going slowly in the course He has place before us;
- the wind can change directions in an instant – then we need to change directions.

b. The *Strengthening*.

...will come upon you mightily... - the verb upon, *salah*, it has the idea of "to rush upon."

Then the Spirit of the LORD will rush upon you... 1 Samuel 10:6 (ESV)

Then the Spirit of the LORD will rush upon you with power... 1 Samuel 10:6 (NCV)

The Old Testament records many instances of the Spirit coming upon individuals to anoint them for special service, including:

- Moses (Num. 11:17),
- Joshua (Num. 27:18),
- the seventy elders of Israel (Num. 11:25),
- Gideon (Judg. 6:34),

- Jephthah (Judg. 11:29),
- Samson (Judg. 13:25),
- Saul (1 Sam. 10:1, 6),
- David (1 Sam. 16:13), Elijah (1 Kings 18:12; 2 Kings 2:16),
- Azariah (2 Chron. 15:1),
- Zechariah (2 Chron. 24:20),
- Ezekiel (Ezek. 2:1-2),
- and Micah (Mic. 3:8).

All those men, however, were limited in their ability to be empowered by the Spirit by their sinful, fallen human natures. But since Jesus was God in human flesh, God gave Him the Spirit without measure (John 3:34). We need to draw upon the power of the Holy Spirit, allow Him to control us and thus lead us into His will (2 Cor. 3:5-6).

On February 10, 2013, a fire broke out in an engine room of the Carnival cruise ship, Triumph. The fire knocked out the ship's power, leaving the vessel drifting in Gulf of Mexico currents. The more than 4,200 passengers and crew were left in limbo. The lost power made it impossible to operate the flush toilets, keep cool in the un-shaded waters of the deep sea, and preserve and cook all the perishable food on board. Passengers reported long lines for food, shortages of fresh water, illnesses, and widespread boredom. Many passengers slept in hallways or outside to escape the odors and heat below decks. CNN dubbed the Triumph "the cruise ship from hell."

Without the Holy Spirit we are powerless, just drifting though life without any real sense of purpose and meaning.

c. The *Speaking* of God's Word.

and you shall prophesy with them – naba [naw-baw], the Holy Spirit would enable Saul to declare the Word of the Lord with the prophets.

"The Scriptures teach that the prophets received their communications by the agency of the Spirit of God. When the seventy elders were appointed the Lord said to Moses, "I will take of the Spirit who is upon you, and will put Him upon them" (Numbers 11:17, 25). Samuel said to Saul, "Then the Spirit of the Lord will come upon you mightily, and you shall prophesy with them and be changed into another man" (1 Samuel 10:6)... According to Peter (2 Peter 1:21), "no prophecy was ever made by an act of human will, but men moved by the Holy Spirit spoke from God." [Unger Bible Dictionary]

Today the Holy Spirit illuminates God's written Word and gives us insight into its meaning. The Spirit working through God's Word is our main source of guidance.

George Mueller noted, "I will seek the will of the Spirit of God through, or in connection with, the Word of God. The Spirit and the Word must be combined. If I look to the Spirit alone without the Word, I lay myself open to great delusions also. If the Holy Ghost guides us at all, He will do it according to the Scriptures and never contrary to them."

d. The *Salvation?*

and be changed into another man – hapak [haw-fak] means to turn or overthrow. Here it is used in the positive sense of turning Saul into another man. It is used of turning the mourning into being joyful, the bad into the good. Cf. "I will turn their mourning into joy" (Jeremiah 31:13 and also Psalm 30:11. "He turned the curse of Balaam into a blessing" (Deut. 23:5 and Neh. 13:2).

Before you know it, the Spirit of GOD will come on you and you'll be prophesying right along with them. And you'll be transformed. You'll be a new person! 1 Samuel 10:6 (MSG)

Is this a reference to regeneration? 2 Cor. 5:21

I do not know…

One thing we can say, when we are exposed to God's Spirit and His Word we cannot help but be transformed, this transformation always gives us insight into God's will for our lives (Rom. 12:1-2).

David Seamands told of a huge man with his arm in a sling who had accepted Christ as his

Savior on the first night of a prison crusade in the South. He was one of the prison's tough guys. A few days later, he said:

"You know, something's happening to me. I don't really understand it and I sure can't explain it. I got up this morning and I didn't scream and holler like I usually do. Even my cellmates commented about it. The only way I can describe it is its like someone took the old tape that had been playing in my mind since I was a kid and put a new tape in and it's playing new talk and new music."

Salvation brings a transformation, a transformation that we need to feed by abiding in the Vine; by being filled and staying in His Word. I thought it was enlightening that the prisoner made this comment later:

"But you know, I've got to keep working on it and see to it that the right tapes are playing."

2. The *Signs*.

[7] *"It shall be when these signs come to you, do for yourself what the occasion requires…* - all of these things were confirmation that Saul was chosen by God to be king of Israel.

3. The *Secret*.

…for God is with you – this is everything! God with us!

[23] "BEHOLD, THE VIRGIN SHALL BE WITH CHILD AND SHALL BEAR A SON, AND THEY

SHALL CALL HIS NAME IMMANUEL," which translated means, "GOD WITH US." Matthew 1:23

God's presence is what leads us as we go through life (Psa. 23/Ex. 33:12-14).

His presence gives us rest, reminds me of something Sherri Yates shared:

"Seth, our curious 5-year-old, was with us during a recent communion service. He watched intently as I received the elements and bowed my head to pray. A few seconds later, I stole a peek at our unusually quiet son to see what he was up to. He was by then intently watching his daddy at prayer after taking communion. I was delighted that he was observing the solemnity of the occasion. "Good parental example," I thought. My gratification was short-lived as Seth leaned toward me and whispered: "What's in that stuff? You eat it and go right to sleep."

4. The *Sacrifices.*

[8] *"And you shall go down before me to Gilgal; and behold, I will come down to you to offer burnt offerings and sacrifice peace offerings –* the OT sacrifices should always remind us of the substitutionary death of Christ. Without that death the only place we would be led would be to hell! This is what gives us such superior assurance of God's favor, love, and continual guidance. They could only look forward to Christ coming, but we live in days

when He has already come! Why is this so important? Because of the fact that He died for all of our sin and failures, we can be assured of His love and acceptance even when we get out of His perfect will (Isa. 53:6/1 Pet. 3:18).

Mackintosh, "I must know, upon divine authority, that all my sins are put away forever out of God's sight…He has glorified Himself in the putting away of my sins, in a far higher and more wonderful manner than if He had sent me to an everlasting hell on account of them…I know I am a sinner – it may be the chief of sinners. I know my sins are more in number than the hairs of my head; that they are black as midnight – black as hell itself…I have not a word to say in excuse for a single sinful thought, to say nothing of a sin-stained life from the first to the last – yes, a life of deliberate, rebellious, high-handed sin…But – eternal hallelujahs to the God of all grace! Instead of sending us to hell because of our sins, He sent His Son to be the propitiation for those sins…[Since] God says to us, "Your sins and iniquities I will remember no more" what could we desire further as a basis for our conscience?...If they were not put away by the atoning death of Christ, they will never be put away. If He did not bear them on the cross, you will have to bear them in the tormenting flames of hell forever, and ever, and ever…But glory to God, His own testimony assures us that Christ has once suffered for sins…He brings us to God without spot or stain or charge. He brings us to God in all His own acceptableness. Is there any guilt on Him? No – it is gone – gone forever – cast as lead into the unfathomable waters of divine forgetfulness...The Christian reader is not to be satisfied with anything less than this...Don't [allow yourself to be driven back to the] bondage of Judaism – that system which God found fault with, and which He has forever abolished, because it did not give the worshipper perfect peace, perfect nearness to Himself, and that forever...[How often we place ourselves under] the Mosaic economy. It grieves the Holy Spirit, wounds the heart of Christ, dishonors the grace of God...If, therefore, we are not in the enjoyment of peace of conscience, it can only be because we are not resting on the finished work of Christ; and if the heart is not at ease, it proves that we are not satisfied with Christ Himself...In general, Christians are not a whit in advance of the condition of the OT saints. They do not know the blessedness of an accomplished redemption. They are not in the enjoyment of a purged conscience...They are, as to their experience, under law. They have never really entered into the deep blessedness of being under the reign of grace."

5. *Shown* what to do.

You shall wait seven days until I come to you and show you what you should do." [9] *Then it happened when he turned his back to leave Samuel, God changed his heart; and all those signs came about on that day* – as we rest in the sufficiency of the Lord Jesus Christ, the Holy Spirit through the Word of God will show us what we are supposed to do. And sometimes it is simply to wait! We are raising a society that simply refuses to wait for anything.

In 1960 McDonald's operated 200 restaurants. By 2012 they had 31,000 restaurants. In 2012 there were more than a quarter-million fast-food restaurants in America, and on any given day 1 in 4 Americans will eat at least one meal at a fast-food restaurant. For many people around the world fast-food symbolizes speed, efficiency, and convenience. Sanford DeVoe, a researcher at the University of Toronto, wanted to explore if our "fast-food culture" was changing our lives in ways beyond just our eating habits. So DeVoe and another colleague conducted a series of experiments in which researchers subliminally flashed corporate logos for McDonald's, KFC, Taco Bell, Burger King, Subway, and Wendy's.

A control group saw other images but no fast-food logos. When the two groups were asked to do an unrelated task, the fast-food group tried to complete it much faster than the non-fast-food group. In another experiment, flashes of fast-food images made students less able to sit back and enjoy music. A third experiment found that people exposed to fast-food logos showed a greater reluctance for saving. Based on these experiments, DeVoe has concluded that fast food helps us save time, but even just thinking about fast food restaurants make us live with more speed and less patience. DeVoe said:

"Fast food culture ... doesn't just change the way we eat but it can also fundamentally alter the way we experience our time."

This impatience spills over in relationship with God, we have almost no concept of waiting on the Lord.

6. The *Summation.*

10 When they came to the hill there, behold, a group of prophets met him; and the Spirit of God came upon him mightily, so that he prophesied among them

7. The *Saying.*

11 It came about, when all who knew him previously saw that he prophesied now with the prophets, that the people said to one another, "What has happened to the son of Kish? Is Saul also among the prophets?" 12 A man there said, "Now, who is their father?" Therefore it became a proverb: "Is Saul also among the prophets?" 13 When he had finished prophesying, he came to the high place – I see nothing to indicate that Saul was not a true believer in spite of his eventual rebellion. One thing for sure salvation gets people's attention.

John Newton, who wrote the beloved song "Amazing Grace," never took lightly the fact of his conversion. He said, "People stare at me and well they may. I am indeed a wonder to many, and a wonder to myself. Especially I wonder that I wonder no more."

B. He does not cause our personalities to *Cease.* 14-16

14 Now Saul's uncle said to him and his servant, "Where did you go?" And he said, "To look for the donkeys. When we saw that they could not be found, we went to Samuel." 15 Saul's uncle said, "Please tell me what Samuel said to you." 16 So Saul said to his uncle, "He told us plainly that the donkeys had been found." But he did not tell him about the matter of the kingdom which Samuel had mentioned –Saul continued to be shy and unassuming.

21 Then he brought the tribe of Benjamin near by its families, and the Matrite family was taken. And Saul the son of Kish was taken; but when they looked for him, he could not be found. 22 Therefore they inquired further of the LORD, "Has the man come here yet?" So the LORD said, "Behold, he is hiding himself by the baggage." – this was an asset! It was only later when he becomes filled with pride that things go badly. I had someone tell me the other day that I should stop demeaning myself. I told them the problem is not with people demeaning themselves but with a narcissistic generation that is self-absorbed.

VII. SEVENTH, UNDERSTAND GOD'S *PERFECT AND PERMISSIVE* WILL. 17-20, 23-26

¹⁷ Thereafter Samuel called the people together to the LORD at Mizpah; ¹⁸ and he said to the sons of Israel, "Thus says the LORD, the God of Israel, 'I brought Israel up from Egypt, and I delivered you from the hand of the Egyptians and from the power of all the kingdoms that were oppressing you.' ¹⁹ "But you have today rejected your God, who delivers you from all your calamities and your distresses; yet you have said, 'No, but set a king over us!' Now therefore, present yourselves before the LORD by your tribes and by your clans… ²³ So they ran and took him from there, and when he stood among the people, he was taller than any of the people from his shoulders upward. ²⁴ Samuel said to all the people, "Do you see him whom the LORD has chosen? Surely there is no one like him among all the people." So all the people shouted and said, "Long live the king!" ²⁵ Then Samuel told the people the ordinances of the kingdom, and wrote them in the book and placed it before the LORD. And Samuel sent all the people away, each one to his house. ²⁶ Saul also went to his house at Gibeah; and the valiant men whose hearts God had touched went with him – it was not God's perfect will for Israel to ask for a king with their motive or at this time, but God allowed.

Most people divide God's will into His Perfect will and His Permissive will. For example it was God's perfect will that David not commit adultery with Bathsheba, but obviously he allowed it. But the truth is the Bible never speaks of God's perfect verses His permissive will. I don't know, I do know we cannot make Him the author of sin.

Augustine, "Nothing, therefore, happens unless the Omnipotent will it to happen: He either permits it to happen or he brings it about Himself."

Philip Hughes, "Under God, however, all things are without exception fully controlled – despite all appearances to the contrary."

VIII. FINALLY, LOOK FOR SOME *PRESSURE.* 27

[27] But certain worthless men said, "How can this one deliver us?" And they despised him and did not bring him any present. But he kept silent – even when we do God's will, we can expect opposition.

Con:

1. God's will, will ultimately find us!

2. That does not eliminate our responsibility to look to His Providence; Precepts; Pray; claim His Promises; follow His peace or lack of it; consider His Presence; recognize His Permissive will; and expect some Pressure.

3. I hate traffic! If I am going to go somewhere I would rather take 30 minutes going through the back roads then get on the highway. One thing I don't like about the highway is the on and off ramps. When I am getting on, I know I am supposed to merge with the traffic but there are no hard and fast rules. Sometimes you have to slow down, other times you have to speed up. I want the cars to just stop and let me on the highway, but that is not how it works!

God's plan for us is always moving, always going on; He is like the main highway. We have to merge with Him, that is something that we have to learn to do.

Chapter Thirteen

COPING IN THE CRISIS OF LIFE

1 Sam. 11

Intro:

1. Spurgeon, "When a field is on fire people see sheets of flames shooting up into the sky, and in haste they flee before the devouring element. Yet they have one hope – in the distance is a lake of water. They reach it, they plunge into it, and they are safe."

2. We are going to experience the fiery trials of this life, but we are ultimately safe in Christ.

I. FIRST, THE *EMERGENCY.* 11:1-3

A. They were *Surrounded.*

Now Nahash the Ammonite came up and besieged Jabesh-gilead – they surround them.

About a month later Nahash the Ammonite and his army surrounded the city of Jabesh in Gilead... 1 Samuel 11:1 (NCV)

The dangers posed by Nahash ("snake"), an Ammonite, they were descendants of Abraham's nephew Lot (Gen. 19:30-38) and therefore related to the Jewish people. They were neighbors to their southeast. He surrounded Jabesh Gilead, a city about 25 miles south of the Sea of Galilee, east of the Jordan River, in the territory belonging to Gad, a city about fifty miles from Saul's home.

Trans: We are also surrounded by enemies! Satan, sinful people, a sin nature, the world system.

They surrounded me like bees; They were extinguished as a fire of thorns; In the name of the LORD I will surely cut them off.
Psalm 118:12

I remember once, as I was with my son, a bee stung him I threw an apple at an old doghouse and before we knew it there were bees everywhere!

Ruby Bridges is the true story of the 6-year-old black girl who became the first black person in the U.S., by federal law, to attend an all-white school in 1960 segregationist New Orleans, Louisiana. In one scene, as Ruby's mother kisses her good night, she says, "You know Momma's got to go back to work tomorrow. And Daddy's working. So do you think you can be a brave girl and go to school by yourself with the big men?" Ruby stops smiling and hesitates for a moment, clutching her doll closer. Finally she shrugs a shoulder and agrees, "Okay." Her mother tries to reassure her, saying, "You know Jesus faced the mob too, baby. Just like you. You know what he did? He prayed for them. Because the Bible says, 'Bless them that persecute you. Bless and curse not.'" The next day an angry crowd in front of the school waved Confederate flags and hollered, "Go on home!" Bravely, Ruby stepped out of the car with the four federal agents that surrounded her. One of them reminded her, "Ruby, remember what I told you. Keep looking straight ahead." As they walked through the crowd, one woman spit on the ground; another yelled that she was going to hang Ruby. Ruby's eyes were fixated on a point by the front door as she recalled her parents' words of encouragement: "You are Daddy's brave little girl. Remember, God loves you, Ruby."

B. They *Surrendered.*

...and all the men of Jabesh said to Nahash, "Make a covenant with us and we will serve you." – unfortunately they tried to cave in and

compromise. We are not to make peace with our enemies but stand firm in our separation.

Barnhouse said, "Some of you have just enough Christianity to be miserable in a nightclub, and not enough to be happy in a prayer meeting."

David H. Petraeus, the former director of the C.I.A. one of America's most-decorated four-star generals, resigned on Friday, November 10th after the F.B.I. discovered that he had been involved in an extramarital affair. President Obama accepted his resignation; it opens the door to security issues such as the possibility of blackmail. Compromise with our enemies opens the door for them to get a strong hold in our lives.

C. They were *Superscared.* 2

But Nahash the Ammonite said to them, "I will make it with you on this condition, that I will gouge out the right eye of every one of you, thus I will make it a reproach on all Israel." – compromise is always costly!

The gouging out of the right eye was designed to incapacitate the men of war and bring reproach and shame on the nation. [The Moody Bible Commentary]

There is also a spiritual blindness that takes place when we compromise. When we compromise we hinder our growth and that causes a blindness.

For he who lacks these *qualities* is blind *or* short-sighted, having forgotten *his* purification from his former sins. 2 Peter 1:9

Because you say, "I am rich, and have become wealthy, and have need of nothing," and you do not know that you are wretched and miserable and poor and blind and naked, Revelation 3:17

You have heard the expression, money doesn't grow on trees," I'm sure. Well, even if it did, many of us might not notice it. That's the conclusion from a team of researchers who were studying something called "inattentional blindness."

According to the study, inattentional blindness occurs when "people fail to become aware of objects unrelated to their current task," even when those objects are "interesting or surprising." Two researchers from Western Washington University clipped money on a tree and then observed the reaction of the passersby. The branch of the tree with the money was bent so that it hung over the path at head height. So the unwitting participants in the study practically bonked their heads on the tree money. Here are the results:

- overall, 396 people were observed walking down the path.

- Only 12 people failed to see and avoid the tree.

- but most people failed to see the money in the tree.

- And a whopping 94 percent of people on a cell phone were so distracted that they didn't spot the money.

The authors of the study ended the study with a rather obvious but important conclusion: "Becoming aware of an object is generally assumed to require focused attention."

When we compromise God's Word we have a similar response to God and spiritual things! We become blind to what is really important in life.

D. The sentence was *Suspended* for seven days. 3

The elders of Jabesh said to him, "Let us alone for seven days, that we may send messengers throughout the territory of Israel. Then, if there is no one to deliver us, we will come out to you." - Again instead of crying out to God they sought help from man (Jer. 17:5-8).

Trans: Israel was facing an Emergency, they are part of life. But not just Israel's life but ours as well. If you were ever affected by a natural disaster, in the middle of an emergency situation, or stranded in the wilderness, would you know what to do to survive?

- Would you know how to treat a snake bite while on a hike?

- If you were lost in the woods would know how to make a fire without matches or how to track and hunt wild animals for food?

- What would you do in case of a terrorist attack?

- Would you know how to escape or forage for food?

- How would you survive major disasters like floods, avalanches, hurricanes, tornadoes, earthquakes, and nuclear aftermaths?

Well, now there's an app to help you with all of these crucial questions. The *SAS Survival Guide* iPhone app takes the bestselling book by John "Lofty" Wiseman and puts it into digital form. Wiseman was a British soldier of the Special Air Service who wrote a best-selling book on SAS Survival. Truth is, the only real ultimate eternal *SAS Survival Guide* is the Savior's Abiding *Strength!*   Phil. 4:13

II. NEXT, THE *ENDURABILITY.* 11:4-13

A. First, we need the *Saint.*

1. The *Request* was *Shared*.

⁴ Then the messengers came to Gibeah of Saul and spoke these words in the hearing of the people... - God is our ultimate source but He usually works through people. When we go through difficult times, we need to share that with other believers.

The movie *Star Trek V: The Final Frontier* begins with this mysterious scene. A human-looking alien named J'onn is toiling beneath a blazing sun. Ragged and malnourished, he drills in vain for water. There are hundreds of holes in the earth around him. Suddenly, he hears the heavy pounding of hooves. A caped rider on horseback thunders ominously toward him. J'onn releases his drilling device, hurries toward his rifle, and raises his gun toward the fast approaching rider. The rider pulls up short and after a few moments of silence says, "I thought weapons were forbidden on this planet." Powerfully built, the rider swings down from the saddle. He continues, "Besides, I can't believe you'd kill me for a field of empty holes." Pathetically, J'onn replies, "It's all I have." He seems to sag under the exhausting weight of his burdens. The rider says, "Your pain runs deep," Sobbing, J'onn says, "What do you know of my pain?" The rider replies, "Let us explore it together." J'onn begins to tremble, and tears flood down his dirty cheeks. The rider continues, "Each man hides a secret pain. It must be exposed and reckoned with. It must be dragged from darkness and forced into the light. Share your pain. Share your pain with me, and gain strength from the sharing."

Bear one another's burdens, and thereby fulfill the law of Christ. Galatians 6:2

2. The Response was they *Prayed*.

and all the people lifted up their voices and wept. ⁵ Now behold, Saul was coming from the field behind the oxen, and he said, "What is the matter with the people that they weep?" So they related to him the words of the men of Jabesh – while we need each other we ultimately need God to intervene. We need both the Saints and Supplication in our crisis!

If ever Genelle Guzman McMillan needed to know she was being held in the strong arms of a God she couldn't see, it was now.

It was just after 12:30 p.m. on September 12, 2001. The towers had fallen 27 hours earlier. Amazingly, Genelle was still alive. Although the 30-year-old Port Authority clerk had fallen from the 64th floor of the North Tower of the World Trade Center, she had survived. But what were her chances of being rescued from the 10 stories of smoking rubble in which she was entombed. Her head was squeezed between chunks of concrete while her legs were sandwiched by pieces of a stairway. Because her right hand was pinned under her leg, only her left hand was free. With that free hand she reached in the darkness, hoping to find something to hold on to physically as well as emotionally. But Genelle could not grasp anything. In the depths of despair and smoking debris, she began to pray. She recalls:

"I kept my hand out there, praying to God, *Show me a sign. Show me a miracle. Show me that you're out there. Show me that you are listening to me.*"

Not long after, someone grabbed her hand. A man's voice identified himself as Paul. Although Genelle tried to open her eyes, she could not. Paul reassured her that she would be fine. He encouraged her to hold on to his hand. According to a newspaper account, "She grabbed his hand. She remembers he was not wearing gloves unlike the firefighter who found her. She also remembers he grabbed her hand with two hands.

She says, "He was holding my hand for a long time, and then other workers came and pulled me out." Genelle Guzman McMillan was the last person pulled alive from the collapsed towers. But she is not the last person to experience being held by God when there seemed to be no hope of survival (Psa. 73:21-23/Isa.41:10-13).

B. Furthermore we need the *Spirit* of God. 6-13

We must keep in mind that without the Spirit of God we cannot even pray to begin with! Rom. 8:26

1. The *Source.* 6a

Then the Spirit of God came upon Saul mightily when he heard these words... - we have seen this before! Ac. 1:8

If you get off at the Johnson Exit when heading for Fayetteville, there is the *James at the Mill*, it is a big round wheel that goes around and around. As long as the water is flowing it's moving. God's Spirit is a river of living water that is always flowing with power and wisdom. All we have to do is go with the flow!

2. The *Sequence.* 6b-13

a. Righteous *Indignation.* 6b

…and he became very angry – this is a godly anger (Jn. 2:14-16/Eph. 4:26).

Once Jack Hyles' child was assigned to read a book at school with foul language in it. He went to the Principle and said, "My son is not going to read that book!" The Principle said, "All right but I don't understand, there are worse words on the bathroom walls?" Jack snapped back, "Yes, and when that becomes required reading, I'll be back!"

b. Righteous *Inclination.* 7

- The Solicitation.

⁷ He took a yoke of oxen and cut them in pieces, and sent them throughout the territory of Israel by the hand of messengers, saying, "Whoever does not come out after Saul and after Samuel, so shall it be done to his oxen." - This anger led Saul to cut a pair of oxen—valuable agricultural animals—into pieces and to send the pieces throughout the borders of

Israel to call the Lord's army together. Saul promised the same fate for the oxen of those who refused to come and follow Saul and Samuel (v. 7). A similar act was performed by a Levite in the book of Judges (Judg. 19:29).

- The Reaction.

Then the dread of the LORD fell on the people, and they came out as one man – this got people's attention.

c. Righteous *Instructions.* 8-11

- *An Assessment. 8*

He numbered them in Bezek; and the sons of Israel were 300,000, and the men of Judah 30,000.

- *An Assurance. 9-10*

⁹ They said to the messengers who had come, "Thus you shall say to the men of Jabesh-gilead, 'Tomorrow, by the time the sun is hot, you will have deliverance.'" So the messengers went and told the men of Jabesh; and they were glad. ¹⁰ Then the men of Jabesh said, "Tomorrow we will come out to you, and you may do to us whatever seems good to you."

- Assignments. 11

The next morning Saul put the people in three companies; and they came into the midst of the camp at the morning watch and struck down the Ammonites until the heat of the day. Those who survived were scattered, so that no two of them were left together – everybody had their assigned place.

Trans: We find our instructions, as we let God's Spirit work through God's Word. We are in a war, and we need to learn to hear and respond to God speaking to us through His Word.

The movie *War Horse* weaves the story of a special bond between a boy and his horse. The film begins in 1912 when a teenager named Albert witnesses the birth of a thoroughbred on a farm in Devon, England. As the foal grows, Albert is touched by the special tie the young horse has with its mother. Then, much to his delight, Albert's father buys the thoroughbred at an auction and Albert vows to train the colt to do all that a workhorse could accomplish. He names the horse Joey and then spends a great deal of time transforming the animal into a useful asset for his family farm. In the midst of training Joey, Albert creates a special bond with the beast. The unique relationship is represented by a distinctive whistle. Whenever Albert cups his hands and blows through his fingers (creating the sound of an owl), Joey comes to his master. When World War I breaks out, Joey is sold to the British army to become one of 8 million horses employed in the war effort. Albert also enlists but has no idea where his beloved horse is. They are separated by hundreds of miles. As the war draws to a close, a group of soldiers discover Joey brutally tangled in barbed wire. After the soldiers untangle Joey and bring him to a British encampment, a military doctor determines Joey's wounds are so bad that he should be put down. As a sergeant raises his pistol and takes aims at Joey's head, a commotion is heard among the troops. Albert, with bandaged eyes from an explosion, hears his fellow soldiers talking about a horse. He wonders if it is possible that this war horse could possibly be his horse. Cupping his hands to his mouth, Albert begins his special whistle. Immediately, Joey's ears perk up and his head turns toward his master. With the recognition of the whistle, Albert is able to save Joey's life.

d. Righteous *Intervention.* 12-13

- The Request. 12

Then the people said to Samuel, "Who is he that said, 'Shall Saul reign over us?' Bring the men, that we may put them to death." – this goes back to 10:27

- *The Restraint. 13a*

But Saul said, "Not a man shall be put to death this day… - when the Holy Spirit is in control hate will be replaced with loving forgiveness.

- The *Right* response.

for today the LORD has accomplished deliverance in Israel." – not Saul who gave them deliverance but the Lord! We should always give God all the glory and credit because without Him there would be no deliverance! 1 Cor. 15:57

Ramon Piaguaje, a Secoya Indian born and raised in the rain forest of Ecuador, won the Winsor & Newton Millennium Art Competition, the largest painting competition in the world. His painting "Eternal Amazon" was selected from over 22,000 entries by professionals and amateur artists from 51 countries and was on display at the United Nations this past summer.

Ramon, who started drawing as a teenager over 30 years ago, was not introduced to oil painting until 1993 in Quito. The young man who has captured the attention of the art world was first encouraged in his efforts by Orville and Mary Johnson, Wycliffe Bible Translators working in his village. Since then, Ramon has met the Prince of Wales and the secretary general of the United Nations, and "Eternal Amazon" has been viewed by ambassadors, artists, dignitaries, and members of the press and public from around the world. Ramon is quick to give the Lord credit for the acclaim he has received. He said,

"I can't take pride of the gift that I have as an artist, for it is God that has given me this talent, and I want to use it for his glory."

III. FINALLY, THE *ECSTASY.* 14-15

A. Remembering. 14a

Then Samuel said to the people, "Come and let us go to Gilgal – Gilgal was like Ebenezer, a place of remembering what the Lord had done for them. It was there that Joshua had set up the 12 stones of remembrance.

B. *Renewing*. 14b

and renew the kingdom there – of Saul as their king.

C. *Rejoicing.* 15

¹⁵ *So all the people went to Gilgal, and there they made Saul king before the LORD in Gilgal. There they also offered sacrifices of peace offerings before the LORD; and there Saul and all the men of Israel rejoiced greatly* – a time of great celebration.

Trans: If we would endure our emergencies God's way we would also experience great joy. Part of the joy is knowing that we are in the process of becoming what we already are.

George MacDonald tells of a woman who cried out, "I wish I'd never been made!" He replied, "My dear, you're not made yet, you're being made – and this is the Maker's process!"

Con:

1. How to Cope in a Crisis? Basically we need two things – God's Spirit and the Saints.

2. The safe place when the fiery trial hits is just where we are – in Christ. Now our only need is to abide in Christ. Jn. 15

3. On Oct. 27, 1993, a series of fires hit parts of southern California. One area hit especially hard was Laguna Hills. The fire jumped from roof top to roof top, being fueled by the cedar shingles. But there was one exception, one house stood, the builder had constructed his roof with concrete and tile. Newspapers across the country showed the dramatic photo of that one house standing. Christ is our Rock!

Chapter Fourteen

A GODLY GOOD-BYE FROM GOD'S MAN SAMUEL

1 Sam. 12

Intro:

1. Samuel Brooks was president of Baylor University from 1902 until his death in 1931. His farewell message to the class of 1931 was in part:

"I stand on the border of mortal life but I face eternal life I look backward to the years of the past to see all pettiness...shrink into nothing and disappear. Adverse criticism has no meaning now, only the worthwhile things, the constructive things done for the glory of God count now. There is beauty, there is joy, and there is laughter in life – as there ought to be, but remember, my students, not to regard lightly, nor to ridicule the sacred things, those worthwhile things. Hold them dear; cherish them, for they alone will sustain you in the end."

2. In our passage another Samuel, is giving his farewell speech, saying the same thing – take God seriously and you will never be disappointed when you come to the end of your life.

I. FIRST, SAMUEL'S *TESTIMONY*. 12:1-5, 23

A. For starters, he has not been *Insubordinate*. 1-2a

¹ Then Samuel said to all Israel, "Behold, I have listened to your voice in all that you said to me and I have appointed a king over you. ² "Now, here is the king walking before you, but I am old and gray, and behold my sons are with you…- it is one thing to submit to God when you want to, but real obedience is demonstrated when we obey when we disagree with the Lord!

Samuel did not want to give Israel a king but he knew it was from the Lord (8:22).

Years ago there was a preacher named Tau*ler* who tells of meeting a *beggar*. He bid him, "May God give you a good day." The beggar replied, "I thank God that I have never had a bad one." Tau*ler* said, "Well, may you have a happy life my friend." Beggar replied, "I have never really been unhappy." Tau*ler* asked for an explanation, and the beggar said:

"Well, when the weather is good, I thank God and when it pours down rain, I thank Him also. When I have plenty, I thank God and when I am hungry as well. Since God's will is my will, whatever pleases Him pleases me, why should I say I am unhappy when I am not?"

The preacher astonished at all of this asked, "Who are you?" The beggar said, "I am a king!" Tau*ler* asked, "And where is your kingdom?" To which he replied, "In my heart."

Samuel was like that, they rejected him and made Saul their king – but his king remained on the throne of his heart!

B. Furthermore, he was a man of *Integrity*. 2b-5

...And I have walked before you from my youth even to this day. ³ "Here I am; bear witness against me before the LORD and His anointed. Whose ox have I taken, or whose donkey have I taken, or whom have I defrauded? Whom have I oppressed, or from whose hand have I taken a bribe to blind my eyes with it? I will restore it to you." ⁴ They said, "You have not defrauded us or oppressed us or taken anything from any man's hand." ⁵ He said to them, "The LORD is witness against you, and His anointed is witness this day that you have found nothing in my hand." And they said, "He

is witness." – it makes their choice to want a human king even more sinful. God had placed before them an honorable man of God!

George Sweeting a past president of Moody Bible Institute tells of a Trigo*nome*try professor who upon giving an exam would say:

"Today I am giving you two exams. The first is trig*onome*try; the second is honesty. I hope you can pass them both. However, if you are going to fail one, fail trig*onome*try. There are many good people in this world who have failed trigonometry but there are no good people in the world who have failed the test of honesty." Ac. 24:16/1 Tim. 1:19

What is involved in integrity?

- Our *Mind.* [Thoughts] 2 Cor. 10:5
- What comes out of our *Mouth* (Mat. 12:36).
- Our *Ministry*. [works] 2 Cor. 5:10
- Our *Motive* (Jer. 17:9-10).

C. Next, he *Interceded in their behalf.* 23a

23 *"Moreover, as for me, far be it from me that I should sin against the LORD by ceasing to pray for you* – since we are commanded to pray, praylessness is a sin!

I fear the church knows very little about real time consuming intercession these days.

Reminds me of something Tonya Singo shared, she said:

"One Wednesday night, I was teaching the third- through sixth-graders at my church about prayer...I asked the kids if anyone knew what *intercession* means. One boy said, "Yeah, that's when the other team catches the football."

D. Finally, he *Instructed* them. 23b

but I will instruct you in the good and right way – we do this today by sharing the Word of God. The basic trouble with both the church and the Nation is that we are neglecting the Word of God. But it is filled with wonderful and fascinating treasures. According to the huge online bookseller AbeBooks.com, they've found a host of strange and exciting objects in used books, including:

- forty $1,000 bills
- a Mickey Mantle rookie baseball card
- a marriage certificate from 1879
- a baby's tooth
- a diamond ring
- social security cards
- credit card receipts, shopping lists, business cards, postcards a World War II

US ration book (with stamps remaining), etc.

Adam Tobin, owner of Unnameable Books in Brooklyn, New York, has created a display inside his bookstore dedicated to objects discovered in books. Tobin said,

It's a motley assortment. We've been doing it for about two years since opening the store. The display quickly took over the back wall and now it's spreading to other places, and there's a backlog of stuff that we haven't put up yet. There are postcards, shopping lists, and concert tickets but my favorites are the cryptic notes. They are often deeply personal and can be very moving. The Bible is like that, it is full of amazing and delightful discoveries.

Notice how Prayer and Proclamation of God's Word go together? Ac 6:4/Jn. 15:7/Eph. 6:17-18

Kent Hughes, "What experience God so far has given me in preaching and praying, has brought a conviction. Should I write a book on essentials for preaching, I know now that I would devote at least a third of it to spiritual preparation in matters such as prayer. This would be the first third."

Charles Finney, "Without this prayer you are weak, as weakness itself. If you lose your spirit of prayer, you will do nothing, or next to nothing, though you had the intellectual endowment of an angel. The blessed Lord deliver and preserve His dead church from the guidance and influence of men who know not what it is to pray."

Thomas Armitage, "A sermon steeped in prayer on the study floor, like Gideon's fleece saturated with dew, will not lose its moisture between that and the pulpit. The first step towards doing anything in the pulpit must be to kiss the feet of the Crucified, as a worshipper, in the study."

Whitesell, "The preacher must be a man of prayer. He should pray for his messages, soak them in prayer, pray as he goes into the pulpit, pray as he preaches insofar as that is possible, and follow up his sermons with prayer."

Paxson, "If we should do much for God, we must ask much from God...I cannot insist on this too much. Prayer is the first thing, the second thing, and the third ting necessary for a minister, especially in seasons of revival. Pray then my dear brother – pray, pray, pray!"

Trans: Samuel had a wonderful Testimony! And how did Israel respond? They fired him!

The website *Business Insider* ran an article titled "7 Brutally Honest Job Rejection Letters." Here are two examples of how *not* to confront someone. Sub Pop, an independent record label in Seattle, sent the following rejection letter:

Dear Loser, Thank you for sending your demo materials to Sun Pop for consideration. Presently, your demo package is one of a massive quantity of material we receive everyday at Sub Pop World Headquarters. [Your material] is on its way through the great lower intestines that is the talent acquisitions process. We appreciate your interest and wish the best in your pursuit. Kind regards. P.S. This letter is known as a "rejection letter."

New Delta Review, a literary magazine in Baton Rouge, sent the following rejection letter:

Thank you for submitting. Unfortunately, the work you sent is quite terrible. Please forgive the form rejection, but it would take too much of my time to tell you exactly how terrible it was. So again, sorry for the form letter.

Israel wasn't quite that brutal but in spite of Samuel's perfect resume and ministry to them they rejected him. And before we leave this planet we will be rejected many times as well – regardless of how hard we try to minister to people.

II. NEXT, WE HAVE ISRAEL'S *HISTORY.* 12:6-18

A. The *Cycle*: one of persistent disobedience.

⁶ *Then Samuel said to the people, "It is the LORD who appointed Moses and Aaron and who brought your fathers up from the land of*

*Egypt. ⁷ "So now, take your stand, that I may plead with you before the LORD concerning all the righteous acts of the LORD which He did for you and your fathers. ⁸ "When Jacob went into Egypt and your fathers cried out to the LORD, then the LORD sent Moses and Aaron who brought your fathers out of Egypt and settled them in this place. ⁹ **"But they forgot the LORD** their God, so He sold them into the hand of Sisera, captain of the army of Hazor, and into the hand of the Philistines and into the hand of the king of Moab, and they fought against them. ¹⁰ "They cried out to the LORD and said, 'We **have sinned because we have forsaken the LORD** and have **served the Baals and the Ashtaroth**; but now deliver us from the hands of our enemies, and we will serve You.' ¹¹ "Then the LORD sent Jerubbaal and Bedan and Jephthah and Samuel, and delivered you from the hands of your enemies all around, so that you lived in security. ¹²*

 *"When you saw that Nahash the king of the sons of Ammon came against you, you said to me, 'No, but **a king shall reign over us,' although the LORD your God was your king**.* – Israel's history is characterized by sinful disobedience. One of the most common phrases used to describe Israel was that of being stiff-necked! Before we stick our chest out too far, we also have a history of rebellion! We have all spent far too much time in Rom. 7! We have to face the facts – we have an old sin nature and we must die to self and let the Holy Spirit work through our new nature – but we

do not do that by denying that the sin nature exists.

Fantastic Mr. Fox is a 2009 American animated comedy film based on the children's novel of the same name. This story is about crafty Mr. Fox, who steals food from farmers. While raiding a farm one day, Mr. Fox and his wife Felicity trigger a trap and become caged. Felicity tells Fox that she is pregnant, and she pleads with him to find a safer job once they escape. Fox becomes a newspaper columnist and moves his family into a big home at the base of a tree.

But two years (or 12 "Fox years") after promising Felicity that he would quit stealing, Fox returns to his old ways. Every night, he sneaks out to steal from local farmers. The farmers eventually get fed up with Mr. Fox's thieving ways, so they dig their way into the Foxes' home. Fox and his family huddle underground with nowhere to go. One night, Felicity tells Fox:

"Twelve fox years ago, you made a promise to me, while we we're caged inside that fox trap, that if we survived, you would never steal another chicken, turkey, goose, duck, or a squab, whatever they are, and I believed you. Why did you lie to me?" Fox replies, "Because I'm a wild animal." His wife counters, "But you are also a husband and a father!" Mr. Fox says, "I'm just trying to tell you the truth about myself."

There is a lot of truth there! We need to realize the truth that we do have a sin nature – but we also need to acknowledge we are also united with Christ and thus have a new nature, are indwelt by the Holy Spirit and do not have to be a slave to sin.

B. The *Simple*: decide to obey or suffer misery! 13-15

13 "Now therefore, here is the king whom you have chosen, whom you have asked for, and behold, the LORD has set a king over you. 14 "If you will fear the LORD and serve Him, and listen to His voice and not rebel against the command of the LORD, then both you and also the king who reigns over you will follow the LORD your God. 15 "If you will not listen to the voice of the LORD, but rebel against the command of the LORD, then the hand of the LORD will be against you, as it was against your fathers – We need to choose to listen to God because if we don't our disobedience will sooner or later cause an explosion!

Stuart Moffatt awoke on the Saturday before Easter, loaded up his wife and three kids in the family car, and headed to the annual Easter Egg Hunt in the British town of Holford, Somerset. About 25 children participated in the egg hunt in the field beside the busy road. As the hunt was drawing to an end, the parents began counting the gathered eggs to see if all had been found. Stuart looked out and noticed a three-year-old little boy had wandered out toward the road, and had apparently found another egg. Not recalling placing an egg that close to the road, Stuart walked out to the child, who was now standing on top of the egg. Impressed that the egg did not crack, Stuart walked up and noticed the egg was oddly shaped and textured. It wasn't until he knelt beside the little boy, still standing on top of the egg, that Stuart realized it was not an egg at all. It was a hand grenade. In fact, it was a live, fully-functional World War 2 grenade. Stuart picked the boy up off the grenade and backed away. A bomb disposal unit was called in, and destroyed the grenade in a controlled explosion.

Disobedience is a sin, and we're not talking about like that boy who ignorantly grabbed that grenade. We choose to sin, and are crazy to stand on it, when we can dispose of it by confessing and forsaking it – if not needless suffering and misery will become part of our lives.

C. The Divine *Approval*: of Samuel. 16-18

16 "Even now, take your stand and see this great thing which the LORD will do before your eyes. 17 "Is it not the wheat harvest today? I will call to the LORD, that He may send thunder and rain. Then you will know and see that your wickedness is great which you have done in the sight of the LORD by asking for yourselves a king." 18 So Samuel called to the

LORD, and the LORD sent thunder and rain that day; and all the people greatly feared the LORD and Samuel – a confirmation not only of Samuel's farewell speech but of his entire life.

McGee noted, "Elijah was not the first man that could "preach up a storm" -- he brought in a thunderstorm, but Samuel did it before Elijah did. And this is God's seal, I think, upon Samuel's life. The thunder and rain were God's great "amen" on Samuel's career as God's spokesman."

This was not the season for thunder and rain – it would be something like me saying in July, if my message is true, God is going to send 2 feet of snow!

III. FINALLY, THE LORD'S *MERCY.* 19-25

A. First, *Realize* we don't come *Faultlessly.* 19

Then all the people said to Samuel, "Pray for your servants to the LORD your God, so that we may not die, for we have added to all our sins this evil by asking for ourselves a king." – we have all sinned! Everyone of us still needs to apply 1 Jn. 1:9 to our lives.

Thomas Kempis was an Augustinian monk who served Christ for more than 90 years. He wrote:

"We cannot trust much to ourselves. There is but little in us, and that which we have we quickly lose by our negligence. Oftentimes too, we do not perceive our own inward blindness, how great it is. We reprehend small things in others, and pass over greater matters in ourselves. We quickly feel and weigh what we suffer at the hands of others; but we mind not, what others suffer from us. He that will rightly consider his own works will find little cause to judge hardly of another."

B. Furthermore, *Return* in spite of your *Folly*. 20

[20] *Samuel said to the people, "Do not fear. You have committed all this evil, yet do not turn aside from following the LORD, but serve the LORD with all your heart* – how many people quit serving God because of sin! The truth is if sin kept us from serving God, we would have never served God in the first place.

Spurgeon, "Thirst makes a person pant for water, and pain reminds man of the need of a physician. Let your needs likewise lead you to Jesus. Go, poor Christian, let your poverty be the rope that pulls you to your rich Brother. Rejoice that your weaknesses make room for grace to rest upon you, and be glad that you have constant needs that perpetually compel you to have fellowship with your Redeemer."

The principle is found in Jer. 18:1-10

If we get marred, we are still in His hands and He can make us another vessel that seems good to Him...

C. Third, *Resolve* to turn from *Futility.* 21

"You must not turn aside, for then you would go after futile things which can not profit or deliver, because they are futile –the futile things he is talking about is idols.

- If we don't trust the Lord we will trust in something else;

- If we don't trust in the Lord to take care of us we will trust in our money or jobs or friends;

- If we do not draw upon the Lord's wisdom then we will depend upon our own plans;

- If we do not appropriate the Lord's strength we will look to unreliable resources. Ultimately they will let us down!

D. Fourth, *Rely* upon God to act *Faithfully.* 22

"For the LORD will not abandon His people on account of His great name, because the LORD has been pleased to make you a people for Himself – Lam. 3:22-23/2 Tim. 2:13/Heb. 13:5-6.

Tozer, "Men become unfaithful out of desire, fear, weakness, loss of interest, or because of some strong influence from without. Obviously none of these forces can affect God in any way. He is His own reason for all He is and does. He cannot be compelled from without, but ever speaks and acts from within Himself by His own sovereign will, as it pleases Him."

And He has clearly promised that it pleases Him never to forsake one of His own...

E. Fifth, *Respond Fearfully.* 24a

"Only fear the LORD and serve Him in truth with all your heart – fear means to reverently trust the Lord. Prov. 3:5-6

F. Sixth, *Remember* Him *Fondly.* 24b

...for consider what great things He has done for you – we can all give a hearty amen to that!

G. Finally, *Repent* lest we enter *Foreign Captivity.* 25

"But if you still do wickedly, both you and your king will be swept away." – talking about Israel being swept away into captivity by foreign nations. Wiersbe notes, "Samuel may have been referring especially to the warning given by Moses in Deut. 28:36, written into the covenant centuries before Israel had a king:

"The Lord will drive you and the king you set over you to a nation unknown to you or your fathers" (niv).

Unfortunately, Israel did disobey the terms of the covenant and God had to send them in exile to Babylon."

Con:

1. Samuel gives us a Godly Good-bye.

2. In essence he was encouraging them to go with God and thus turn from self and idolatry.

3. The origin of our English word "good-bye" comes from the phrase "God be with you." Unfortunately the meaning of the term has become lost in our day. We should revive its true meaning – good-bye should be a sincere wish that God be with us – the alternative is not what any of us need or want.

Chapter Fifteen

THE DANGER OF DISHONEST DISOBEDIENCE

1 Sam. 13:1-15

Intro:

1. Attorney A.M. "Marty" Stroud III, of Shreveport, Louisiana was the lead prosecutor in the December 1984 first-degree murder trial of Glenn Ford, who was sentenced to death for the death of a Shreveport jeweler. Ford was released from prison March 11, 2014, after the state admitted new evidence proving Ford was not the killer. A year later (March 2015), Stroud wrote a brutally honest apology for *The Shreveport Times*.

In 1984, I was 33 years old. I was arrogant, judgmental, narcissistic and very full of myself. I was not as interested in justice as I was in winning. To borrow a phrase from Al Pacino in the movie "And Justice for All," "Winning became everything." ... [As a result], Mr. Ford spent 30 years of his life in a small, dingy cell .... Lighting was poor, heating and cooling were almost non-existent, food bordered on the uneatable. After the death verdict [was handed down], I went out with others and celebrated with a few rounds of drinks. That's sick. I had been entrusted with the duty to seek the death of a fellow human being, a very solemn task that certainly did not warrant any "celebration." In my rebuttal argument during the penalty phase of the trial, I mocked Mr. Ford, stating that this man wanted to stay alive so he could be given the opportunity to prove his innocence. ... How totally wrong I was....I apologize to Glenn Ford for all the misery I have caused him and his family. I apologize to the [victim's family] for giving them the false hope of some closure. I apologize to the members of the jury for not having all of the story that should have been disclosed to them. I apologize to the court in not having been more diligent in my duty ..."

2. There is an indispensable requirement for a man or woman to be used by God – brutal honesty! The basic problem of king Saul was not his iniquity but his deceptive dishonesty.

I. FIRST, THE *REVELATION.* 10:8

"And you shall go down before me to Gilgal; and behold, I will come down to you to offer burnt offerings and sacrifice peace offerings. You shall wait seven days until I come to you and show you what you should do." – the prophet Samuel was clear as to what Saul was supposed to do. He was to *wait* at Gilgal until Samuel came. We have become an impatient generation that has no concept of waiting on anything - let alone God!

An article in *The Boston Globe* claims that our "demand for instant results is seeping into every corner of our lives." The need for instant gratification is not new, but our expectation of "instant" has become faster. The article states:

Retailers are jumping into same-day delivery services. Smartphone apps eliminate the wait for a cab, a date, or a table at a hot restaurant. Movies and TV shows begin streaming in seconds. But experts caution that instant gratification comes at a price: It's making us less patient...Christopher Muther noted:

We've come to expect things so quickly that researchers found people can't wait more than a few seconds for a video to load. One researcher examined the viewing habits of 6.7 million internet users. How long were subjects willing to be patient? Two seconds. After that they started abandoning the site. After five seconds, the abandonment rate is 25 percent. When you get to 10 seconds, half are gone."

The results offer a glimpse into the future. As Internet speeds increase, people will be even less willing to wait for that cute puppy video. The researcher, who spent years developing the study, worries someday people will be too impatient to conduct studies on patience.

Impatience and a refusal to wait on God is sin.

II. NEXT, SAUL'S *REIGN.* 13:1

Saul was thirty years old when he began to reign, and he reigned forty two years over Israel – we may not be patient with the Lord but He is certainly patient with us! He put up with Saul for some 40 years!

Note: First Samuel as preserved in the Masoretic or Received Text has lost the number that must have been included in the original manuscript. The Revised translation translates it literally:

Saul was...years old when he began to reign; and he reigned... and two years over Israel. 1 Samuel 13:1 (NRSV)

"Then they asked for a king, and God gave them Saul the son of Kish, a man of the tribe of Benjamin, for forty years." Acts 13:21

Since we tend to make God in our own image we usually view God as being impatient with us – but that is not true. While 2 Pet. 3:9 is usually applied to the lost, Peter is writing to the saved not the lost!

The Lord is not slow about His promise, as some count slowness, but is patient toward **you**, not wishing for any to perish but for all to come to repentance. 2 Peter 3:9

⁹ The Lord does not delay *and* is not tardy *or* slow about what He promises, according to some people's conception of slowness, but He is long-suffering (extraordinarily patient) toward you, not desiring that any should perish, but that all should turn to repentance. 2 Peter 3:9 (AMP)

Our impatience does not negate God's patience (Ex. 34:6/Neh.9:16-17/Psa.86:14-15).

Packer gives some good advice, "Think how he has borne with you, and still bears with you, when so much in your life is unworthy of him and you have so richly deserved his rejection. Learn to marvel at his patience, and seek grace to imitate it in your dealings with others; and try not to try his patience any more."

III. THIRD SAUL'S *REGIMENT.* 2

Now Saul chose for himself 3,000 men of Israel, of which 2,000 were with Saul in Michmash and in the hill country of Bethel, while 1,000 were with Jonathan at Gibeah of Benjamin. But he sent away the rest of the people, each to his tent - Having learned from his recent experience with the Ammonites, Saul set about to create a standing army of 3,000 trained troops—2,000 under his direct control and 1,000 under his son Jonathan.

These he stationed at Micmash and Gibeah respectively, in order to avert Philistine attacks.

IV. FOURTH, SAUL'S SON'S *REPOSSESSION* OF THEIR LAND. 3a

Jonathan smote the garrison of the Philistines that was in Geba, and the Philistines heard of it – Geba was a Levitical town (Josh. 18:24). Originally allotted to the tribe of Benjamin. This was land that God had given to them so Jonathan was taking back what rightfully belonged to Israel.

V. FIFTH, SAUL'S *REACTION*. 3b-4

Then Saul blew the trumpet throughout the land, saying, "Let the Hebrews hear." 4 All Israel heard the news that Saul had smitten the garrison of the Philistines, and also that Israel had become odious to the Philistines. The people were then summoned to Saul at Gilgal – notice his dishonesty. It was Jonathan, not Saul, that smote the Philistines.

Application Bible, "Saul's growing pride started out small—taking credit for a battle that was won by his son. Left unchecked, his pride grew into an ugly obsession; thus, it destroyed him, tore his family apart, and threatened the well-being of the nation. Taking credit for the accomplishments of others indicates that pride is controlling your life."

Mattoones, "Saul gets the credit for what Jonathan accomplished. Pride begins to surface in Saul's life. Getting the glory was important to Saul and it becomes a snare to him. Later, Saul will become enraged with David when the women sing, "Saul has slain his thousands and David his ten thousands!" His anger will motivate him to try to kill David."

Pride *goes* before destruction, And a haughty spirit before stumbling. Proverbs 16:18

A military expert was scheduled to deliver a speech in St. Louis Missouri. But he was bumped" from the plane in Washington D.C. on his way to Missouri. The one who "bumped" him was a General, who later realized that he had bumped his main speaker! If we are not careful we can bump the glory of God by taking credit for what He had done.

VI. SIXTH, THE *RETALIATION.* 5

Now the Philistines assembled to fight with Israel, 30,000 chariots and 6,000 horsemen, and people like the sand which is on the seashore in abundance; and they came up and camped in Michmash, east of Beth-aven – it become abundantly clear that Saul is vastly outnumbered.

But one with God is a majority! Clearly Jonathan understood that, "Then Jonathan said to the young man who was carrying his armor, "Come and let us cross over to the garrison of these uncircumcised; perhaps the LORD will work for us, for the LORD is not restrained to save by many or by few." 1 Samuel 14:6

Gideon found this out, "⁴ Then the LORD said to Gideon, "The people are still too many; bring them down to the water and I will test them for you there. Therefore it shall be that he of whom I say to you, 'This one shall go with you,' he shall go with you; but everyone of whom I say to you, 'This one shall not go with you,' he shall not go." ⁵ So he brought the people down to the water. And the LORD said to Gideon, "You shall separate everyone who laps the water with his tongue as a dog laps, as well as everyone who kneels to drink." ⁶ Now the number of those who lapped, putting their hand to their mouth, was 300 men; but all the rest of the people kneeled to drink water. ⁷ The LORD said to Gideon, "I will deliver you with the 300 men who lapped and will give the Midianites into your hands; so let all the *other* people go, each man to his home." Judges 7:4-7

¹¹ Then Asa called to the LORD his God and said, "LORD, there is no one besides You to help *in the battle* between the powerful and those who have no strength; so help us, O LORD our God, for we trust in You, and in Your name have come against this multitude. O LORD, You are our God; let not man prevail against You." 2 Chronicles 14:11

What then shall we say to these things? If God *is* for us, who *is* against us? Romans 8:31

John Oxenham wrote, "Thanks be to God for a life full-packed with things that matter crying to be done--a life, thank God, of never-ending strife against the odds. ... Just enough time to do one's best, and then pass on, leaving the rest to Him."

VII. SEVENTH, THE *REDUCTION*. 6-7

A. The *Distress*. V. 6

When the men of Israel saw that they were in a strait (for the people were hard-pressed), then the people hid themselves in caves, in thickets, in cliffs, in cellars, and in pits – it was a, feet don't fail me now, moment!

B. The *Desertion*. 7a

⁷ Also some of the Hebrews crossed the Jordan into the land of Gad and Gilead – they went AWOL!

C. The *Dread*. 7b

But as for Saul, he was still in Gilgal, and all the people followed him trembling – they panicked and were terrified. Let's face it we have all, at one time or another, allowed fear to make cowards of us! We need to take Josh. 1:8-9 to heart. Fear is often due to a overconfidence in ourselves. Perhaps Israel was placing their confidence in king Saul instead of King Yahweh!

On July 21, 1861, raw Union recruits marched toward the Confederate Army camping at Bull

Run, 30 miles southwest of Washington. These Union soldiers were overconfident and acted like they were headed toward a sporting event. Congressmen, ladies, and all sorts of spectators trailed along with lunch baskets to observe the fun. But the courage of the Confederates and the arrival of Confederate reinforcements threw the Union forces into a panic even though the Union had superior forces! One observer wrote:

"We called to them, tried to tell them there was no danger, called them to stop, implored them to stand. We called them cowards, denounced them in the most offensive terms but all in vain; a cruel crazy, mad hopeless panic possessed them."

Fear can overwhelm us especially if we get our eyes off the Lord. But we can ignore our feelings and by faith place our trust in the Lord. Prov. 3:5-6

Frederick Buechner was parked by the roadside, depressed and afraid because of a problem that he was facing. About that time a car drove by with a license place that had in capital letters: T.R.U.S.T. The owner of the car was a trust officer in a bank, but God used that plate to encourage Frederick and renew his trust in the Lord. Isa. 41:10

III. EIGHTH, THE *REBELLION.* 8-10

A. The *Delay.* 8

Now he waited seven days, according to the appointed time set by Samuel, but Samuel did not come to Gilgal; and the people were scattering from him – God often delays to teach us who is in control.

In the daily devotional book Streams in the Desert, on January 26, said:

"The Bible has a great deal to say about waiting for God, and the teaching cannot be too strongly emphasized. We so easily become impatient with God's delays. Yet much of our trouble in life is the result of our restless, and sometimes reckless, haste. We cannot wait for the fruit to ripen, but insist on picking it while it is still green. We cannot wait for the answers to our prayers, although it may take many years for the things we pray for to be prepared for us. We are encouraged to walk with God, but often God walks very slowly."

B. The *Disobedience.* 9-10

⁹ So Saul said, "Bring to me the burnt offering and the peace offerings." And he offered the burnt offering. ¹⁰ As soon as he finished offering the burnt offering, behold, Samuel came; and Saul went out to meet him and to greet him – he was told to wait until Samuel arrived.

Trans: Disobedience is sin but it was not Saul's basic problem. This seems small compared to what king David did in committing adultery and murder. Yet he was restored.

IX. NINTH, THE *RATIONALIZATION*. 11-12

A. He blamed the *People*.

11 But Samuel said, "What have you done?" And Saul said, "Because I saw that the people were scattering from me... - it is easy to blame others for our sin.

B. He blamed the *Prophet*.

...and that you did not come within the appointed days - since Samuel was God's representative, to blame Samuel was the same as blaming the Lord.

C. He blamed the *Philistines*.

...and that the Philistines were assembling at Michmash 12 therefore I said, 'Now the Philistines will come down against me at Gilgal, and I have not asked the favor of the LORD.' So I forced myself and offered the burnt offering." – he blamed everybody but himself and therefore refused to confess his sin.

Trans: We likewise blame our sin nature or Satan or the government or family or friends for our sin. But we will never get right with God unless we take full responsibility for our sin.

Dietrich Bonheoffer, "In confession the light breaks into the darkness and seclusion of the heart. The sin must be brought into the light.

The unexpressed must be openly spoken and acknowledged. All that is secret and hidden must be made manifest. It is a hard struggle until the sin is openly admitted."

Paul Claudel, "The greatest sin is to lose the sense of sin...We see ourselves as basically nice, benevolent people with minor hang-ups and neuroses that are the common lot of humanity. We rationalize and minimize our terrifying capacity to make peace with evil and thereby reject all that is not nice about us...If we gloss over our selfishness and rationalize the evil within us, we only pretend we are sinners and therefore only pretend we have been forgiven."

X. TENTH, THE *REJECTION.* 13:13-14

A. The *Problem: Dishonest disobedience!*

Samuel said to Saul, "You have acted foolishly; you have not kept the commandment of the LORD your God, which He commanded you – there was neither obedience nor confession of disobedience. Unconfesssed sin is always a problem!

Rod Cooper, shared this:

After I graduated from Dallas Seminary, waiting on my first ministry, I went home to live with my mother. My mom gave me chores. She said, "One of your jobs is to take out the trash, Son." So every week I put out the garbage. One week I forgot to put out the garbage. Garbage has a way of making itself known. It began to smell. Every day we kept piling more garbage onto it. It even began to spill over, and it was right where you came into the back of the house. Every time we went into the house we would get a whiff of it. The aroma began to seep into the house and infected the atmosphere. Then it started to infect my mom's relationship with me. Every time she looked at me, it was as if she were saying, "Why don't you take out the garbage?" The next week, I took out the garbage. The atmosphere cleaned up. Our relationship was better. Everything was okay.

That is the way unconfessed sin works, it stinks and effects our fellowship with God and with one another.

B. The *Promise: Disavowed.*

...for now the LORD would have established your kingdom over Israel forever – some promises are conditional. [14] *"But now your kingdom shall not endure. The LORD has sought out for Himself a man after His own heart, and the LORD has appointed him as ruler over His people, because you have not kept what the LORD commanded you."* [15] *Then Samuel arose and went up from Gilgal to Gibeah of Benjamin. And Saul numbered the people who were present with him, about six hundred men* – some promises of God have conditions.

Holman OT commentary notes, "Saul's disobedience produced two consequences (13:14). First, God had intended to give Saul a dynasty, but now because of his sin his dynasty would not endure. Saul would be the last of his line to rule over Israel. Second, the Lord had already taken measures to seek out a man after his own heart. This individual would be appointed as leader of his people. The same word leader (Hb. nagid) used to describe Saul's position (9:16; 10:1) is used here. Clearly, Saul's leadership position was based on his faithful obedience."

- Some promises are conditional – God's manifested presence is conditioned on obedience (Jn. 14:21)….

- We have to submit to God before resisting the devil is effective (Ja. 4:7)…

- We have to pray according to God's will before we can have confidence of being heard (1 John 5:14-15)

These are just a few examples….

Trans: Nobody gets so big that they do not need to obey God! Neither Israel's king nor the president of the United States for that matter.

James VI of Scotland was known for his rudeness during the worship service. The king was once talking while Robert Bruce was preaching. So Robert stopped preaching and the king stopped talking; then Robert continued preaching and the king then started talking again. So Robert stopped preaching and the king stopped talking. The Robert said, "It is said, to have been an expression, of the wisest of kings – When the Lion roars, all the beasts of the field are quiet – the Lion of the tribe of Judah is now roaring in the voice of the gospel, and it becomes all the petty kings of the earth to be silent!" Saul seems to have forgotten that even the king of Israel is subject to the King of kings!

Con:

1. The Danger – not so much of Disobedience – but Dishonest Disobedience. We have all disobeyed God, but God promised that if we would Admit it; Quit it; and Forget it, we can confess and press (1 Jn. 1:9). If not – all we can expect is continued chastisement until we do.

2. Grover Cleveland was known to be brutally honest. During one of his campaign's for the presidency, the *Buffalo* newspaper reported that as a young bachelor Grover had had an adulterous relationship with Maria Halpin. His campaign manager came to him with the article and asked, "What are we going to do?" Grover replied, "We are going to tell the truth!" He was elected.

If walking with God required sinlessness none of us would make it – but if we will get honest with God by confessing sin and depending upon God we will sin less.

Chapter Sixteen

PRINCIPLES OF FAITH

1 Sam. 13:16-14:23

Intro:

1. Google has digitized 30 million unique books. According to author Christian Rudder:

"This body of data has created a new field of quantitative cultural studies called culturomics; its primary method is to track changes in word use through time. The long reach of the data (it goes back to 1800) allows an unusual look at people and what's important to them." For example, "'Ice cream' took off in the 1910s—right when GE introduced the powered home icebox," while the word 'pasta' nose dived in the late 1990s when the Atkins diet became popular. The study reveals what's deeply important to us. "The data shows that with each passing year, we're getting more wrapped up in the present." And what does it show for the word "God"? That word "has been in steady decline for decades and is now used only about a third as much in American writing as it was in the early 1800s."

2. Since the object of faith is God, a disappearance of God means the disappearance of Biblical faith, a mistrust of God or a trust in something other than God.

I. FIRST, FAITH IS NOT *INTIMIDATED* BY OBSTACLES. 16-23

A. The Philistine *Army.* Vv. 5, 16-18

16 Now Saul and his son Jonathan and the people who were present with them were staying in Geba of Benjamin while the Philistines camped at Michmash. 17 And the raiders came from the camp of the Philistines in three companies: one company turned toward Ophrah, to the land of Shual, 18 and another company turned toward Beth-horon, and another company turned toward the border which overlooks the valley of Zeboim toward the wilderness – The combined forces of Saul and Jonathan at Gibeah numbered only in the hundreds (14:2), while those of the Philistines at Micmash scarcely four miles to the northeast numbered in the thousands (v. 5). Philistine "raiding parties" (14:15) left camp in three detachments, a common military strategy in those days (11:11; Jdg 7:16; 9:43; 2Sa 18:2) since it provided more options and greater mobility. They headed off in three different directions:

- One group went toward Ophrah in Benjamin (cf. Jos 18:23),

- a second went toward (Upper) Beth Horon in Ephraim (cf. Jos 16:5),

- and the third went an undetermined distance eastward toward the Valley of Zeboim.

B. The Philistine *Armor*. 19-23

19 Now no blacksmith could be found in all the land of Israel, for the Philistines said, "Otherwise the Hebrews will make swords or spears." 20 So all Israel went down to the Philistines, each to sharpen his plowshare, his mattock, his axe, and his hoe. 21 The charge was two-thirds of a shekel for the plowshares, the mattocks, the forks, and the axes, and to fix the hoes. 22 So it came about on the day of battle that neither sword nor spear was found in the hands of any of the people who were with Saul and Jonathan, but they were found with Saul and his son Jonathan. 23 And the garrison of the Philistines went out to the pass of Michmash – The Philistines had been in such complete control for so long that they had removed every blacksmith from Israel. The Hebrews had to come to them to get their farm implements sharpened. Only a few men had swords. Things looked grim indeed.

Israel had bronze, which was a mixture of copper alloyed with tin. This was used to make military weapons such as spears, bows, and shields. But the Philistines had discovered the skill of iron weaponry. The skill of smelting, a process which separated iron from its mixes. Thus even if it had a smaller army, which it did not, it would have been superior to the Israelites.

Sort of like North Korea, they are feared because they had nuclear warheads. That gives them an advantage over larger nations that don't possess them.

Trans: Jonathan was a man of faith, and therefore was not intimidated by these obstacles, he knew the object of his faith was God Himself and no army is a match for God.

God is greater than our health problems, or lack of money, or boss, or Isis or whatever. The Philistines had iron but Israel had God!

C.S. Lewis, "In God you come up against something which is in every respect immeasurably superior to yourself. Unless you know God as that…you do not know God at all!"

Satan doesn't want us to see that he is a totally defeated foe, he tries to intimidate us into thinking that he is bigger than he really is.

In his book *Head Game*, author Tim Downs writes:

Psyops stands for Psychological Operations, a form of warfare as old as the art of war itself. An early example of this can be found in the battle strategies of Alexander the Great. On one occasion when his army was in full retreat from a larger army, he gave orders to his armorers to construct oversized breastplates and helmets that would fit men 7 or 8 feet tall. As his army would retreat, he would leave these items for the pursuing army to discover. When the enemy would find the oversized gear, they would be demoralized by the thought of fighting such giant soldiers, and they would abandon their pursuit. Satan likes to play head games with us, trying to make himself bigger or greater than he really is. And the quickest way to thwart our Enemy's psy-ops is to gaze upon the greatness of our God.

II. NEXT, FAITH IS NOT *INHERITED* BY OTHERS. 14:1b, 16-19

Now the day came that Jonathan, the son of Saul, said to the young man who was carrying his armor, "Come and let us cross over to the Philistines' garrison that is on the other side." But he did not tell his father – Jonathan knew that his father would not approve because he was known for trusting either in himself or favorable circumstances.

Look at verses 16-19:

16 Now Saul's watchmen in Gibeah of Benjamin looked, and behold, the multitude melted away; and they went here and *there.* 17 Saul said to the people who *were* with him, "Number now and see who has gone from us."

And when they had numbered, behold, Jonathan and his armor bearer were not *there.* ⁱ⁸ Then Saul said to Ahijah, "Bring the ark of God here." For the ark of God was at that time with the sons of Israel. ¹⁹ While Saul talked to the priest, the commotion in the camp of the Philistines continued and increased; so Saul said to the priest, "Withdraw your hand." – this is another example of how fickle Saul was. He asks for the "ark of God", the LXX translates this "ephod" which was used to discover God's will.

Then Saul said to Ahijah, "Bring the priestly ephod," because Ahijah carried the ephod in front of Israel that day. 1 Samuel 14:18 (GW)

So Saul said to Ahijah, "Bring near the ephod," for he was at that time wearing the ephod. 1 Samuel 14:18 (NET1)

The NET Bible note, "*Heb* "the ark of God." It seems unlikely that Saul would call for the ark, which was several miles away in Kiriath-jearim (see 1 Sam 7:2). The LXX and an Old Latin ms have "ephod" here, a reading which harmonizes better with v. 3 and fits better with the verb "bring near" (see 1 Sam 23:9; 30:7) and with the expression "withdraw your hand" in v.19."

When they called the roll, Jonathan and his armor bearer turned up missing. Saul ordered Ahijah, "Bring the priestly Ephod. Let's see what GOD has to say here." (Ahijah was responsible for the Ephod in those days.) 1 Samuel 14:18 (MSG)

An ephod is used to consult the divine will.

But notice, when the circumstances change, he immediately says forget about asking God! "Withdraw you hand" from the ephod.

Trans: Faith is not dependent upon others, Saul clearly knew little about walking by faith, but that did not stop his son Jonathan from trusting God. If we don't trust God we cannot blame our parents or circumstances or anything else – we choose to either trust God or we do not.

Cymbala notes, "Let us never accept the excuse that God cannot work in our situation, . . .that our particular people are too rich, or too poor, . . . too inner-city or too suburban, . . .That kind of thinking is never found in the Word of God. . . .We can see God do things just as he did in the book of Acts since He has never changed."

III. THIRD, FAITH IS NOT *INFLUENCED* BY NUMBERS. 1-7

A. The *People*. 1-2

1 Now the day came that Jonathan, the son of Saul, said to the young man who was carrying his armor, "Come and let us cross over to the Philistines' garrison that is on the other side." But he did not tell his father. 2 Saul was staying in the outskirts of Gibeah under the pomegranate tree which is in Migron. And the people who were with him were about six hundred men – the people were with Saul not Jonathan – he only had one person with him. Faith is never in numbers but in God, and God has not changed in His ability to deliver us.

A "Letter from a Birmingham Jail," by Martin Luther King Jr., written to Christian leaders:

"Whenever the early Christians entered a town, the people in power became disturbed and immediately sought to convict the Christians for being "disturbers of the peace" and "outside agitators." But the Christians pressed on, in the conviction that they were a "colony of heaven" called to obey God rather than man. Small in number, they were big in commitment. They were too God-intoxicated to be "astronomically intimidated."

Oh that we would be God-intoxicated!

B. The *Priest*. 3

and Ahijah, the son of Ahitub, Ichabod's brother, the son of Phinehas, the son of Eli, the priest of the LORD at Shiloh, was wearing an ephod. And the people did not know that Jonathan had gone – Wiersbe, "Saul had a priest of the Lord attending him, a man named Ahijah from the rejected line of Eli (v. 3), but the king never waited for the Lord's counsel (vv. 18-20). Saul is a tragic example of the popular man of the world who tries to appear religious and do God's work, but who lacks a living faith in God and a heart to honor Him."

How easy it is to look like we want God's will, but like Saul we go ahead and do what we want without waiting for God to really lead us. How many people *say* that they are praying about God's will but in reality are doing exactly what they want to do.

In the movie, *Hoosiers,* Coach Norman Dale (played by Gene Hackman) knew that Strap, a backup power forward, had a quirky way of expressing his religious fervor. As the Huskers began to trot out of the locker room for the tip-off of the season opener, he noticed that Strap who always kneeled in prayer before each game wasn't moving. With Strap frozen on bended knee, Dale asked one of his other players, "How long is he going to be like that?" "Until he gets ready," was the matter-of-fact reply. Three-fourths of the way through the season and in a game with playoff implications, the Huskers find themselves in a tight spot. Near the end of the fourth quarter, Everett, one of the starters, is injured; they signal a time out. Coach Dale looks down at the end of the bench and calls out, "Strap, you're going in for Everett." Then, remembering Strap's difficulty getting the ball in the hoop, he adds, "And don't shoot the ball unless you're under the basket all by yourself." Breaking the huddle, the Huskers jog back onto the court. But Strap doesn't budge, kneeling on the hardwood next to the bench with his head bowed. The gym reverberates with fans cheering and coaches screaming. The referees blow their whistles to get the game moving again. It's chaos, but Strap just kneels there.

Dale testily urges, "Let's go, Strap," and then again, louder and more insistent, "Let's go!" Strap doesn't budge. Deliberately, Dale comes up beside him, kneels down, and whispers in his ear, "Strap, God wants you on the floor." Strap looks up, a broad smile breaking across his face. He rushes onto the court. Apparently, God had more in mind than just having him on the floor, because Strap scores the next two baskets and helps lead the Huskers to a win. That real prayer not just some religious ritual, he didn't care if the whole team had to wait, he was waiting on God!

C. The *Philistines*. 4-5, 14

[4] Between the passes by which Jonathan sought to cross over to the Philistines' garrison, there was a sharp crag on the one side and a sharp crag on the other side, and the name of the one was Bozez, and the name of the other Seneh. [5] The one crag rose on the north opposite Michmash, and the other on the south opposite Geba

[14] That first slaughter which Jonathan and his armor bearer made was about twenty men within about half a furrow in an acre of land – this victory clearly proves that numbers had nothing to do with it – if that were true the

Philistines would have killed Jonathan and his armor bearer.

D. The *Principle*. 6-7

6 Then Jonathan said to the young man who was carrying his armor, "Come and let us cross over to the garrison of these uncircumcised; perhaps the LORD will work for us, for the LORD is not restrained to save by many or by few." 7 His armor bearer said to him, "Do all that is in your heart; turn yourself, and here I am with you according to your desire." – one with God is a majority. Later we will see just one lad trusting God, will slay an enormous giant! People today are more focused on numbers than on God Himself. NOTHING is impossible for God to do (Gen. 18:13-14/Job 42:1-2/Jer. 32:17/Lu. 1:36-37/Mk. 14:36).

In his book *An Unstoppable Force,* Erwin McManus shares the story of how prayers resulted in what can only be called a miraculous recreation. Through prayer, an impossibility was changed to a fulfillment. While ministering in South Dallas, McManus's small congregation began to grow. Looking for a place to build a larger church building, the leadership spotted an acre of land for sale. Given its location near downtown Dallas, it seemed strange that the property was available. Excited at their good fortune, this small group of people, many on welfare, began to pray that the site would soon be theirs. Eventually, they were able to purchase the property after receiving financial help from an association of churches. As the congregation began the process of obtaining building permits, they discovered the property had been declared unacceptable for construction by the city of Dallas. The acre of land in a prime location was nothing more than a worthless landfill. McManus grieved over this waste of precious time and money. He writes:

We had bought an acre of garbage. Several core samples were taken. From what I understood, they went at least twenty-five feet deep and found nothing but trash. All I could do was ask our congregation to pray with me and believe that God was with us, and that He would even use the worst of human mistakes to perform the greatest of miracles. After months of prayer, a woman from the congregation told McManus that since they had asked God to turn the land into something useful, surely it had been taken care of. Feeling God's confirmation of her words, McManus asked for more core samples to be taken. This time the researchers did their tests again and found soil.

McManus writes:

How did this happen? Was it because the core sample was in a different part of the land or could it be that God had actually performed a miracle and changed the landfill to good land? What I do know is that the same realtor who sold the property to me came back and offered me three times the amount he had sold it for once he heard the clearance to build had actually come through. What I do know is that the previous owners could not build on the property, but we could. What I do know is that we were told the property was worthless and unusable. What I cannot tell you is what happened beneath the ground at 2815 South Ervay Street. All I can tell you is what I know—and that is that God took my failure and performed a miracle. Today Cornerstone Church worships on that acre of land in a sanctuary built by our own hands. Beloved, with God all things are possible.

IV. FOURTH, FAITH IS NOT *INSPIRED* BY HUMAN LOGIC. 8-14

A. The *Element* of surprise was *Denied.* 8

Then Jonathan said, "Behold, we will cross over to the men and reveal ourselves to them - At an appropriate distance, somewhere in the valley, the two would come out from the cover of the rocky crags and see what reaction they provoked from the Philistines and take that reaction as guidance for what to do next.

B. The *Exhaustive* climb would make their strength *Depleted.* 8-14

9 "If they say to us, 'Wait until we come to you'; then we will stand in our place and not go up to them. 10 "But if they say, 'Come up to us,' then we will go up, for the LORD has given them into our hands; and this shall be the sign to us." ⁱⁱ When both of them revealed themselves to the garrison of the Philistines, the Philistines said, "Behold, Hebrews are coming out of the holes where they have hidden themselves." ¹² So the men of the garrison hailed Jonathan and his armor bearer and said, "Come up to us and we will tell you something." And Jonathan said to his armor bearer, "Come up after me, for the LORD has given them into the hands of Israel." ¹³ Then Jonathan climbed up on his hands and feet, with his armor bearer behind him; and they fell before Jonathan, and his armor bearer put some to death after him. ¹⁴ That first slaughter which Jonathan and his armor bearer made was about twenty men within about half a furrow in an acre of land – imagine how exhaustived they would have been after making such a climb. It is good when our strength is depleted because it forces us to depend upon God's strength.

"From a human perspective, two men climbing up a cliff to fight with several soldiers waiting for them when they arrive at the top appears to be the height of foolishness, but Jonathan is assessing the situation from the perspective of faith."

Trans: Point is, faith often seems foolish and unreasonable. It says silly things like:

- We give to get.
- We are strong through weakness.
- We humble ourselves to be lifted up.

- We die to live.

God told Joshua to walk around Jericho and the walls would come tumbling down...

God told Naaman to dip 7 times in the Jordan River and his leprosy would cleansed. Many times obeying God seems downright foolish, I just put 5,000 dollars on my credit card to get this new book published...seems rather foolish when our congregation is dwindling. But I have followed God's lead as far as I know.

Jonathan was simply obeying God - [15] Now a day before Saul's coming, the LORD had revealed *this* to Samuel saying, [16] "About this time tomorrow I will send you a man from the land of Benjamin, and you shall anoint him to be prince over My people Israel; and he will deliver My people from the hand of the Philistines. For I have regarded My people, because their cry has come to Me." 1 Sam. 9:15-16

John Wesley, "I am a creature of a day. I am a spirit come from God, and returning to God. I want to know one thing: the way to heaven [he could have also said, the way to walk by faith on the way to heaven]. God Himself has condescended to teach me the way. He has written it down in a book. Oh, give me that book! At any price give me the book of God. Let me be a man of one book!"

Faith must be tied into God's Word...Rom. 10:17

Joe Boggs, is a private pilot, meaning he flies occasionally for pleasure and for family trips. It is amazing how many instruments it takes to fly a plane - instruments for measuring his altitude, his fuel supply, his horizontal equilibrium, and his air speed.

Joe has his "IFR" rating, which stands for "Instrument Flight Rules". This means that he can fly the plane without seeing the ground or horizon. If he is surrounded by thick clouds and can see nothing of the sky or ground, he can rely solely on the instruments of the plane to navigate.

In order to qualify for his IFR rating, his instructor put a visor over his head blocking his view through the windshield. He had to prove he could fly in complete dependence on the instrument panel. Christians need to have their IFR rating [An Insistence on a Faith that Relies on God]! Joe's dependence and faith in his instruments and their ability to keep him from crashing illustrate how Christians should rely on God as the source of direction in our lives. We simply must believe that God is trustworthy.

V. FIFTH, FAITH GETS GOD *INVOLVED*. 15-22

A. The *Consternation.* 15a

And there was a trembling in the camp, in the field, and among all the people. Even the garrison and the raiders trembled - Why? God put fear into their hearts.

B. The *Convulsion*. 15b

and the earth quaked so that it became a great trembling – Who was doing this? It was God!

Chishold noted, "In the Hebrew text the noun translated "panic" occurs twice and its verbal root once. The repetition emphasizes the supernatural fear that the Lord sends upon the Philistines… Prior to this the verb translated "melting away" appears only in Exodus 15: 15 and Joshua 2: 9, 24, where it describes the fear of the Canaanites at the news of the Lord's great victory over the Egyptians at the Red Sea."

C. The *Confusion*. 20

Then Saul and all the people who were with him rallied and came to the battle; and behold, every man's sword was against his fellow, and there was very great confusion – the Philistines started killing each other!

D. The *Conversion*. 21-22

21 Now the Hebrews who were with the Philistines previously, who went up with them all around in the camp, even they also turned to be with the Israelites who were with Saul and Jonathan. 22 When all the men of Israel who had hidden themselves in the hill country of Ephraim heard that the Philistines had fled, even they also pursued them closely in the battle – faith is contagious! People began to change.

Trans: Faith gets God involved! Hudson Taylor, the great missionary to China, said, "Many Christians estimate difficulty in the light of their own resources, and thus they attempt very little, and they always fail. All giants have been weak men who did great things for God because they reckoned on His power and His presence to be with them." 6,000 Plus Illustrations for Communicating Biblical Truths.

VI. FINALLY, FAITH IS ONLY *INTERESTED* IN GIVING GLORY TO GOD. 23

So the LORD delivered Israel that day, and the battle spread beyond Beth-aven – if it is Biblical faith, then God is the object, and if He is the object then He should obviously get the glory. God is acknowledged as the one who delivered them (Deut. 20:4/Josh.10:13-14, 42

If we don't realize this truth we will seek ourselves and steal God's glory. The self-seekers are self-losers and self-destroyers:

- Absalom and Judas sought themselves, and hanged themselves.
- Saul seeks himself, and kills himself.
- Pharaoh seeks himself, and overthrows himself and his mighty army in the Red Sea.
- Cain sought himself, and slew two at once – his brother and his own soul.

- The princes and residents sought the ruin of Daniel, but ruined themselves.

We must always give God the glory!

Jonathan Edwards drew up a list of resolutions, committing himself to a God-centered life lived in harmony with others. The list, excerpted here, was probably first written down in 1722 and added to at several times in his lifetime. There are seventy resolutions in all. He writes, "Being sensible that I am unable to do anything without God's help, I do humbly entreat Him by His grace to enable me to keep these resolutions, so far as they are agreeable to His will, for Christ's sake. His very first resolution is:

Resolved, That I will do whatsoever I think to be most to God's glory, and my own good, profit and pleasure, in the whole of my duration.

Con:

1. Our culture has been slowly getting rid of God, and the problem is we have to trust in someone or something – anyone outside of God – and that will leave us empty and without a firm foundation.

2. David Hume was a philosopher and skeptic who influenced many people to abandon their faith in God.

One of his converts was his own mother, who on her death bed said to him, "Son, you have taken away my faith, and now you have nothing to give me in its stead!"

Nothing in life, death, or eternity can replace faith in God.

Chapter Seventeen

THE FLESH: THE WAY TO TURN DELIVERANCE INTO DEFEAT

1 Sam. 14:24-52

Intro:

1. Historian William H. Prescott's account of an incident in the career of General Francisco Pizarro, Spanish invader of Peru: At a moment of crisis Pizarro drew his sword and traced a line with it on the sand from East to West. Then, turning toward the South, "Friends and comrades," he said, "on that side are toil, hunger, nakedness, the drenching storm, desertion, and death; on this side ease and pleasure. There lies Peru with its riches; here, Panama and its poverty. Choose, each man, what best becomes a brave Castilian. For my part, I go to the South."

2. As we compare Saul with his son Jonathan, we realize that they made two different choices: Jonathan chooses to walk by *faith*; while *Saul* chooses to walk according to the

flesh. We must also make a choice – faith life or fleshly living...

I. FIRST, FLESH MAKES *STUPID* DECISIONS. 14:24a

Now the men of Israel were hard-pressed on that day, for Saul had put the people under oath, saying, "Cursed be the man who eats food before evening – this was a dumb move! Had they taken advantage of God's provisions they would have eliminated the Philistines (v. 30). We are not capable of making wise decisions when we are walking according to the flesh. The flesh trades divine Revelation for human Reasoning.

I know, O LORD, that a man's way is not in himself, Nor is it in a man who walks to direct his steps. Jeremiah 10:23

J. Vernon McGee, "No man can walk aright apart from the revelation of God in His Word. The minute a man turns from the Word of God, he is on a detour. That is our natural course. In fact, we begin that way. I used to take my little grandson for a walk around the block when he was learning to walk. He was a wonderful little fellow, but he wore me out because he wanted to walk up the sidewalk of every house we passed; and when we came to a driveway, he would want to run out in the street, and when we would get to a corner he would want to go the wrong way. I have never seen a little fellow who wanted to go in as many wrong ways as he did. One day when we finally got home, I said to him, "Kim, you're just like your grandfather. When he gets away from the Word of God, he always goes down a detour."

II. SECOND, THE FLESH WILL *STEAL* GOD'S GLORY. 24b

and until I have avenged myself on my enemies." – notice the "I" problem! What a contrast with the truth:

Then Jonathan said to the young man who was carrying his armor, "Come and let us cross over to the garrison of these uncircumcised; perhaps the LORD will work for us, for the LORD is not restrained to save by many or by few." 1 Samuel 14:6

Then David said to the Philistine, "You come to me with a sword, a spear, and a javelin, but I come to you in the name of the LORD of hosts, the God of the armies of Israel, whom you have taunted. 1 Samuel 17:45

A huge clock was built and placed in the tower of the Pottsdam Garrison Church by the Emperor Frederick the Great of Prussia. This magnificent timepiece would chime out the hymn, "Praise Ye the Lord" every half hour. One day the melody ceased. Repairmen opened the gearbox of the massive clock. To their amazement, they discovered that a brown butterfly found its way into the intricate gears and stopped the music!

Saul was like that little brown bug! He was a hindrance to give all the praise to God. Likewise, we need to get the bugs out of our lives! Anything that is drawing attention to us instead of God needs to be removed.

III. NEXT, THE FLESH WILL CAUSE US TO *STARVE* IN THE MIDST OF PLENTY. 24b-26

So none of the people tasted food [25] *All the people of the land entered the forest, and there was honey on the ground.* [26] *When the people entered the forest, behold, there was a flow of honey; but no man put his hand to his mouth, for the people feared the oath* – here is God's provision all around them but they refuse to partake of it! We are likewise blessed with all spiritual blessings but we refuse to partake of it when we are in the flesh! I do not know how many times on a major holiday I have lost my appetite for the main meal because of eating junk food. On holidays, like Thanksgiving, the meal is usually late, and so I eat junk food and by the time the meal is ready I am already full!

In the spiritual realm if we feed on junk food, things related to the flesh we will lose our appetite for God's Word. We may feel full but in reality, we will be starving spiritually. The flesh, will crowd out the spiritual, if we let it, every time.

The famous cuckoo bird never builds its own nest. It flies around until it sees another nest with eggs in it and no mother bird around. The cuckoo quickly lands, lays its eggs there, and flies away. The thrush, whose nest has been invaded, comes back. Not being very good at arithmetic, she gets to work hatching the eggs. What happens? Four little thrushes hatch, but one large cuckoo hatches. The cuckoo is two or three times the size of the thrushes. When Mrs. Thrush brings to the nest one large, juicy worm, she finds four petite thrush mouths, one cavernous cuckoo mouth. Guess who gets the worm? A full-sized thrush ends up feeding a baby cuckoo that is three times as big as it is. Over time, the bigger cuckoo gets bigger and bigger, and the smaller thrushes get smaller and smaller. You can always find a baby cuckoo's nest. You walk along a hedgerow until you find dead little thrushes, which the cuckoo throws out one at a time.

Paul teaches that spiritually speaking, you've got two natures in one nest. The nature that you go on feeding will grow, and the nature that you go on starving will diminish.

IV. FOURTH, FLESH ALWAYS BRINGS *STRIFE*. 27-30

[27] But Jonathan had not heard when his father put the people under oath; therefore, he put out the end of the staff that was in his hand and dipped it in the honeycomb, and put his hand to his mouth, and his eyes brightened. [28] Then one of the people said, "Your father strictly put the people under oath, saying,

'Cursed be the man who eats food today.'" And the people were weary. ²⁹ Then Jonathan said, "My father has troubled the land. See now, how my eyes have brightened because I tasted a little of this honey. ³⁰ "How much more, if only the people had eaten freely today of the spoil of their enemies which they found! For now the slaughter among the Philistines has not been great." – the flesh doesn't get along with anybody! Saul's carnality was causing trouble among God's people and causing a division between him and his own son (1 Cor. 3:1-3).

Stephen Brown explains that when a group of thoroughbred horses face attack, they stand in a circle facing each other and, with their back legs, kick out at the enemy. Donkeys do just the opposite; they face the enemy and kick each other! The spirit-filled believers act like a majestic thoroughbred; but when we get in the flesh we act like a bunch of jack-assesses!

The Lord deserves better than a church that is filled with strife and fleshly members. In her book *"The Key to a Loving Heart,"* Karen Mains includes a parable about the church. It was entitled *"The Brawling Bride."* It tells about the most climactic moment in a wedding ceremony. The families have been seated. The groom and his attendants are in their places. The pastor is waiting, Bible in hand. The bridesmaids have come down the aisle. The organ begins the bridal march, and everyone rises. When the guests turn to view the bride, a gasp bursts from the crowd. The bride is limping down the aisle. Her gown is ripped and covered with splatters of mud. Bruises are visible on her arms. Blood is trickling down her nose. One eye is purple and swollen. Her hair is mussed like she stuck her finger in an electrical socket.

In this parable, the groom is the Lord Jesus Christ. The author asks, "Doesn't He deserve better than this?" His bride, the church, has been fighting again. Ridiculous? Not when we hear of churches with factions that sit on opposite sides of the aisle. Not when one part of the congregation meets upstairs at the same time the rest meet in the basement. Division in the church is an indication of carnality in some of the believers.

V. FIFTH, THE FLESH *STUBBORNLY* REJECTS GOD'S WORD. 31-32

31 They struck among the Philistines that day from Michmash to Aijalon. And the people were very weary. 32 The people rushed greedily upon the spoil, and took sheep and oxen and calves, and slew them on the ground; and the people ate them with the blood – these people knew that God's Word forbid eating meat with the blood (Gen. 9:4/See Leviticus chps 3, 7, and 17).

The flesh never submits to God's Word (Rom. 8:7-8). Our flesh will never obey God (Rom. 7:14-19). We must reckon upon the fact that the flesh has been crucified with Christ, make a firm choice to say no to it and by faith depend upon the Holy Spirit (Gal. 5:16).

Spurgeon, "A greater and more *all-pervading fullness of the Holy Spirit's residence* is another condition of growth...You cannot have it too thoroughly impressed upon you that every step in the Christian life is to be taken under the influence of the Holy Spirit. The thing to be attained is the universal teaching and guidance of the Holy Spirit, so that in all things you shall be led by the Spirit of God. "If ye are led by the Spirit, ye shall not fulfill the lusts of the flesh," (Galatians 5:16) "If through the Spirit ye do mortify the deeds of the body, ye shall live." (Romans 8:13) "To be spiritually minded is life and peace, but to be carnally minded is death." (Romans 8:6). Always remember, therefore, that to grow in grace, you must grow in the possession of the fullness of the Holy Ghost in your heart."

VI. SIXTH, THE FLESH IS NEVER *STRAIGHTFORWARD* ABOUT SIN. 33-35

A. He *Blamed* the *Congregation*. 33

Then they told Saul, saying, "Behold, the people are sinning against the LORD by eating with the blood." And he said, "You have acted treacherously; roll a great stone to me today."
– There is an old saying, "The buck stops here!" He was their leader, and besides his foolish oath encouraged them to sin.

Wayne Dyer wrote, "All blame is a waste of time. No matter how much fault you find with another, and regardless of how much you blame him, it will not change you. The only thing blame does is to keep the focus off you when you are looking for external reasons to explain your unhappiness or frustration. You may succeed in making another feel guilty of something by blaming him, but you won't succeed in changing whatever it is about you that is making you unhappy."

B. He *Bypassed Confession.* 34-35

*34 Saul said, "Disperse yourselves among the people and say to them, 'Each one of **you** bring me his ox or his sheep, and slaughter it here and eat; and do not sin against the LORD by eating with the blood.'" So all the people that night brought each one his ox with him and slaughtered it there. 35 And Saul built an altar to the LORD; it was the first altar that he built to the LORD* – the Bible is clear that the first thing we do when we sin is confess it (1 Jn. 1:9). Notice, he instructs the people to deal with their sin, but seems to refuse to include himself as one who sinned.

Trans: Flesh can always see sin in somebody else's life, but tends to excuse our own sin. As one noted:

"Have you noticed when others are set in their ways, they're obstinate; when you are, it is godly conviction. When your neighbor doesn't like your friend, he's prejudiced; but when you don't like his, you are a good judge of human nature. When he takes his time doing something, he is lazy; but, when you do, you're deliberate and thoughtful. When he says what he thinks, he is mean-spirited; but when we do we are just being honest."

We all need to come to grips with sin in our lives. Susannah Wesley defined sin as:

"Whatever weakens your reasoning, impairs the tenderness of your conscience, obscures your sense of God or takes away your relish for spiritual things; in short, if anything increases the authority and power of the flesh over the spirit, that to you becomes sin, however good [it appears to be] in itself."

VII. SEVENTH, THE FLESH *STOPS* FELLOWSHIP WITH GOD. 36-37

36 Then Saul said, "Let us go down after the Philistines by night and take spoil among them until the morning light, and let us not leave a man of them." And they said, "Do whatever seems good to you." So the priest said, "Let us draw near to God here." 37 Saul inquired of God, "Shall I go down after the Philistines? Will You give them into the hand of Israel?" But He did not answer him on that day – God doesn't waste time revealing things to those, He knows, are not going to obey Him (Jam. 4:3).

Bounds, "Obedience is faith in action...If you have an earnest desire to pray well, you must learn how to obey well. Nowhere does He approve of sin and excuse disobedience. To excuse sinning by the logic that obedience to God is not possible is to discount the new birth, the indwelling Holy Spirit, the intercession of Christ, and the woodshed of the Father and takes us to a place where effective praying is not possible. He who prays must obey."

[22] Samuel said, "Has the LORD as much delight in burnt offerings and sacrifices As in obeying the voice of the LORD? Behold, to obey is better than sacrifice, *And* to heed than the fat of rams. 1 Samuel 15:22

VIII. EIGTH, FLESH ALWAYS *STRIKES* OUT IN ANGER. 38-46

A. A *Losers Indignation.* 38-39

[38] Saul said, "Draw near here, all you chiefs of the people, and investigate and see how this sin has happened today. [39] "For as the LORD lives, who delivers Israel, though it is in Jonathan my son, he shall surely die." But not one of all the people answered him – death for eating some honey! Keep in mind he didn't know about the king's foolish oath to begin with.

B. *Lots* are cast for *Identification.* 40-44

[40] Then he said to all Israel, "You shall be on one side and I and Jonathan my son will be on the other side." And the people said to Saul,

"Do what seems good to you." ⁴¹ *Therefore, Saul said to the LORD, the God of Israel, "Give a perfect lot." And Jonathan and Saul were taken, but the people escaped.* ⁴² *Saul said, "Cast lots between me and Jonathan my son." And Jonathan was taken.* ⁴³ *Then Saul said to Jonathan, "Tell me what you have done." So Jonathan told him and said, "I indeed tasted a little honey with the end of the staff that was in my hand. Here I am, I must die!"* ⁴⁴ *Saul said, "May God do this to me and more also, for you shall surely die, Jonathan."* – people who walk by faith and have a clear conscience before God are never afraid to die!

C. The *Lord's Intervention.* 45-46

⁴⁵ *But the people said to Saul, "Must Jonathan die, who has brought about this great deliverance in Israel? Far from it! As the LORD lives, not one hair of his head shall fall to the ground, for he has worked with God this day." So the people rescued Jonathan and he did not die.* ⁴⁶ *Then Saul went up from pursuing the Philistines, and the Philistines went to their own place* – God overruled Saul's stupidity!

Trans: The flesh always strikes out in anger! Gal. 5:19-20

Mary Gordon shares how fleshly anger makes us beast like:

"I became an animal. It was a hot August afternoon. I was having 10 people over for dinner that evening. No one was giving me a bit of help. I was feeling like a victim. It is important to remember that the angry person's habit of self-justification is often connected to his habit of seeing himself as a victim. I had been chopping, stirring, bending over a low flame, and all alone, alone! My mother and my children thought this was a good time for civil disobedience. They positioned themselves in the car and refused to move until I took them swimming. They leaned on the horn and shouted my name out the window. I lost it. I lost myself. I ran out and literally jumped on the hood of my car. I pounded on the windshield. I told my mother and my children that I was never, ever going to take any of them anywhere and none of them were ever going to have one friend in any house of mine until the hour of their death, which I said, I hoped would be soon! I couldn't stop pounding on the windshield. Then the frightening thing happened, I *became a huge bird.* My legs became hard stalks; my eyes were sharp and vicious. I developed a murderous beak. Greasy black feathers took the place of arms. I flapped and flapped. The taste of blood entranced me. I wanted to peck and peck forever. I wanted to carry them all off in my bloody beak and drop them on a rock where I would feed on their battered corpses till my bird stomach swelled. When I came back to myself I was appalled. I realized that I had frightened my children; they could no longer even recognize me. Because of that experience and others that I won't tell you about, I understand the deadly nature of the sin of anger."

Fleshly anger is more dangerous than any of us ever imagined.

IX. FINALLY, THE FLESH *STAYS* IN CONTINUAL CONFLICT. 47-52

47 Now when Saul had taken the kingdom over Israel, he fought against all his enemies on every side, against Moab, the sons of Ammon, Edom, the kings of Zobah, and the Philistines; and wherever he turned, he inflicted punishment. 48 He acted valiantly and defeated the Amalekites, and delivered Israel from the hands of those who plundered them. 49 Now the sons of Saul were Jonathan and Ishvi and Malchi-shua; and the names of his two daughters were these: the name of the firstborn Merab and the name of the younger Michal. 50 The name of Saul's wife was Ahinoam the daughter of Ahimaaz. And the name of the captain of his army was Abner the son of Ner, Saul's uncle. 51 Kish was the father of Saul, and Ner the father of Abner was the son of Abiel. 52 Now the war against the Philistines was severe all the days of Saul; and when Saul saw any mighty man or any valiant man, he attached him to his staff – just as Saul was in continual conflict with the enemy, so we will remain in continual conflict with our inward enemy – the flesh. As long as we are in this body, we must be prepared to fight against it!

Con:

1. Choosing to live according to the flesh, guarantees that we will turn our Deliverances into Defeats.

2. We all have the flesh, but we do not have to live according to the flesh. We can live like Saul or Jonathan.

3. I have to confess I feel like the little boy in Sunday school class. The teacher asked him, "If all the good people in the world were purple, and all the bad people in the world were orange, what color would you be?" He thought for a few moments and then gave an honest answer, "I'd be streaky!"

Some days I am like Jonathan, but other days like Saul. But by God's grace we can progressively be more like Jesus than self – by an act of our will renouncing self and relying upon the Holy Spirit.

Chapter Eighteen

GOD'S DIRECTIVES ARE NOT AN INVITATION FOR DISCUSSION

1 Sam. 15

Intro:

1. Gen. Montgomery came into command in North Africa, to find the allied forces in defeat

and disarray. He took them from losing every battle to victory – by adding one ingredient: *Obedience.* He noted:

"Orders no longer formed the basis for discussion, but for action...Previously orders had generally been questioned by subordinates right down the line. I was determined to stop this state of affairs at once."

2. All of our defeats and confusion could be solved by one simple principle: Unquestioning obedience to God's Word.

Trans: 1 Sam. 15. King Saul has demonstrated a pattern of questioning God; excusing his sin; and blaming others for his clear disobedience.

I. FIRST, THE *VOICE* OF GOD. 15:1, 3

A. It is supposed to be *Heeded.* V. 1

Then Samuel said to Saul, "The LORD sent me to anoint you as king over His people, over Israel; now therefore, listen to the words of the LORD – end of discussion! When God speaks, obey! We are an, *I'll do it my way* generation! We don't like to think that we need God's help or instructions, but disobedience will always remove our peace and bring disaster. One of Lowe's [Hardware] commercials shows a proud do-it-yourselfer installing a new ceiling fan in his family's living room. He proudly gives the fan one last little turn, climbs off the aluminum ladder, and steps aside to turn on the switch. After he turns it on, he stands with his hands on his hips, satisfied with his brilliant, money-saving work. Within a second of the first rotation of the blades, the central motor sparks and the entire fan crashes to the floor, crushing a small table on its way down. The scene cuts away to the outside of the house, looking at the clear bay window of the room where the man stands. It's quiet and bright outside. Suddenly, the ceiling fan comes flying through the picture window and lands in the yard, disrupting the peaceful moment. The words flash on the screen: "Need help?"

B. God's Word was clearly *Heard.* 3

'Now go and strike Amalek and utterly destroy all that he has, and do not spare him; but put to death both man and woman, child and infant, ox and sheep, camel and donkey.'" – the message was not complicated or hard to understand but crystal clear – utterly destroy all...spare not!

Trans: God's Word is just as clear today and it must be obeyed or it is of little value to our lives. *Owning a Bible is not the same as Obeying the Bible.* Haddon Robinson noted:

"Since 1955 knowledge has doubled every 5 years: libraries groan with the weight of new books...Our generation possesses more data about the universe and human personality than all previous generations put together. In terms of *facts alone* neither Moses nor Paul could pass a college entrance exam today. Yet the result has been a bumper crop of *brilliant failures!* Let's face it. Knowledge is not enough to meet life's problems..."

Knowledge of God's Word, has to be wedded to obedience to God's Word (Jer. 7:23-24/Lu.6:46/1 Pet. 1"13-14).

II. NEXT, THE *VENGENCE* OF GOD. 2, 32-33

A. First, it is always *Reasonable.* 2

"Thus says the LORD of hosts, 'I will punish Amalek for what he did to Israel, how he set himself against him on the way while he was coming up from Egypt – God had every reason to punish Amalek.

1. The *Previous* generation.

Then Amalek came and fought against Israel at Rephidim. Exodus 17:8

[17] "Remember what Amalek did to you along the way when you came out from Egypt, [18] how he met you along the way and attacked among you all the stragglers at your rear when you were faint and weary; and he did not fear God. Deuteronomy 25:17-18

2. The *Present* generation. 18

and the LORD sent you on a mission, and said, 'Go and utterly destroy the sinners, the Amalekites, and fight against them until they are exterminated.' – they were unrepentant sinners who would experience God's judgment.

It was not because of Israel personal righteousness that they were spared extermination, but because of God's mercy and grace in choosing that nation; it is the same with us, it is not that we have some personal righteousness that exceeds the lost man (Deut. 9:1-6).

B. Furthermore, it is always *Merciful.*

1. God waited some 300 years before wiping them out (Gen. 15:16).

Unfortunately this merciful delay is often used by the wicked to think that they have gotten away with their sins (Eccles. 8:11/Rom.2:3-5).

London held its breath in June 1987. While working on a building site, a construction foreman thought his workers had hit a cast iron pipe while using a pile driver. After picking up and then dropping the huge object, they realized the pipe looked like a bomb. It was a 2,200-pound World War II bomb, one of the largest the Germans dropped during the blitz which killed more than 15,000 Londoners. After evacuating the area, a 10-man bomb disposal unit worked 18 hours before deactivating the seven-foot device. God's judgment is like an unexploded bomb, if people refuse to repent and turn to God, the only thing that can deactivate it, there will be an explosion!

2. God remembered the Kenites. V. 6

Saul said to the Kenites, "Go, depart, go down from among the Amalekites, so that I do not destroy you with them; for you showed kindness to all the sons of Israel when they came up from Egypt." So the Kenites departed from among the Amalekites. - the Kenites were spared since they had shown kindness to Israel in the wilderness wandering (Ex. 18:9-10), Jethro was a Kenite (Judges 1:16).

C. Yet, vengeance is always *Inevitable.* 32-33

³² Then Samuel said, "Bring me Agag, the king of the Amalekites." And Agag came to him cheerfully. And Agag said, "Surely the bitterness of death is past." ³³ But Samuel said, "As your sword has made women childless, so shall your mother be childless among women." And Samuel hewed Agag to pieces before the LORD at Gilgal

Trans: How many today have rejected the gospel time and time again. They think because nothing has happened they are safe – they are wrong judgment is coming! Never take your own revenge, beloved, but leave room for the wrath *of God,* for it is written, "VENGEANCE IS MINE, I WILL REPAY," says the Lord. Romans 12:19

Just because everything is rosy now as one rejects the Lord Jesus doesn't mean those roses will not one day turn to wrath. Heliogabalus was a Roman Emperor, who ruled between 218 and 222 A.D. It is said that he invited some to be his dinner guests. During the feast he quietly sneaked out and had all of the entrances locked. While those invited were getting drunk and engaging in immoral behavior, he opened a ceiling window and had flowers thrown down upon his dinner guests. They poured down like rain until the people were shouting, "Enough! Enough!" But he continued until they literally suffocated in a sea of flowers!" [boston.com]

Sin is like that, it looks like a rose garden but it will ultimately turn out to be a God's just judgment.

III. THIRD, THE *AVOIDANCE* OF GOOD. 15:7-23

Saul is about to learn that partial obedience is really total disobedience!

A. The *Conquest.* 7

So Saul defeated the Amalekites, from Havilah as you go to Shur, which is east of Egypt – of course in reality it was God not Saul who was defeating them.

B. The *Compromise.* 8-9

⁸ He captured Agag the king of the Amalekites alive, and utterly destroyed all the people with the edge of the sword. ⁹ But Saul and the people spared Agag and the best of the sheep, the oxen, the fatlings, the lambs, and all that was good, and were not willing to destroy them utterly; but everything despised and worthless, that they utterly destroyed - he did not utterly destroy all. He was living by reason instead of revelation – why not save the good stuff? If God calls something bad and fitted for destruction, then we are fools to call it "the best of..."

²⁰ Woe to those who call evil good, and good evil; Who substitute darkness for light and light for darkness; Who substitute bitter for sweet and sweet for bitter! ²¹ Woe to those who are wise in their own eyes And clever in their own sight! Isaiah 5:20-21

St. Francis took a couple of men who were being considered for the monastery out to plant a row of cabbages. He began planting them with the head into the ground and the roots sticking straight up! Immediately one of them protested, "That is not the way to make cabbages grow!" He was immediately dismissed as unfit for their order. Our place is not to question God!

C. The *Candor.* 10-11

¹⁰ Then the word of the LORD came to Samuel, saying, ¹¹ "I regret that I have made

Saul king, for he has turned back from following Me and has not carried out My commands." And Samuel was distressed and cried out to the LORD all night – our disobedience grieves the heart of God, and will distress the man of God also.

"The Lord revealed that the source of his grief was Saul's failure to follow his instructions completely. Saul's partial obedience might have been acceptable to his contemporaries, but when weighed in the divine balances, it was found wanting. Nothing short of strict obedience to the Lord's instructions was acceptable; anything less produced grief in heaven and pain and loss on earth. Samuel, who was uniquely in tune with God's heart, "was troubled" (lit., "became angry") when the Lord informed him of Saul's actions. In a sleepless, agonizing night "he cried out to the Lord." The term translated "cried out" (Hb. zā'aq) refers to an intense expression of grief or anxiety (cf. 1 Sam 4:13; 7:8; 8:18; 12:8, 10), doubtlessly mirroring the Lord's displeasure. [New American Commentary - New American Commentary – Volume 7: 1, 2 Samuel, Robert D. Bergen]

D. The *Concern.* 11b, 34-35

And Samuel was distressed and cried out to the LORD all night – what a contrast with an *"I told you so!"* attitude.

³⁴ Then Samuel went to Ramah, but Saul went up to his house at Gibeah of Saul. ³⁵ Samuel did not see Saul again until the day of his death; for Samuel grieved over Saul. And the LORD regretted that He had made Saul king over Israel - Do we take a little delight when some well known preacher falls? Are we even concerned when a fellow Christian stops walking with God?

E. The *Confrontation.* 12-23

Notice that being grieved over someone's sin does not mean that we accept their sins as acceptable. Sin needs to be confronted!

1. Notice Saul's self *Exaltation.* 12

Samuel rose early in the morning to meet Saul; and it was told Samuel, saying, "Saul came to Carmel, and behold, he set up a monument for himself, then turned and proceeded on down to Gilgal." – talk about an idiot!

2. Notice also his *Exuberance.* 13

Samuel came to Saul, and Saul said to him, "Blessed are you of the LORD! I have carried out the command of the LORD." – like most Baptist we can come to Church 1 Sunday of the month and sing, "*Blessed Be the Name*" and never come to Sunday School Class or attend the Sunday evening service, or tithe or share the gospel with the lost, have no time for prayer…but how we can sing "*Have Thine own way Lord!*"

3. Then we have Samuel's *Excuse me!* 14

But Samuel said, "What then is this bleating of the sheep in my ears, and the lowing of the oxen which I hear?" – funny how those dead sheep and oxen are still bleating! When we seek to cover instead of confess our sin, we will always hear our sin calling us out.

4. The *Excuses.* 15

Saul said, "They have brought them from the Amalekites, for the people spared the best of the sheep and oxen, to sacrifice to the LORD your God; but the rest we have utterly destroyed." – how easy it is to justify and rationalize and excuse our sin!

5. The *Exasperation.* 16-21

a. *Shut-up!* 16a

Then Samuel said to Saul, "Wait… - it means desist! Stop! Be quiet! Enough! Shut up! How is that for tact and diplomacy!

b. *Listen-up!* 16b-19

…and let me tell you what the LORD said to me last night." And he said to him, "Speak!"

- You have become *Arrogant.* 17

Samuel said, "Is it not true, though you were little in your own eyes, you were made the head of the tribes of Israel? And the LORD anointed you king over Israel – he went from a *little shot,* to a *big shot,* and now one who ought to be shot!

- You have been *Disobedient.* 18-19

18 and the LORD sent you on a mission, and said, 'Go and utterly destroy the sinners, the Amalekites, and fight against them until they are exterminated.' 19 "Why then did you not obey the voice of the LORD, but rushed upon the spoil and did what was evil in the sight of the LORD?"

c. Hey *Lighten-up!* 20-21
20 Then Saul said to Samuel, "I did obey the voice of the LORD, and went on the mission on which the LORD sent me, and have brought back Agag the king of Amalek, and have utterly destroyed the Amalekites. 21 "But the people took some of the spoil, sheep and oxen, the choicest of the things devoted to destruction, to sacrifice to the LORD your God at Gilgal." – typical Saul response, lighten-up its no big deal we can offer these to the Lord! Sort of like when Aaron make the golden calf and then said they could use it to worship the Lord!

6. The *Excluded.* 22-23

²² Samuel said, "Has the LORD as much delight in burnt offerings and sacrifices As in obeying the voice of the LORD? Behold, to obey is better than sacrifice, And to heed than the fat of rams. ²³ "For rebellion is as the sin of divination, And insubordination is as iniquity and idolatry. Because you have rejected the word of the LORD, He has also rejected you from being king." – this is not related to salvation but service. Again, do NOT miss Saul's real problem! It was NOT related to his sin but refusal to come clean and confess and forsake his sin!

- David committed gross sin but died as king because he ultimately confessd his sin.

- Peter denied the Lord but went out and wept with bitter tears and thus was the keynote speaker on the Day of Pentecost.

- Moses murdered a man but was used by God to lead the children of Israel out of Egyptian bondage because he was the most humble man on the planet.

Saul had the same problem that Ananias and Sapphira had, they called partial obedience total obedience but God always calls partial obedience total disobedience!

IV. FINALLY, THE *VICE* OF UNGODLINESS. 15:24-31

A. That of *Fearing the People.* 24

24 Then Saul said to Samuel, "I have sinned; I have indeed transgressed the command of the LORD and your words, because I feared the people and listened to their voice – fear of man and faith in God never mix! Prov. 29:25

B. That of *Feeding on* human *Praise.* 25-31

25 "Now therefore, please pardon my sin and return with me, that I may worship the LORD." 26 But Samuel said to Saul, "I will not return with you; for you have rejected the word of the LORD, and the LORD has rejected you from being king over Israel." 27 As Samuel turned to go, Saul seized the edge of his robe, and it tore. 28 So Samuel said to him, "The LORD has torn the kingdom of Israel from you today and has given it to your neighbor, who is better than you. 29 "Also the Glory of Israel will not lie or change His mind; for He is not a man that He should change His mind." 30 Then he said, "I have sinned; but please honor me now before the elders of my people and before Israel, and go back with me, that I may worship the LORD your God." 31 So Samuel went back following Saul, and Saul worshiped the LORD – there it is in a nutshell – "please honor me before the people (Jn. 5:41,44; 8:54; 12:42-43/Gal.1:10).

We cannot seek God's face and save our own at the same time…

Swindoll, "The more you use Scripture, the less you worry about pleasing the flock. The more you care about presenting what God said in His Word, the less interested you are in human opinion. A minister who has reverted to flattery has drifted from a proper emphasis on the Scriptures. Show me a pastor who tells the congregation what they want to hear and I'll show you a man who has stopped expositing the Book. When you teach, commit yourself to the Book, you find that you pay less and less attention to both strokes and attacks from others."

Con:

1. Let's get it straight – there is no substitute for obedience!

2. Is our obedience up-to-date? Have we formed the hellish habit of arguing with God, striving with our Maker?

3. Sir Leonard Wood visited the King of France, and the king enjoyed his company so much that he invited him for dinner the next day. Leonard showed up at the palace at the appointed time. The king was delighted and said, "Why, Sir Leonard, I did not expect to see you. You did not answer my invitation." I think Leonard's answer is a classic, one we should learn in our response to the King of kings. It was, "You Majesty, a king's invitation is never to be answered, but to be obeyed!"

It is high time we stopped answering God and started obeying Him.

Chapter Nineteen

THE KIND OF PERSON GOD CHOOSES AND USES.

1 Sam. 16

Intro:

1. Paul Tan tells of a girl who wanted to marry a Seminary student. Her parents were opposed to it because they how little most preachers made and were afraid that he would not be able to provide for her. She persisted and they finally agreed to hear him preach. After hearing him, they gave their blessing to them being married. He asked them what convinced them to allow them to get married – was it his preaching? They said, "Yes, after hearing you preach we are convinced that you will never make it as a preacher!"

2. I have a feeling those parents are going to be sorely disappointed, because God usually uses those who seem most unqualified to preach his Word.

I. FIRST, GOD'S *COMMUNICATION* TO SAMUEL. 16:1-3

A. It was *Needed.*

1. Because of *Cowardice*. 1

¹ Now the LORD said to Samuel, "How long will you grieve over Saul, since I have rejected him from being king over Israel? Fill your horn with oil and go; I will send you to Jesse the Bethlehemite, for I have selected a king for Myself among his sons." – two questions come to mind:

- Why is Samuel so upset over Saul's removal?

Could it be that he is afraid of what's going to happen to Israel? He knows that Israel needs strong leadership lest they rebel against God.

- Why is he afraid to go down to Bethlehem?

Because to go to Bethlehem he has to pass through Gibeah, which is where Saul lives. He was afraid that when Saul found out he was going to select another king, Saul would kill him!

Trans: At first this shocks us because Samuel is such a godly man, a prayer warrior – but he is still a man. And if truth be known those "No Fear" stickers are a lie! We all wrestle with fear of some kind.

- George Washington was scared to death of being buried alive.

- Richard Nixon was terrified of hospitals.
- Napoleon Bonaparte, the military and political genius, feared cats.
- Jennifer Aniston, Cher, and Whoopi Goldberg are all afraid of flying.
- Barbra Streisand is uncomfortable around strangers.
- Michael Jackson was haunted by the fear of contamination, infections, and diseases.
- Woody Allen. He's afraid of insects, sunshine, dogs, deer, bright colors, children, heights, small rooms, crowds, and cancer.

We must recognize fears but then refuse to give into them.

2. Because of *InCompetence.* 2

But Samuel said, "How can I go? When Saul hears of it, he will kill me." And the LORD said, "Take a heifer with you and say, 'I have come to sacrifice to the LORD.' – Samuel needs to hear from God because he has no idea who was the one God had chosen. V. 6

B. God's communication was *Limited.* 3

"You shall invite Jesse to the sacrifice, and I will show you what you shall do; and you shall

anoint for Me the one whom I designate to you." – it is limited to those who the Lord knows will obey. Notice, Saul was the king but God did not speak to him about it. Why? Because Saul was not one who had a track record of obeying God. God never wastes time revealing truth that He knows will be rejected. 14:37

Trans: God's Communication is Needed by all but Limited to those who have already decided they are going to obey.

"You call me Master and yet obey me not,
 You call me Light and see me not,
 You call me the Way, and walk in me not,
 You call me Wise, and yet do not follow me;
 If I am silent, blame me not!"

II. NEXT, THE ELDER'S *CONCERN*. 4-5

⁴ So Samuel did what the LORD said, and came to Bethlehem. And the elders of the city came trembling to meet him and said, "Do you come in peace?" ⁵ He said, "In peace; I have come to sacrifice to the LORD. Consecrate yourselves and come with me to the sacrifice." He also consecrated Jesse and his sons and invited them to the sacrifice – I think Saul had everybody on edge! "Consecrate" meant that each of the guests would take a bath and change clothes (Ex. 19:10-15), because nobody ceremonially unclean could partake of the sacrificial feast (Lev. 7:19-21). For Jesse and his sons to be invited to this feast was a high honor, and, of course, nobody but Samuel knew why they were included.

III. THIRD, GOD'S *CHOOSEN*. 6-13

A. First, he was *Spiritual*. 13:14

*"But now your kingdom shall not endure. The LORD has sought out for Himself **a man after His own heart**, and the LORD has appointed him as ruler over His people, because you have not kept what the LORD commanded you." –* Ac. 13:22

NIV Commentary, "The term "heart" connotes "will" or "choice" in this context and emphasizes Yahweh's freedom in selecting a replacement for Saul rather than continuing Saul's line.[10] While this phrase primarily emphasizes Yahweh's choice of David, it also connotes something positive about David's character over against Saul's. The new king will genuinely act in accordance with Yahweh's wishes in a way that Saul does not. He will exhibit a certain "like-mindedness" with Yahweh."

That is the essence of being a man after God's heart:

[22] "After He had removed him, He raised up David to be their king, concerning whom He also testified and said, 'I HAVE FOUND DAVID the son of Jesse, A MAN AFTER MY HEART, **who will do all My will.**' Acts 13:22

That does not mean that he was perfect, after all he was guilty of adultery (2 Sam. 11:1-4), and murder (2 Sam. 12:9). But he was a man who confessed his sin and turned from it. (Psa. 32, 38, 51); He allowed divine chastisement to do a transforming work. David may justly be termed a man after God's heart because (unlike Saul) his greatest desire was that he wanted to do God's will. In 1970, while Bob Russell was a graduate student at Temple University in Philadelphia, his 1967 Austin Healey sports car was stolen. Over the years, Russell kept the original title to the car and the keys, and he memorized the vehicle identification number. During a sleepless night on May 11, 2012, Russell got out of bed and began surfing the internet. While browsing eBay, he saw his old car for sale. After contacting the seller, getting a copy of the old police report through the National Crime Information Center, securing the assistance of the Philadelphia Police Department, and haggling with the seller over the buy-back price, Bob Russell and his wife Cynthia (who had gone on their first dates together in that car over forty years earlier), flew to California and took back ownership of the car on June 18, 2012. Though the VIN plate had been removed, and the glove box lock had been broken, and the lock to the trunk was missing, he was delighted to get his car back. Russell commented, "When it was stolen it was pristine; now it's going to need a lot of work.

On the other hand, it's been more than 40 years. It's very gratifying to get it back."

Bob was a man with a heart after a sports car – David was a man with a heart after God! When we want God and His will like Bob wanted that sports car we will find Him!
[1] As the deer pants for the water brooks, So my soul pants for You, O God. [2] My soul thirsts for God, for the living God; When shall I come and appear before God? Psalm 42:1-2

Tozer, "O God, I have tasted Your goodness and it has both satisfied me and made me thirsty for more. I am painfully conscious of my need of further grace, I am ashamed of my lack of desire. O God, I want to want You; I long to be filled with longing for you; I thirst to be made more thirstily still."

B. Second, he was outwardly *Simple.* 6-10

He was unimpressive, common, ordinary.

1. For starters, the human *Genus.*

- Eliab the *Athletic.* 6

When they entered, he looked at Eliab and thought, "Surely the LORD'S anointed is before Him."

Peterson, "Eliab, the eldest son, and a swaggering body was first. His mountainous size and rough-hewn good looks commanded attention. Samuel was impressed!"

Someone noted, "This big old farm boy probably stood 6' 2" and weighed 225 pounds, muscles bulging. Likely a wide receiver for Bethlehem High, no doubt made the All-Judean All star team, a future Mr. Universe if ever there was one."

- Abidadab, the *Intellect.* 8

Then Jesse called Abinadab and made him pass before Samuel. And he said, "The LORD has not chosen this one either." – letting our imagination run just a bit another writes:

"Abidadab the intellectual snob. A tall, stringy bean-pole, he stood before Samuel with sneering arrogance. He used big words, showing off his prestigious learning every chance he got. Samuel dismisses him with a gesture."

- Shammah the *Sophisticate.* 9

Next Jesse made Shammah pass by. And he said, "The LORD has not chosen this one either." – again just having some fun, one imagines:

"Here comes a mincing little sophisticate wearing the latest Calvin Klein jeans and alligator cowboy boots. He hated living in the backwoods of Bethlehem. Samuel looked to him like a ticket to the lifestyle of the rich and the famous!"

- The rest were inwardly *Insignificant.*

Davis, makes a good point, when he observed, "We must not conclude from verse 7 that God opposes fine appearance. The comment about David in verse 12 should knock out that notion. Rather the idea is that external appearances neither qualifies nor disqualifies; it simply does not matter!"

Man always focuses on the wrong thing – thin is in! Beauty is best. But we need to see things as God does.

Jeff Pierce was the 1994 captain of the Chevrolet-L.A. Sheriff professional cycling team and a top competitor. In 1987 he won one stage of the Tour de France. But in 1994, according to *USA Today,* he accepted an interesting and potentially dangerous assignment. To prepare for an article he planned to write for a magazine called *Bicycle Guide,* Pierce worked for a month as a *bike messenger* in downtown New York. On the streets for eleven hours a day, he dodged taxis and buses, sometimes reaching a speed of thirty-nine miles an hour on his *custom-made, $2,500 racing bike*. Was he worried about this expensive bike being stolen as he dashed into buildings to deliver his packages? You bet he was. To thwart thieves, Pierce wrapped duct tape around the frame of his bike and spray-painted it black. His bike looked like a piece of junk, and his plan worked. No one touched it.

How many people look like a piece of junk but inwardly they are like David – they have a heart for God. We need to learn not to evaluate people based on outward appearances.

2. Furthermore, the *Mysterious.* 7, 10

[7] But the LORD said to Samuel, "Do not look at his appearance or at the height of his stature, because I have rejected him; for God sees not as man sees, for man looks at the outward appearance, but the LORD looks at the heart." 1 Samuel 16:7

[10] Thus Jesse made seven of his sons pass before Samuel. But Samuel said to Jesse, "The LORD has not chosen these." 1 Samuel 16:10

Since God's choice is based upon one's heart, that choice will always remain mysterious to us, because we do not have the privilege of looking into one's heart.

[8] "For My thoughts are not your thoughts, Nor are your ways My ways," declares the LORD. [9] "For *as* the heavens are higher than the earth, So are My ways higher than your ways And My thoughts than your thoughts. Isaiah 55:8-9

In 2004, nine year old Devon Rivers of Gresham, Oregon collapsed in a seizure during a phys-ed class. He lapsed into a coma and doctors were at a loss of what to do. Medics took samples of Devon's spinal fluid trying to figure out what was causing his illness. But every test—from West Nile virus to lead poisoning—came back negative. For twenty-two months he languished in a "persistent vegetative state." His mother, Carla Rivers, visited him regularly and, in addition to physical therapy by his pediatric nursing home to keep his limbs supple, she talked to him in the belief that coma patients can retain their hearing and some understanding. "For two years the doctors said there was no hope," said Carla Rivers. But during those two years, his family and church prayed for him. Then, in August 2006 his mother, Carla Rivers, noticed that he began turning his head to follow movement; instead of a blank stare, he was reacting to his environment. Days later Devon was breathing without a respirator. In October 2006, Devon was alert, able to play, and was making a remarkable progress in his recovery. Carla said, "Devon may make a full recovery or what we see today may be what we get... God's plan is greater than ours. There's nothing we can do to force it any sooner or hold it back."

No matter what we think, or believe, or try to do, we will never demystify God. My point is that *compared to* his brothers, David was just a simple, ordinary boy. But God sees things that nobody else does!

C. He was a *Social* low-life. 11

[11] *And Samuel said to Jesse, "Are these all the children?" And he said, "There remains…* - he is

viewed as nothing more than remains! Someone observed, "It is a word that carries undertones of insignificance, of not counting for very much – certainly not a prime candidate for prestigious work. The family runt!"

Then he asked Jesse, "Is this it? Are there no more sons?" "Well, yes, there's the runt. But he's out tending the sheep." Samuel ordered Jesse, "Go get him. We're not moving from this spot until he's here." 1 Sam.16:11 (MSG)

…yet the youngest, and behold, he is tending the sheep."Then Samuel said to Jesse, "Send and bring him; for we will not sit down until he comes here." – tending sheep was the lowest of all jobs on the farm. It's like baby-sitting for a living, or seeing a 40 year old man bagging groceries at the family owned supermarket.

You might be at the bottom of the social ladder, but if you're in Christ, you couldn't be higher or more prosperous (Eph. 1:3).

Indra B. Tamang, who grew up in a mud house in a farming village in Nepal, has reached a pinnacle of society after more than three decades of loyal service as a butler, cook and caretaker to a socially prominent American family. Mr Tamang became Ruth Ford's trusted assistant and companion in 2002, she was a film and stage actor, after the death of her brother Charles. She named him as the sole beneficiary when she died in August, 2014 at the age of 98. He is now a multi-millionaire.

David is about to go from a lowly servant of man, to God's anointed king!

D. He was *Incidental.* 12-13

- He was *Uninvited.* All the other brothers were invited but David was not even thought important enough to fool with!

- He was *Unidentified* – until verse 13. Jesse's other sons are introduced by name; David is just called the youngest.

Peterson notes, "The plain folk, the undistinguished in the eyes of their neighbors, those lacking social status and peer recognition. Which is to say, the overwhelming majority of all wo have lived on this old planet earth. Election into God's purposes isn't by popular vote. Election into God's purposes isn't based on proved ability or potential promise."

We may be ugly as sin, or have the lowest job on the planet, don't worry about it! You're just the one that God has been looking for!

26 Take a good look, friends, at who you were when you got called into this life. I don't see many of "the brightest and the best" among you, not many influential, not many from high-society families. 27 Isn't it obvious that God

deliberately chose men and women that the culture overlooks and exploits and abuses, [28] chose these "nobodies" to expose the hollow pretensions of the "somebodies"? [29] That makes it quite clear that none of you can get by with blowing your own horn before God. [30] Everything that we have—right thinking and right living, a clean slate and a fresh start—comes from God by way of Jesus Christ. [31] That's why we have the saying, "If you're going to blow a horn, blow a trumpet for God."
1 Corinthians 1:26-31 (MSG)

Trans: God's chosen one is rarely what we think they should be. Lorne Sanny writes:

"Before I met Charlie Riggs, he had worked for seven years as a roughneck in the oil fields of Pennsylvania. Social graces weren't particularly prominent in his life. He could hardly talk without stuttering. But God picked him out. He has trained several hundred thousand people in personal counseling all over the world through his work with the Billy Graham team. When Charlie first came into my home, I was disappointed. I had scheduled a Bible class for servicemen, and he was the only one who showed up. One man! In those days I didn't realize the importance of helping just one fellow. I was forced into it. He would come to these meetings and sit without a smile, looking tough and rugged. We would have our Bible class, and then he would leave. But it wasn't long before Charlie came in one night and said,

"Lorrie, let me show you something God gave me out of the Scripture." I also remember the night when he said, "Lorrie, I've been getting up to meet the Lord in the morning at six, and then a quarter to six, and then five-thirty, but it still isn't time enough. I just feel I ought to get up and start my devotions at five." Soon I found out he was reviewing two or three hundred memorized verses a day. To me it's astounding what God has done with that fellow. I would never have picked him out for it. In fact, I've quit picking out people for what God wants to do with them. But I am having an ever-increasing vision of the possibilities of *every* individual as a channel of blessing through the transforming power of Christ."

III. FINALLY, DAVID IS UNDER CONSTRUCTION. 16:13-23

A. For starters, the *Ability.* 13

Then Samuel took the horn of oil and anointed him in the midst of his brothers; and the Spirit of the LORD came mightily upon David from that day forward. And Samuel arose and went to Ramah – only the Holy Spirit can enable us to serve God. Ac. 1:8

On Wednesday, October 11, 1994, NASA's *Magellan* space explorer fell silent. The *Magellan* had circled Venus more than fifteen thousand times since arriving at the planet in 1990, but on this day NASA scientists intentionally changed the satellite's course and sent it veering into the planet where it burned to a crisp in the atmosphere. Why would NASA send the *Magellan*—which cost nine hundred million dollars—plummeting into the planet? Because the *Magellan* was virtually out of power. One final experiment had drained its batteries to the point where it could no longer transmit data. Without power, even the highest technology is worthless. Without the power of God's Spirit, even the most committed Christian can bear no fruit.

B. Furthermore, the *Inactivity.*

He was anointed to be the king of Israel – yet he would not be recognized as king for another 25 years or so! God's power does not always manifested itself in outward success but often works quietly in solitude and obscurity before showing itself to others.

C. Third, the *Ambiguity.* 14-23

1. His working with *Sheep!*

David went back to the boring, routine job of taking care of those sheep…

Barber, "In the providence of God, even his experience as a shepherd was preparing David for his future service. His duties to watch over his flock, to feed and protect them, to heal and bind up the broken, and to bring back those that wandered away corresponded to the responsibilities of a faithful and godly ruler."

2. His using a musical instrument.

*14 Now the Spirit of the LORD departed from Saul, and an evil spirit from the LORD terrorized him. 15 Saul's servants then said to him, "Behold now, an evil spirit from God is terrorizing you. 16 "Let our lord now command your servants who are before you. Let them seek a man who is a skillful player on the harp; and it shall come about when the evil spirit from God is on you, that he shall play the harp with his hand, and you will be well." 17 So Saul said to his servants, "Provide for me now a man who can play well and bring him to me."
18 Then one of the young men said, "Behold, I have seen a son of Jesse the Bethlehemite who is a skillful musician, a mighty man of valor, a warrior, one prudent in speech, and a handsome man; and the LORD is with him." 19 So Saul sent messengers to Jesse and said, "Send me your son David who is with the flock." 20 Jesse took a donkey loaded with bread and a jug of wine and a young goat, and sent them to Saul by David his son.
21 Then David came to Saul and attended him; and Saul loved him greatly, and he became his armor bearer. 22 Saul sent to Jesse, saying, "Let David now stand before me, for he has found favor in my sight." 23 So it came about whenever the evil spirit from God came to Saul, David would take the harp and play it with his hand; and Saul would be refreshed and be well, and the evil spirit would depart from him* – notice.

- God will get us where he wants us to be. David doesn't have to fret and scheme. God can get us where He wants us without our trying to make things happen.

- God uses everything in our lives. David's ability to play a musical instrument before a bunch of sheep seemed insignificant but God used it.

The key is just to relax, rely upon the Holy Spirit and wait on His timetable to make things happen. Too often, we are like Don Young, Sr's., daughter. He writes:

"When our eldest daughter was old enough to understand what saving money was all about, my wife and I sat down with her and explained the value of money. We explained how you save, and when the piggybank was full, you take the money out and deposit it in a commercial bank so that it might draw interest. We thought we had done a thorough job. She seemed to understand and couldn't wait to open a savings account in our local bank by herself. I called the banker in our little town and told him our daughter was on the way to open her savings account. We would stop in later and sign the necessary papers. What a thrill! She got the president of the bank himself to wait on her. She handed over her savings, and he gave her a receipt and thanked her for her business. But she wouldn't leave. She just stood there like she was waiting on something else. He asked her, "Is there anything else that I can help you with?" "Yes," she said, "I want my interest."

D. Finally, his *Adversity.*

If we think being empowered by the Holy Spirit means that we will never experience opposition and suffering we are thinking wrongly! In fact Spirit filled living doesn't eliminate opposition it guarantees it.

Davis notes, "No sooner does the Spirit touch David then he is catapulted into endless trouble – the envy, anger, and plots of Saul now begin. David the man with the Spirit will be hunted and betrayed, trapped and escaping, hiding in caves, living in exile, driven to the edge – right to the end of first Samuel."

Con:

1. The kind of person God uses and chooses – not outwardly dynamic but inwardly has a desire for God.

2. David Livingstone's first attempt to preach ended in utter failure. He got to the pulpit and said, "Friends, I have forgotten all I had to say." In embarrassment, he sat down. But who hasn't heard of David Livingstone? His heart was on fire for God. And make no mistake about it; this truth is not just for preachers.

Howard Butt was right on target when he wrote:

"God doesn't issue a special call to pastors and leave everyone else uncalled. Every Christian should think of himself as having a divine call for glorifying God as a full-time career."

Chapter Twenty

WHAT HAVING A HEART AFTER GOD OUTWARDLY LOOKS LIKE?

1 Sam. 17

Intro:

1. I read a rather strange story about a widow named Marguerite Therese. She lived in France for many years. When her husband died, she had his heart encased in a glass case. For the next 29 years until her death she spent 7 hours every day sitting and gazing upon it.

2. That strikes me as very weird, but it was an outward display of her inward heart for her husband. David was a man after God's heart, and it showed outwardly, revealing that he no doubt invested many hours in gazing at the heart of God.

I. FIRST, IT IS A HEART OF *HUMILITY.* 17:12-15

¹² Now David was the son of the Ephrathite of Bethlehem in Judah, whose name was Jesse, and he had eight sons. And Jesse was old in the days of Saul, advanced in years among men. ¹³ The three older sons of Jesse had gone after Saul to the battle. And the names of his three sons who went to the battle were Eliab the firstborn, and the second to him Abinadab, and the third Shammah. ¹⁴ David was the youngest. Now the three oldest followed Saul, ¹⁵ but David went back and forth from Saul to tend his father's flock at Bethlehem – David is now employed in the palace, he is destined to be the next king and he knows it. Yet he leaves the place of influence and comfort and goes back and takes care of those lowly smelly sheep. I think that demonstrates humility…David does not view himself as too important to tend the sheep. Though Saul has been rejected and David anointed, he still is not yet on the throne and has to play second fiddle to him.

Leonard Bernstein, the late conductor of the New York Philharmonic orchestra, was once asked to name the most difficult instrument to play. Without hesitation, he replied, "The second fiddle. I can get plenty of first violinists, but to find someone who can play the second fiddle with enthusiasm—that's a problem. And if we have no second fiddle, we have no harmony."

No church or person will ever be in harmony until we all learn the value of humility. Humility is an attitude that has no problem rightly evaluating ourselves. On his way to a reception held in his honor, Ulysses S. Grant got caught in a shower and offered to share his umbrella with a stranger walking in the same direction. The man said he was going to Grant's reception out of curiosity; he had never seen the general. "I have always thought that Grant was a much overrated man," he said. Grant replied, "That's my view also."

Paul was such a man (1 Cor. 15:9/Eph.3:8/ 1 Tim. 1:15).

George Washington Carver, the scientist who developed hundreds of useful products from the peanut:

"When I was young, I said to God, 'God, tell me the mystery of the universe.' But God answered, 'That knowledge is reserved for me alone.' So I said, 'God, tell me the mystery of the peanut.' Then God said, 'Well, George, that's more nearly your size.' And he told me."

A man after God's heart has to be a person of humility if he wants to have intimacy with Deity.

C. S. Lewis, "We must not think Pride is something God forbids because He is offended at it, or that humility is something He demands, as due to His own dignity – as if, God Himself was proud. He is not in the least worried about His dignity. The point is, He wants you to know Him; He wants to give you,

Himself. And He and you, are two things of such a kind, that if you really get in touch with Him, you will in fact be humble – delightedly humble, feeling the infinite relief, of having once and for all, got rid of all the silly nonsense about your own dignity, which has made you restless and unhappy all of your life. He is trying to make you humble in order to make this moment possible."

II. FURTHERMORE HE DID HIS DUTIES FAITHFULLY. 16-20a

16 The Philistine came forward morning and evening for forty days and took his stand. 17 Then Jesse said to David his son, "Take now for your brothers an ephah of this roasted grain and these ten loaves and run to the camp to your brothers. 18 "Bring also these ten cuts of cheese to the commander of their thousand, and look into the welfare of your brothers, and bring back news of them. 19 "For Saul and they and all the men of Israel are in the valley of Elah, fighting with the Philistines." 20 So David arose early in the morning and left the flock with a keeper and took the supplies and went as Jesse had commanded him... - he is given a new assignment, bring the boys a sack lunch. Notice he does not neglect the sheep! He could have had the attitude, "Dad told me to take the boys their lunch, let somebody else worry about the sheep!"

See, Lu. 16:10-12/1 Corinthians 4:2/2 Timothy 2:2.

David was faithful in the little things and therefore could be trusted with bigger things. Admiral William H. McRaven, a 36-year Navy SEAL veteran, gave the commencement address to the Class of 2014 at the University of Texas in Austin. He titled his talk "10 Lessons to Change the World." Here's his first lesson about how to change the world:

Every morning in basic SEAL training, my instructors ... would show up in my barracks room and the first thing they would inspect was your bed. If you did it right, the corners would be square, the covers pulled tight, the pillow centered just under the headboard and the extra blanket folded neatly at the foot of the rack—rack—that's Navy talk for bed. It was a simple task—mundane at best. But every morning we were required to make our bed to perfection. It seemed a little ridiculous at the time, particularly in light of the fact that we were aspiring to be real warriors, tough battle hardened SEALs—but the wisdom of this simple act has been proven to me many times over. If you make your bed every morning you will have accomplished the first task of the day ...By the end of the day, that one task completed will have turned into many tasks completed. Making your bed will also reinforce the fact that little things in life matter. If you can't do the little things right, you will never do the big things right. And, if by chance you have a miserable day, you will come home to a bed that is made—that you made—and a made bed gives you encouragement that tomorrow will be better. If you want to change the world, start off by making your bed.

III. THIRD, HE WALKED WITH GOD *PRIVATELY*. 17:20b-21, 1-11, 22-37.

A. First, the *Stand-off.* 20b-21, 1-3

[20]...And he came to the circle of the camp while the army was going out in battle array shouting the war cry

[1] Now the Philistines gathered their armies for battle; and they were gathered at Socoh which belongs to Judah, and they camped between Socoh and Azekah, in Ephes-dammim. [2] Saul and the men of Israel were gathered and camped in the valley of Elah, and drew up in battle array to encounter the Philistines. [3] The Philistines stood on the mountain on one side while Israel stood on the mountain on the other side, with the valley between them – we have the typical stand-off. Reminds me of the civil war with the North and the South coming at each other.

B. Then, the one who *Stands-out.* 4-10

1. The *Champion*. 4-7

[4] Then a champion came out from the armies of the Philistines named Goliath, from Gath, whose height was six cubits and a span. [5] He had a bronze helmet on his head, and he was clothed with scale-armor which weighed five

thousand shekels of bronze. ⁶ He also had bronze greaves on his legs and a bronze javelin slung between his shoulders. ⁷ The shaft of his spear was like a weaver's beam, and the head of his spear weighed six hundred shekels of iron; his shield-carrier also walked before him – The word translated "champion" literally means "the man of the between," a vivid way of describing "anyone who comes forward from the front line [and] becomes a 'man between the battle lines' and is thus a sort of 'challenger' or 'champion.'" Out from the Philistine camp, then, came "the man of the between."

This is a monster! He is about 9 foot, 9 in. with 125 lbs. of armor, including a 15 lb. tipped spear. This is a big man! Yao Ming, the Chinese giant, plays center for the Houston Rockets. He was the first draft pick last year and came in second for the NBA Rookie of the Year award in 2002-03. No one would argue that he isn't a large man, but at just 7 foot 6 inches, he would be no match for Goliath who had 18 inches on him. Since most door jams are 6 foot 8 inches tall, the top of the jam would hit him about chest high and since most ceilings are at 8 foot, his head would be in the attic.

2. The *Challenge*. 8-10

⁸ He stood and shouted to the ranks of Israel and said to them, "Why do you come out to draw up in battle array? Am I not the Philistine and you servants of Saul? Choose a man for yourselves and let him come down to me. ⁹ *"If he is able to fight with me and kill me, then we will become your servants; but if I prevail against him and kill him, then you shall become our servants and serve us."* ¹⁰ *Again the Philistine said, "I defy the ranks of Israel this day; give me a man that we may fight together."* – his challenge is bring out your best man, winner take all!

C. The *Stand-still*. 11

When Saul and all Israel heard these words of the Philistine, they were dismayed and greatly afraid – they are paralyzed with fear.

The phrase "Be afraid, be very afraid" was a tagline from the 1986 horror flick *The Fly*. Google the phrase and you'll get about 183 million results for that phrase. But what people commonly fear is not always what they *should* be afraid of. For example:

- Are you afraid to fly? You have a 0.00001% chance of dying in an airplane crash.

- Are you afraid of a car crash? The car insurance industry estimates that the average driver will be involved in three or four car crashes in their lifetime and the odds of dying in a car crash are one to two percent.

- Are you afraid of heights? It's the second most reported fear. Your chance of being injured by falling, jumping, or being pushed from a high place is 1 in 65,092.

- Afraid of identity thief? The chance of having your identity stolen is 1 in 200.

- Do you fear being killed by a bolt of lightning? The odds of that happening are 1 in 2.3 million. You're much more likely to be struck by a meteorite—those lifetime odds are about 1 in 700,000.

- How about dogs? Their bark really is worse than their bite: Your chance of suffering a dog bite is 1 in 137,694.

- Who is afraid to mow the lawn? Yet, your chance of being injured while mowing the lawn is 1 in 3,623.

- How about sharks? You're much more likely to be killed by your spouse (1 in 135,000) than a shark (1 in 300 million).

- Won't ride a roller coaster? If you have the patience to stand in the line, the chance of a roller coaster injury is 1 in 300 million.

- Fourth of July scare you? If you play with fireworks on the Fourth of July, you're really playing with fire: the chance of injury is 1 in 20,000.

Truth is most of what we fear will never happens to us. In *Scared to Life* (Victor), Douglas Rumford cites a study that explains why we shouldn't allow fear to rule our lives:

- 60% of our fears are totally unfounded
- 20% are already behind us
- 10% are so petty they don't make any difference
- 4-5% of the remaining 10% are real, but we can't do anything about them

That means only 5% are real fears that we can do something about. The only real fear is the fear of God; it is the beginning of wisdom and the end of all other fears. 2 Tim. 1:7

D. Finally the one who *Stands-up* to the giant. 22-37

1. The *Dreadful Situation*. 22-24

22 Then David left his baggage in the care of the baggage keeper, and ran to the battle line and entered in order to greet his brothers. 23 As he was talking with them, behold, the champion, the Philistine from Gath named Goliath, was coming up from the army of the Philistines, and he spoke these same words; and David heard them. 24 When all the men of Israel saw the man, they fled from him and were greatly afraid – the entire Israelite army is in a panic! Goliath is standing taller than God in their minds.

The fear of man brings a snare, but whoever trusts in the LORD shall be safe. Proverbs 29:25

We have to take our eyes off ourselves and our problems and look to the Lord and yield to His wise plan for our lives. Lloyd Ogilvie wrote:

Our need to be in charge of ourselves, others, and situations often makes our relationship with Christ life's biggest power struggle. We are reluctant to relinquish our control and allow Him to run our lives. We may believe in Him and be active in the church and Christian causes, but trusting Him as Lord of everything in life can be scary. Even though we pray about our challenges and problems, all too often what we really want is strength to accomplish what we've already decided is best for ourselves and others. Meanwhile we press on with our own priorities and plans. We remain the script writer, casting director, choreographer, and producer of the drama of our own lives, in which we are the star performer.

2. The *Carnal Solution.* 25

The men of Israel said, "Have you seen this man who is coming up? Surely he is coming up to defy Israel. And it will be that the king will enrich the man who kills him with great riches and will give him his daughter and make his father's house free in Israel – they were looking to man or to money to solve their problem. It sounds a lot like us – we think our military might or throwing money at the enemy will solve all of our problems.

3. The *Supernatural Salvation.* 26-27

²⁶ Then David spoke to the men who were standing by him, saying, "What will be done for the man who kills this Philistine and takes away the reproach from Israel? For who is this uncircumcised Philistine, that he should taunt the armies of the living God?" ²⁷ The people answered him in accord with this word, saying, "Thus it will be done for the man who kills him." – he is saying, "Hey, remember God! He is not dead!"

4. A *Personal Suggestion.* 31-37

³¹ When the words which David spoke were heard, they told them to Saul, and he sent for him. ³² David said to Saul, "Let no man's heart fail on account of him; your servant will go and fight with this Philistine." ³³ Then Saul said to David, "You are not able to go against this Philistine to fight with him; for you are but a youth while he has been a warrior from his youth." ³⁴ But David said to Saul, "Your servant was tending his father's sheep. When a lion or a bear came and took a lamb from the flock, ³⁵ I went out after him and attacked him, and rescued it from his mouth; and when he rose up against me, I seized him by his beard and struck him and killed him. ³⁶ "Your servant has killed both the lion and the bear; and this uncircumcised Philistine will be like one of them, since he has taunted the armies of the living God." ³⁷ And David said, "The LORD who delivered me from the paw of the lion and from the paw of the bear, He will deliver me from the hand of this Philistine." And Saul said to David, "Go, and may the LORD be with you." – Let the Lord cut this big pagan down to size!

- The Story.

He tells about a time when he was alone watching his father's sheep. A lion and a bear came out after the sheep. If he was in the flesh he would have looked for a tall tree! Or said to himself, "Oh well, maybe they will eat a lamb or two, then they will leave the rest alone…not to mention yours truly!" But being empowered by God he was faithful to his job which was defending the sheep.

- The Secrecy.

We do not know if this happened last week or last year. Apparently David told no one. This is the kind of person God is looking for – one who is just as courageous and dedicated to God when there is no one around! Many people will fight a Goliath in public, but run like a scared rabbit before the lion and bear, when there is no one around to praise them. Many will pray up a storm in public but haven't spent 5 minutes in private prayer all week; Easy to do things before man but it is what we do before God that really counts. Easy to be bold in our witnessing when someone is with us but silent when no one is there to admire us for our witness. Mt. 23:2-7

The Sardis church is still alive and well in our day (Rev. 3:1-3).

God is looking for the person who is just as courageous when there is nobody around. It appears that the criminal mind, which seems never to sleep, has devised a new approach to its craft—silicone masks, with a degree of "ultra high realism."

In Ohio, Conrad Zdzierak, pleaded guilty to using one of the masks to transform himself from a 30-year-old white man into a black character he called The Player, who carried out a string of robberies in the state. The disguise was so effective that local police mistakenly arrested a young African American for the crimes.

Detective Keenan Riordan told reporters, "We showed the picture [of the masked perpetrator] to his mother, and even she thought it was him."

The masks came from the Los Angeles company SPFX Masks, which sells "movie quality" silicone masks that incorporate human hair to achieve what its advertisements call "ultra high realism." The company, set up to cater to the film industry, said that they're proud of the fact that the hand-painted products look realistic. However, they're concerned that the masks have been linked to a string of unsolved crimes. We can wear a spiritual mask but the Lord knows who and what we really are.

IV. FOURTH, HIS *HONESTY*. 38-40

^{38} Then Saul clothed David with his garments and put a bronze helmet on his head, and he clothed him with armor.
^{39} David girded his sword over his armor and tried to walk, for he had not tested them. So David said to Saul, "I cannot go with these, for I have not tested them." And David took them off. ^{40} He took his stick in his hand and chose for himself five smooth stones from the brook, and put them in the shepherd's bag which he had, even in his pouch, and his sling was in his hand; and he approached the Philistine – as instructed he put on Saul's armor. Remember Saul was head and shoulders taller then everybody. It obviously didn't fit David and was not David. David was too honest to try to be what he was not – many today are trying to wear Saul's armor, trying to be what they are not! We need to know and cultivate the gifts and talents that God has given us, and stop trying to be like somebody else. Also, since they were in a valley, people from above may have mistaken David for Saul, if he had worn Saul's armor, with the result that Saul might have gotten the glory…We live in days of dishonesty, politicians proudly brag about, how they can solve this nation's entire problem; dating sites are filled with phony people.
One dating website OkCupid revealed how thousands of its users had answered one

particular question in a survey to measure partner compatibility: Are you a genius?

Amazingly, according to OKCupid's blogger Christian Rudder, two in five people (and nearly half of all men!) said yes to that question. Rudder said, "2 out of 5 think they are one in a thousand." To qualify for most high IQ societies—"genius clubs" like MENSA—you usually need to have an IQ *at least* in the 98th to 99th percentile. That's about one in a hundred. So there's something seriously wrong when 50 percent of men think they are geniuses. God doesn't require any of us to be geniuses but He does demand honesty. Paul sarcastically confronts those in the Corinthian church for thinking they are greater than they are (1 Cor. 4:7-10).

V. FINALLY, HIS *DEPENDENCY* ON GOD. 41-54

A. David's *Inability*. 41-44

⁴¹ Then the Philistine came on and approached David, with the shield-bearer in front of him. ⁴² When the Philistine looked and saw David, he disdained him; for he was but a youth, and ruddy, with a handsome appearance. ⁴³ The Philistine said to David, "Am I a dog, that you come to me with sticks?" And the Philistine cursed David by his gods. ⁴⁴ The Philistine also said to David, "Come to me, and I will give your flesh to the birds of the sky and the beasts of the field." – humanly speaking David looked mighty small standing next to Goliath that day. And he was (2 Cor. 3:5).

Apollo 11 landed on the surface of the moon on Sunday, July 20, 1969. Most of us are familiar with astronaut Neil Armstrong's historic statement as he stepped onto the moon's surface: "That's one small step for man; one giant leap for mankind." But few know about the first meal eaten on the moon. Buzz Aldrin had brought aboard the spacecraft a tiny Communion kit provided by his church. Aldrin sent a radio broadcast to Earth asking listeners to contemplate the events of that day and give thanks. Then, in radio blackout for privacy Buzz Aldrin read, "I am the vine, ye *are* the branches: He that abideth in me, and I in him, the same bringeth forth much fruit: for without me ye can do nothing."

B. David's *Sufficiency.* 45-47

45 Then David said to the Philistine, "You come to me with a sword, a spear, and a javelin, but I come to you in the name of the LORD of hosts, the God of the armies of Israel, whom you have taunted. 46 "This day the LORD will deliver you up into my hands, and I will strike you down and remove your head from you. And I will give the dead bodies of the army of the Philistines this day to the birds of the sky and the wild beasts of the earth, that all the earth may know that there is a God in Israel, 47 and that all this assembly may know that the LORD does not deliver by sword or by spear; for the battle is the LORD'S and He will give you into our hands." – David looked him straight in the kneecap and said the Lord will deliver you into my hands! Phil. 4:13

Dr. Cuyler, "I crossed the ocean lately on a powerful steamship, which weighed over twenty thousand tons, and pushed her way against winds and waves at the rate of twenty knots an hour. I could not see the propelling force: that was hidden deep down in the glowing furnaces, heaped constantly with fresh coal. As long as the coal lasted the steamer could hold on her victorious way. That illustrates the spiritual life of every strong, healthy Christian. His strength is measured by his inward supply of Divine [enabling] grace (Phil. 4:13)."

C. David's God-given *Victory.* 48-54

48 Then it happened when the Philistine rose and came and drew near to meet David, that David ran quickly toward the battle line to meet the Philistine. 49 And David put his hand into his bag and took from it a stone and slung it, and struck the Philistine on his forehead. And the stone sank into his forehead, so that he fell on his face to the ground. 50 Thus David prevailed over the Philistine with a sling and a stone, and he struck the Philistine and killed him; but there was no sword in David's hand. 51 Then David ran and stood over the Philistine and took his sword and drew it out of its sheath and killed him, and cut off his head with it. When the Philistines saw that their champion was dead, they fled. ⁵² The men of Israel and Judah arose and shouted and pursued the Philistines as far as the valley, and to the gates of Ekron. And the slain Philistines lay along the way to Shaaraim, even to Gath and Ekron. ⁵³ The sons of Israel returned from chasing the Philistines and plundered their camps. ⁵⁴ Then David took the Philistine's head and brought it to Jerusalem, but he put his weapons in his tent – any time our inadequacy meets God's sufficiency we will have victory (1 Cor. 15:57).

C. Saul wants to know David's *Identity*. 55-58

⁵⁵ Now when Saul saw David going out against the Philistine, he said to Abner the commander of the army, "Abner, whose son is this young man?" And Abner said, "By your life, O king, I do not know." ⁵⁶ The king said, "You inquire whose son the youth is." ⁵⁷ So when David returned from killing the Philistine, Abner took him and brought him before Saul with the Philistine's head in his hand. ⁵⁸ Saul said to him, "Whose son are you, young man?" And David answered, "I am the son of your servant Jesse the Bethlehemite."

Con:

1. Do we have a heart for God?

2. Margaret was the widow of Scot Baliol of Norway. When he died, she had his heart removed and placed in a sealed ivory box. For

some 21 years she carried it with her and called it her "sweet heart and silent companion."

One her death bed she requested that his heart be laid upon her breast, declaring that their hearts would be united throughout eternity.

Lucado makes a needed observation:

"Our hearts seems so far from His. His is pure, we are greedy; He is peaceful, we are hassled; He is purposeful, we are distracted; He is pleasant, we are cranky; He is spiritual, we are earthbound. The distance between our hearts and His seem so immense. How could we ever hope to have the heart of Jesus? Ready for the surprise? As believers we already do! Paul says "Christ lives in me!" (Gal. 2:20). He has moved in and unpacked his bags and is ready to change you into His likeness from one degree of glory to another (2 Cor. 3:18).

Chapter Twenty-One

SAUL, A SMALL HEARTED KING

1 Sam. 18

Intro:

1. "Every Who, down in Who-Ville. Liked Christmas a lot...

But the Grinch, who lived just north of Who-ville, did not!

The Grinch hated Christmas! The whole Christmas season.

Now, please don't ask why. No one quite knows the reason.

It could be his head wasn't screwed on just right.

It could be, perhaps, that his shoes were too tight.

But I think that the most likely reason of all

May have been that his heart was two sizes too small."

2. Most of us are familiar with the Dr. Seuss story, *How the Grinch Stole Christmas,* that poor old Grinch had a heart that was too small – the tragedy of small-hearted people.

I. FIRST, THE BIG HEART'S *LOYALTY.* 18:1-4

A. The *Kinship.* 1-2

¹Now it came about when he had finished speaking to Saul, that the soul of Jonathan was knit to the soul of David, and Jonathan loved him as himself. ² Saul took him that day and did not let him return to his father's house – Jonathan loved David as so did all of Israel (v. 16).

The verb carries the connotation "was loyal to" (cf. vv. 1, 3). This idiom is attested in the broader culture. In the Amarna letters (fourteenth century BC) cities are said to "love" a leader; the term refers to loyalty. This shows Jonathan's heart; remember he would have been the next in line to be the king of Israel, if God had not rejected Saul. He could have resented David and sought to undermine his leadership, but his heart was big and godly. There is a real kinship between David and Jonathan. Everybody needs a Jonathan, someone we feel a kinship with, this goes beyond mere blood ties.

In the movie *Tombstone,* Doc Holliday is out in the wilderness, coughing uncontrollably, he has TB. He is with Wyatt Earps men. One asks him, "Doc, why are you out here, you should be in bed!" He said, "Wyatt's my friend." The man laughs and says, "I've got lots of friends." Doc replied, "I don't!" The truth is we have very few real friends; we have lots of acquaintances but few real friends.

B. The *Kingship.* 3-4

³ Then Jonathan made a covenant with David because he loved him as himself. ⁴ Jonathan stripped himself of the robe that was on him and gave it to David, with his armor, including his sword and his bow and his belt – Jonathan is renouncing his right to be the king because he recognizes that David is God's choice.

Bergens, "The fact that Jonathan gave David the garb and the armaments originally reserved for the heir to Saul's throne clearly posses symbolic significance."

Davis, "If we press the verb, the bond was inaugurated by severing an animal and by both parties passing between the pieces as if to say, "If I am unfaithful to my word in this covenant, may I end up in pieces as this animal…The clothes signify the person and his position – hence Jonathan renounces his position as crown prince and transfers, so far as his own will goes, the right of succession to David."

Trans: Jonathan, unlike his father Saul, had a large heart, one that gladly surrendered to what he knew was God's will. He was loyal to David because he was loyal to God.

According to Zac Levi, the star of the NBC spy comedy *Chuck*, playing the role of an average guy whose life gets turned upside-down as a government spy is not much different than suddenly becoming the star of a TV show. Zac said:

"Just as Chuck was struggling through the newfound world of spydom, I was struggling with a newfound world of celebrity. If you're someone who puts their faith in Jesus, then trust him in being led. To me, it's not rocket science. Go about your day putting your faith in God and standing on truth. It's pretty easy: …Walk in love and that opens some doors of dialogue. How about just starting to talk and see where it goes? I don't think there's any clock on it—your life is God's, so let him do as he wills with it."

II. FINALLY, THE SMALL HEART IS FILLED WITH JEALOUSY. 5-30

A. For starters, the *Case* of Jealousy – the fear of losing something. 5-7

1. Fear of losing *Affection.* 1, 16, 20

[1] Now it came about when he had finished speaking to Saul, that the soul of Jonathan was knit to the soul of David, and Jonathan loved him as himself...[16] But all Israel and Judah loved David, and he went out and came in before them...[20] Now Michal [Mike-el], Saul's daughter, loved David. When they told Saul, the thing was agreeable to him – Saul was afraid that his son, daughter, and the nation loved David more than him!

Jealousy is always afraid of losing someone's affections. I remember reading about Winston Churchill; he had a dog named Rufus. When Churchill came home from a trip, the dog was brought to the station to meet him. On one trip the dog ran over to Norman McGowan. Churchill with a hurt look on his face whispered, "Norman, in the future, I would prefer you stay in the train until I've said hello!"

2. Fear of losing *Acceptance.* 5

⁵ So David went out wherever Saul sent him, and prospered; and Saul set him over the men of war. And it was pleasing in the sight of all the people and also in the sight of Saul's servants – David was immediately accepted by everybody! In Saul's mind, David's acceptance meant Saul's rejection. A small heart filled with jealousy cannot imagine anyone having more than one friend.

In her new book, *Linda Ronstadt: Simple Dreams*, the 11-time Grammy Award singer recalls the first time she heard fellow singer Emmylou Harris.

"My first reaction to it was slightly conflicted. First, I loved her singing wildly. Second, in my opinion, she was doing what I was trying to do, only a whole lot better. Then came a split-second decision that I made that affected the way I listened to and enjoyed music for the rest of my life. I thought that if I allowed myself to become envious of Emmy, it would be painful to listen to her, and I would deny myself the pleasure of it. If I simply surrendered to loving what she did, I could take my rightful place among the other drooling Emmylou fans, and then maybe, just maybe, I might be able to sing with her. I surrendered."

Linda went on to not only sing with Emmy, but also record three award-winning albums with her and Dolly Parton as a trio.

What a wonderful trio, Saul, David, and Jonathan could have made – but Saul's small heart would have no part of it!

3. Fear of losing the place of *Achievement.* 6-7

6 It happened as they were coming, when David returned from killing the Philistine, that the women came out of all the cities of Israel, singing and dancing, to meet King Saul, with tambourines, with joy and with musical instruments. 7 The women sang as they played, and said, "Saul has slain his thousands, And David his ten thousands." – David was achieving more then Saul!

Henry Varley is best known as the man who stated to Dwight Moody, "The world has yet to see what God will do with a man who is fully committed to him." Moody sought to be that man and went on to become the world's most prominent evangelist of his day.

What is not so well known about Varley is that he was himself a powerful evangelist and pastor. But he faced a pitch battle with jealousy when another preacher in his neighborhood began having great success and started drawing some of Varley's members. Varley felt deep resentment toward the other minister and later divulged:

"I shall never forget the sense of guilt and sin that possessed me over that business. I was miserable. Was I practically saying to the Lord Jesus, "Unless the prosperity of [your] church and people comes in this neighborhood by me, success had better not come"? Was I really showing inability to rejoice in another worker's service? I felt that it was a sin of a very hateful character. I never asked the Lord to take away my life either before or since, but I did then, unless his grace would give me victory over this foul image of jealousy."

Trans: Jealousy is the fear of losing something – loosing exclusive rights to someone's affections; fear of others being accepted and out achieving us – it is a sin we all wrestle with from time to time! But few of us will admit it.

Gene Edwards, "Saul is in your bloodstream, in the marrow of your bones. He makes up the very flesh and muscle of your heart. He is mixed into your soul. He inhabits the nuclei of your atoms. King Saul is one with you!"

As long as we still have a sin nature there is a Grinch heart in all of us!

"All the Who girls and boys, Would wake bright and early.

They'd rush for their toys, And then! Oh, the noise! Noise, Noise

Then the Who's, young and old, would sit down to a feast.

And they'd feast! And they'd feast!

They would feast on Who-pudding, and rare Who-roast-beef

Which was something the Grinch couldn't stand in the least!"

Jealousy hates the thought that somebody else might be feasting more then it...

B. Furthermore the *Consequences* of Jealousy – we lose it! 8-30

1. There was *Irritability.* 8a

⁸ *Then Saul became very angry...* – when we turn green with envy, it's not long before we turn red with anger.

Jesus said that anger was the father of murder! If we allow anger to fester in our hearts, we become a murderous time-bomb!

In June of 2012, Carl Ericsson, a 73-year-old South Dakota man, was sentenced to life in prison after admitting to the murder of a former high school classmate. Friends and family members were shocked that the once-successful insurance salesman seemed to snap. Ericsson had been married to his wife for over 44 years. But after the murder, Ericsson's secret finally came out. For over 50 years he had simmered with a belated grudge: He was still mad about a classmate, Norman Johnson who had once pulled a jock strap over his head during a high school locker room prank. After holding the grudge for over 50 years, Carl Ericsson rang Johnson's doorbell and shot him dead. Ericsson told a judge, "I guess it was from something that happened over 50 years ago. It was apparently in my subconscious." During his sentencing, Ericsson turned to Johnson's widow and apologized, saying, "I just wish I could turn the calendar back."

2. The *Insecurity.* 8b-9

⁸ Then Saul became very angry, for this saying displeased him; and he said, "They have ascribed to David ten thousands, but to me they have ascribed thousands. Now what more can he have but the kingdom?" ⁹ Saul looked at David with suspicion from that day on – Saul had nothing to fear from David, but jealousy twists our thinking.

A European city has a statue that is a monument to Envy and Jealousy. It has *crooked legs* symbolizing the way jealousy twists things; the *arms* are unusually long with big rough hands because jealously reaches out to destroy anything that threatens its existence; its *ears* are big and long because they are always suspiciously listening for any tidbit to jump on; the *eyes* are hideous and diseased because jealousy can only see things negatively with a reference point to itself; and from its *mouth* hangs a long tongue – its forked for all its speech is demonic.

3.The demonic *Instability.* 10-12

¹⁰ *Now it came about on the next day that an evil spirit from God came mightily upon Saul, and he raved in the midst of the house, while David was playing the harp with his hand, as*

usual; and a spear *was* in Saul's hand. [11] Saul hurled the spear for he thought, "I will pin David to the wall." But David escaped from his presence twice. [12] Now Saul was afraid of David, for the LORD was with him but had departed from Saul – any time we tolerate sin we open the door for a Satanic stronghold.

[26] BE ANGRY, AND *yet* DO NOT SIN; do not let the sun go down on your anger, [27] and do not give the devil an opportunity. Ephesians 4:26-27

In the story we see the Grinch seething in anger. The narrative says:

"Then he growled, with his Grinch fingers nervously drumming.

I must find some way to stop Christmas from coming…

Then he got an idea! An awful idea!

The Grinch got a wonderful, awful idea!"

He then makes himself a Santa Claus suit and puts antlers on his dog Max and heads for Who-ville.

Saul must stop David and so begins his demonically crafted plan.

4. The temporary *Insanity.* 13-30

That is likely what they would call it these days in a court of law…it was a planned, premeditated murder! We think we are incapable of such planning, but if we allow jealously a place in our hearts, we become capable of doing anything!

a. He tried to murder David by way of the *Military*. 13-19

13 Therefore Saul removed him from his presence and appointed him as his commander of a thousand; and he went out and came in before the people. 14 David was prospering in all his ways for the LORD was with him. 15 When Saul saw that he was prospering greatly, he dreaded him. 16 But all Israel and Judah loved David, and he went out and came in before them. 17 Then Saul said to David, "Here is my older daughter Merab; I will give her to you as a wife, only be a valiant man for me and fight the LORD'S battles." For Saul thought, "My hand shall not be against him, but let the hand of the Philistines be against him." 18 But David said to Saul, "Who am I, and what is my life or my father's family in Israel, that I should be the king's son-in-law?" 19 So it came about at the time when Merab, Saul's daughter, should have been given to David, that she was given to Adriel the Meholathite for a wife – he was simply hoping that David would be killed in a battle against the Philistines.

As for offering him his daughter, she was already rightly his when he killed Goliath (17:25). Apparently, Saul had not kept his word. The fact that David had killed Goliath wasn't enough, for Saul now expected David to "fight the battles of the Lord" in order to gain his wife, Saul's eldest daughter, Merab.

b. He tried through *Matrimony*. 20-30

[20] Now Michal, Saul's daughter, loved David. When they told Saul, the thing was agreeable to him. [21] Saul thought, "I will give her to him that she may become a snare to him, and that the hand of the Philistines may be against him." Therefore Saul said to David, "For a second time you may be my son-in-law today." [22] Then Saul commanded his servants, "Speak to David secretly, saying, 'Behold, the king delights in you, and all his servants love you; now therefore, become the king's son-in-law.'" [23] So Saul's servants spoke these words to David. But David said, "Is it trivial in your sight to become the king's son-in-law, since I am a poor man and lightly esteemed?" [24] The servants of Saul reported to him according to these words which David spoke. [25] Saul then said, "Thus you shall say to David, 'The king does not desire any dowry except a hundred foreskins of the Philistines, to take vengeance on the king's enemies.'" Now Saul planned to make David fall by the hand of the Philistines. [26] When his servants told David these words, it pleased David to become the king's son-in-law. Before the days had expired [27] David rose up and went, he and his men, and struck down two hundred men among the Philistines. Then David brought their foreskins, and they gave

them in full number to the king, that he might become the king's son-in-law. So Saul gave him Michal his daughter for a wife. ²⁸ When Saul saw and knew that the LORD was with David, and that Michal, Saul's daughter, loved him, ²⁹ then Saul was even more afraid of David. Thus Saul was David's enemy continually. ³⁰ Then the commanders of the Philistines went out to battle, and it happened as often as they went out, that David behaved himself more wisely than all the servants of Saul. So his name was highly esteemed - Saul told his servants to tell David that all that the king required for a bride price was 100 foreskins from the "uncircumcised Philistines." Saul was certain that at some point in this endeavor, David would meet his death. David once more survived the battles and he brought the king 200 foreskins. Another of Saul's schemes had failed and he had to give Michal to David as his wife.

Trans: The Consequences of unchecked and unconfessed Jealousy is deadly on others and ultimately on ourselves. There is a Grecian story of a man who killed himself through jealousy. His fellow citizens had erected a statue to a man who was loved, respected, and praised for his military ability. This man was so jealous that he went out every night and under the cover of darkness chipped away at the base of the statue. Finally one night the huge statue fell – right on the man and killed him instantly!

Jealousy does more damage to the one in whom it is stored than the one on whom it is poured.

After the Grinch had taken all the Who's stocking, presents, tree, and food he sat listening above for the cries of woe...

"They're just waking up! I know just what they'll do!

Their mouths will hang open for a minute or two

Then the Who's down in Who-ville will all cry Boo-hoo!

That's a noise, grinned the Grinch, That I simply must hear!

So he paused. And the Grinch put his hand to his ear.

And he did hear a sound rising over the snow.

It started in low. Then it started to grow...

But the sound wasn't sad! Why, this sound sounded merry!

It couldn't be so! But it was merry! Very!

Every Who down in Who-ville, the tall and the small,

Was singing! Without any presents at all!

He hadn't stopped Christmas from coming! It came!

Somehow or other, it came just the same!"

Jealous people are confused when those they hate are just as content when they have nothing left but Jesus!

C. Finally the only *Cure* for Jealousy...Let go!

1. His *Lordship*.

Saul's basic problem was that he forgot who the kingdom belonged to in the first place! He forgot that there was a king higher than his kingship! Like the Supreme Court these days, they have forgotten there is one more supreme then they are!

Lutzer, "Saul's one fatal flaw: He saw the kingdom as belonging to Himself and not to God! He would not recognize God's authority as owner over the kingdom. He would not resign even though the Almighty had spoken. Saul hoped to manipulate instead of celebrate God's will!"

Have we sought to trade our God's kingdom for our little self-kingdom? Jealousy is the fear of losing something, once we realize it all belongs to Him; jealousy loses its power over us. We do not fear losing that which is not ours to begin with!

2. His *Love*.

Notice Jonathan never had a problem with David's position as the next king because he loved both God and David. Jealousy is self-love, we need to replace it with love for God and others.

Con:

1. While it is true, we all still have a small heart like that of Saul. None of us have lost the sin nature. It is also equally true that all who are saved have a new nature that loves God and others. We have the desire in our new man, and the power to carry that out by the indwelling Holy Spirit (Gal. 5:16).

2. The same thing happend to us, that happened to that Grinch!

"He puzzled three hours, till his puzzler was sore.

Then the Grinch thought of something he hadn't before.

Maybe Christmas he thought doesn't come from a store.

Maybe Christmas, perhaps, means a little bit more.

And what happened then…? Well, in Who-ville they say

That the Grinch's small heart, grew three sizes that day."

The gospel offers something better, not a re-patching up of the old heart but a new one – one inhabited by God Himself!

Chapter Twenty-Two

THE MARKS OF FRIENDSHIP

1 Sam. 19-20

Intro:

1. "Friendship is a priceless gift,

That cannot be bought or sold,

But its value is far greater, than a mountain of gold.

For gold is cold and lifeless, it can neither see nor hear.

And in the time of trouble, it is powerless to cheer.

It has no ears to listen, or heart to understand.

It cannot bring you comfort or reach out a helping hand.

So when you ask God for a gift, be thankful if He sends,

Not diamonds, pearls or riches,

But the love of real true friends."

2. Friendship in one's life is better than, gold in one's safe! We have before us what real friendship is all about.

I. FIRST, A FRIENDSHIP INVOLVES INTERCESSION. 1-7

A. The *Plot.* 19:1

Now Saul told Jonathan his son and all his servants to put David to death. But Jonathan, Saul's son, greatly delighted in David – Saul had quietly tried to put David to death through others, now he no longer hides the fact that he wants David dead! Five times in this chapter reference is made to Saul's intending to kill David (vv. 1, 2, 5, 11, 15).

B. The secret hiding *Place.* 2-3

² So Jonathan told David saying, "Saul my father is seeking to put you to death. Now therefore, please be on guard in the morning, and stay in a secret place and hide yourself. ³ "I will go out and stand beside my father in the field where you are, and I will speak with my father about you; if I find out anything, then I will tell you." – Jonathan warned David and sent him to a place of safety.

C. The *Plea.* 4-7

⁴ Then Jonathan spoke well of David to Saul his father and said to him, "Do not let the king sin against his servant David, since he has not sinned against you, and since his deeds have been very beneficial to you. ⁵ "For he took his life in his hand and struck the Philistine, and the LORD brought about a great deliverance for all Israel; you saw it and rejoiced. Why then will you sin against innocent blood by putting David to death without a cause?" ⁶ Saul listened to the voice of Jonathan, and Saul vowed, "As the LORD lives, he shall not be put to death." ⁷ Then Jonathan called David, and Jonathan told him all these words. And Jonathan brought David to Saul, and he was in his presence as formerly - Jonathan demonstrated his friendship by interceding in David's behalf.

This is demonstrated by the best friend that we have: Therefore He is able also to save forever those who draw near to God through Him, since He always lives to make intercession for them. Hebrews 7:25

Satan the accuser of the brethren will always bring accusations against us, but the Lord Jesus pleads His blood in our behalf (Rom. 8:31-34/1 Jn. 2:1-2).

Trans: You can look into a dirty mud puddle on a full moon night, and see bright and beautiful stars being reflected in it. No matter how muddy the puddle, it does not affect the brightness of those stars. In the same way, even when a Christian sins and finds himself in the dirt, God sees Christ in our behalf! His blood and His righteousness never wane or diminish.

II. FURTHERMORE, FRIENDSHIP INVOLVES *IMPERFECTION*. 8-17

A. Jonathan was *Away*. 8-10

⁸ When there was war again, David went out and fought with the Philistines and defeated them with great slaughter, so that they fled before him. ⁹ Now there was an evil spirit from the LORD on Saul as he was sitting in his house with his spear in his hand, and David was playing the harp with his hand. ¹⁰ Saul tried to pin David to the wall with the spear, but he slipped away out of Saul's presence, so that he stuck the spear into the wall. And David fled and escaped that night – where was Jonathan? We don't know but he was not there for David when he needed him.

In the movie Cool Hand Luke the other prisoners were supportive of Luke until he broke and then they wanted nothing to do with him. In one scene after an exhaustive time on digging a ditch and then refilling it over and over again, after being beat he comes in and falls to the ground, everybody turns their back on him and he cries out, "Where are you now!"

Truth is all friends are imperfect, I have learned one thing in pastoring, you cannot depend on people! I have found there are two kinds of members, those who have left just when you needed them, and those that are gonna leave. But there is one friend who will never leave or forsake us, who will be there always and forever!

He is never Away (Mat. 28:19-20/Prov.18:24).

B. Michal went *Astray.* 11-16

1. She was guilty of the sin of *Idolatry.* 11-13

¹¹ Then Saul sent messengers to David's house to watch him, in order to put him to death in the morning. But Michal, David's wife, told him, saying, "If you do not save your life tonight, tomorrow you will be put to death." ¹² So Michal let David down through a window, and he went out and fled and escaped. ¹³ Michal took the household idol and laid it on the bed, and put a quilt of goats' hair at its head, and covered it with clothes – David's wife was demonstrated friendship as she foiled Saul's plan to kill David in bed. She used a household idol, something that was forbidden to have.

2. She was also guilty of telling a *Story.* 14-16

¹⁴ When Saul sent messengers to take David, she said, "He is sick." ¹⁵ Then Saul sent messengers to see David, saying, "Bring him up to me on his bed, that I may put him to death." ¹⁶ When the messengers entered, behold, the household idol was on the bed with the quilt of goats' hair at its head – in reality David was not sick. The truth is every earthly friend we have is still a sinner! We may not want to admit it but we have all bowed to an idol and have shaded the truth.

If we claim that we're free of sin, we're only fooling ourselves. A claim like that is errant nonsense. 1 John 1:8 (MSG)

History has shown that George Washington most likely did *not* chop down his father's cherry tree and thus did not say, "I cannot tell a lie." He, like us, is quite capable of telling a lie. One little girl asked her mother, "Do people who never tell lies go to heaven?" Her mother said, "Yes, they are the only ones." The little girl looked sad and said, "Gosh, I'll bet its lonely up there with only God and George Washington!"

C. Michal's loyalty was only *Part Way.* 17

So Saul said to Michal, "Why have you deceived me like this and let my enemy go, so that he has escaped?" And Michal said to Saul, "He said to me, 'Let me go! Why should I put you to death?'" – she was loyal only to a point. When her back was against the wall she leveled a false accusation against David. He had never threatened to kill her. And by saying he did, would only increase Saul's anger against David.

Trans: Bottom line – earthly friends are imperfect. We do know what it is like go Away when people need us or we need them; we have all gone Astray from time to time; and our loyalty is sometimes only part Way. But we do have a friend that is always near and there for us; He is perfectly faithful and sinless. When Ronald Reagan met with the Speaker of the House Tip O'Neil, shortly after being elected, Tip told him, "even though we belong to different parties, and will have many disagreements, I look forward to working together with you." Then he said, "Let's agree to always be friends after five o'clock."

Our friendship with the Lord is *always* and *all the way…*

III. THIRD, FRIENDSHIP MEANS *INTERVENTION.* 18-24

Samuel proved to be a friend of David…

A. You can *go* to a friend *Anytime.* 18a

18 Now David fled and escaped and came to Samuel at Ramah… - he doesn't send a word to Samuel that he is coming, he just shows up and he is welcomed and warmly received.
B. You can also *talk* to a friend about *Anything.* 18b

…and told him all that Saul had done to him – he was allowed to share his heart with him.

B. You are *safe* with a friend, from *Anyone.* 18c-24

1. He had a *Prolonged* stay with Samuel.

And he and Samuel went and stayed in Naioth – stayed in the Hebrew is an *imperfect tense* meaning that he stayed with Samuel a long time. A friend will take you in and help you out long term.

2. He *Prayed* with Samuel.

How do we know that? Because our previous study of Samuel revealed he was constantly in prayer.

3. He was *Protected* by Samuel. 19-24

a. First Wave. 19-20

[19] It was told Saul, saying, "Behold, David is at Naioth in Ramah." [20] Then Saul sent messengers to take David, but when they saw the company of the prophets prophesying, with Samuel standing and presiding over them, the Spirit of God came upon the messengers of Saul; and they also prophesied – these boys were either saved or revived!

b. Second Wave. 21a

[21] When it was told Saul, he sent other messengers, and they also prophesied

c. Third Wave. 21b

So Saul sent messengers again the third time, and they also prophesied

d. Final Wave. 22-24

²² Then he himself went to Ramah and came as far as the large well that is in Secu; and he asked and said, "Where are Samuel and David?" And someone said, "Behold, they are at Naioth in Ramah." ²³ He proceeded there to Naioth in Ramah; and the Spirit of God came upon him also, so that he went along prophesying continually until he came to Naioth in Ramah. ²⁴ He also stripped off his clothes, and he too prophesied before Samuel and lay down naked all that day and all that night. Therefore they say, "Is Saul also among the prophets?" – this is a snapshot of what Saul could have been – broken and blessed by God's Spirit.

Trans: Again, there is only one friend who we can go to *anytime* and share with Him *anything* that is on our hearts. We are invited to abide in Him, have prayer with Him, and know that He will protect us from any and all enemies.

I read about a Mrs. Civilla D.Martin who was seriously ill, she sought the Lord and was supernaturally delivered. She wrote:

"Why should I feel discouraged?
Why should the shadows come?
Why should my heart be lonely?
And long for heaven and home,
When Jesus is my portion,
My constant friend is He;
His eye is on the sparrow,

And I know He watches me!"

Mrs. Booth, wife of William Booth who founded the Salvation Army, when she was a little girl she saw them dragging a prisoner down the street. People were yelling at the prisoner but she walked up to him and walked down the street with him. Later she said, "It seemed to me that he had not a friend in the world. I walk down the street with him determined that he should know that there was one soul that felt for him *whether he suffered for his own fault or that of another.*"

"No longer do I call you slaves, for the slave does not know what his master is doing; but I have called you friends, for all things that I have heard from My Father I have made known to you. John 15:15

The Lord can sing that James Taylor song to all of His own:

When you're down and troubled
and you need a helping hand
and nothing whoa nothing is going right.
Close your eyes and think of me
and soon I will be there
to brighten up even your darkest nights.
You just call out my name
and you know wherever I am
I'll come running...
If the sky above you
should turn dark and full of clouds
and that old north wind should begin to blow

Keep your head together and call my name out loud
and soon I will be knocking upon your door.
You just call out my name and you know wherever I am
I'll come running to see you again.
Winter, spring, summer or fall
all you got to do is call
and I'll be there...
Hey, ain't it good to know that you've got a friend?
People can be so cold.
They'll hurt you and desert you.
Well they'll take your soul if you let them.
Oh yeah, but don't you let them.
You just call out my name and you know wherever I am
I'll come running to see you again...
Winter spring summer or fall,
Hey now, all you've got to do is call.
Lord, I'll be there, yes I will.
You've got a friend.
You've got a friend.
Ain't it good to know you've got a friend.
Ain't it good to know you've got a friend.
You've got a friend.

IV. FOURTH, FRIENDSHIP DOES NOT ELIMINATE *CONFRONTATION*. 20:1-2

A. The *Confusion.* 1

Then David fled from Naioth in Ramah, and came and said to Jonathan, "What have I done? What is my iniquity? And what is my sin before your father, that he is seeking my life?" – he is having a self-pity party! We whine why me Lord? Why can't I get this church off the ground? Why can't I pay my bills" Why can't I get my health back? Why can't I get a job?"

B. The *Correction.* 2

He said to him, "Far from it, you shall not die. Behold, my father does nothing either great or small without disclosing it to me. So why should my father hide this thing from me? It is not so!" – friends love us enough to confront us with the truth. Jonathan said, "David you got it wrong and you should know it! Do you think God anointed you king so you could die before wearing the crown? Get a grip!"

Kingsley, "A blessed thing it is for any man or woman to have a friend; one who knows the best and worst of us, and who loves us in spite of our faults; and yet who will speak honest truth to us."

V. FIFTH, FRIENDSHIP GIVES *INSTRUCTIONS.* 20:3-40

A. The *Certainty.*

³ Yet David vowed again, saying, "Your father knows well that I have found favor in your sight, and he has said, 'Do not let Jonathan know this, or he will be grieved.' But truly as the LORD lives and as your soul lives, there is hardly a step between me and death." – normally this would be true, but before that step he must step upon the throne of Israel because God has promised.

B. *Strategy.*

⁴ Then Jonathan said to David, "Whatever you say, I will do for you." ⁵ So David said to Jonathan, "Behold, tomorrow is the new moon, and I ought to sit down to eat with the king. But let me go, that I may hide myself in the field until the third evening. ⁶ "If your father misses me at all, then say, 'David earnestly asked leave of me to run to Bethlehem his city, because it is the yearly sacrifice there for the whole family.' ⁷ "If he says, 'It is good,' your servant will be safe; but if he is very angry, know that he has decided on evil.
⁸ "Therefore deal kindly with your servant, for you have brought your servant into a covenant of the LORD with you. But if there is iniquity in me, put me to death yourself; for why then should you bring me to your father?" ⁹ Jonathan said, "Far be it from you! For if I should indeed learn that evil has been decided by my father to come upon you, then would I not tell you about it?" ¹⁰ Then David said to Jonathan, "Who will tell me if your father answers you harshly?" ¹¹ Jonathan said to David, "Come, and let us go out into the field." So both of them went out to the field.
¹² Then Jonathan said to David, "The LORD, the God of Israel, be witness! When I have sounded out my father about this time tomorrow, or the third day, behold, if there is good feeling toward David, shall I not then

send to you and make it known to you? ¹³ "If it please my father to do you harm, may the LORD do so to Jonathan and more also, if I do not make it known to you and send you away, that you may go in safety. And may the LORD be with you as He has been with my father. ¹⁴ "If I am still alive, will you not show me the lovingkindness of the LORD, that I may not die? ¹⁵ "You shall not cut off your lovingkindness from my house forever, not even when the LORD cuts off every one of the enemies of David from the face of the earth."
¹⁶ So Jonathan made a covenant with the house of David, saying, "May the LORD require it at the hands of David's enemies."
¹⁷ Jonathan made David vow again because of his love for him, because he loved him as he loved his own life. ¹⁸ Then Jonathan said to him, "Tomorrow is the new moon, and you will be missed because your seat will be empty.
¹⁹ "When you have stayed for three days, you shall go down quickly and come to the place where you hid yourself on that eventful day, and you shall remain by the stone Ezel. ²⁰ "I will shoot three arrows to the side, as though I shot at a target. ²¹ "And behold, I will send the lad, saying, 'Go, find the arrows.' If I specifically say to the lad, 'Behold, the arrows are on this side of you, get them,' then come; for there is safety for you and no harm, as the LORD lives. ²² "But if I say to the youth, 'Behold, the arrows are beyond you,' go, for the LORD has sent you away. ²³ "As for the agreement of which you and I have spoken,

behold, the LORD is between you and me forever." ²⁴ So David hid in the field; and when the new moon came, the king sat down to eat food. ²⁵ The king sat on his seat as usual, the seat by the wall; then Jonathan rose up and Abner sat down by Saul's side, but David's place was empty. ²⁶ Nevertheless Saul did not speak anything that day, for he thought, "It is an accident, he is not clean, surely he is not clean." ²⁷ It came about the next day, the second day of the new moon, that David's place was empty; so Saul said to Jonathan his son, "Why has the son of Jesse not come to the meal, either yesterday or today?" ²⁸ Jonathan then answered Saul, "David earnestly asked leave of me to go to Bethlehem, ²⁹ for he said, 'Please let me go, since our family has a sacrifice in the city, and my brother has commanded me to attend. And now, if I have found favor in your sight, please let me get away that I may see my brothers.' For this reason he has not come to the king's table." ³⁰ Then Saul's anger burned against Jonathan and he said to him, "You son of a perverse, rebellious woman! Do I not know that you are choosing the son of Jesse to your own shame and to the shame of your mother's nakedness? ³¹ "For as long as the son of Jesse lives on the earth, neither you nor your kingdom will be established. Therefore now, send and bring him to me, for he must surely die." ³² But Jonathan answered Saul his father and said to him, "Why should he be put to death? What has he done?" ³³ Then Saul *hurled his spear at him to strike him down; so Jonathan knew that his father had decided to put David to death. ³⁴ Then Jonathan arose from the table in fierce anger, and did not eat food on the second day of the new moon, for he was grieved over David because his father had dishonored him. ³⁵ Now it came about in the morning that Jonathan went out into the field for the appointment with David, and a little lad was with him. ³⁶ He said to his lad, "Run, find now the arrows which I am about to shoot." As the lad was running, he shot an arrow past him. ³⁷ When the lad reached the place of the arrow which Jonathan had shot, Jonathan called after the lad and said, "Is not the arrow beyond you?" ³⁸ And Jonathan called after the lad, "Hurry, be quick, do not stay!" And Jonathan's lad picked up the arrow and came to his master. ³⁹ But the lad was not aware of anything; only Jonathan and David knew about the matter. ⁴⁰ Then Jonathan gave his weapons to his lad and said to him, "Go, bring them to the city."* – he instructs him on a workable plan.

The plan is basically David is not going to show up for supper. Saul will say, "Hey, where's David?" Jonathan will say, "He is going to Bethel to offer a sacrifice." And they observe his father reaction. Saul goes crazy and threatens to kill David and throws a spear at Jonathan! It's obvious that David's life is in jeopardy. David was hiding out in the field, Jonathan's arrow boy shot an arrow and when he went after it, Jonathan shouted "The arrows are beyond you" thus telling David it was not safe to come home. Friends give each other advice and our greatest Friend has given us an instruction Book to live by.

Joseph Scriven had set plans to get married, but she accidently drowned just before the wedding. Some years later his mother became deathly ill. He wrote a letter to her that contained these words:

What a friend we have in Jesus, All our sins and grief's to bear;

What a privilege to carry, Everything to God in prayer.

O what peace we often forfeit, O what needless pain we bear,

All because we do not carry everything to God in prayer.

VI. FINALLY, FRIENDSHIP INVOLVES AFFECTION. 41-42

41 When the lad was gone, David rose from the south side and fell on his face to the ground, and bowed three times. And they kissed each other and wept together, but David wept the more. 42 Jonathan said to David, "Go in safety, inasmuch as we have sworn to each other in the name of the LORD, saying, 'The LORD will be between me and you, and between my descendants and your descendants forever.'"

Then he rose and departed, while Jonathan went into the city – Friends should not be afraid to shed a few tears and say, "I love you."

Gordon MacDonald, shared this, "I was an interior lineman, starting freshman. And I played every game for four years without a serious injury. There were three other guys on the line that played with me almost the entire time. I can't tell you how much we loved each other. We won; we lost; we helped each other through injuries, through good and bad romances, through studies. There wasn't anything we didn't do together. I could cry with those guys. And there wasn't anything we couldn't say to each other. I mean there were some times when we got good and mad at one another. And I'm thirty-eight. I'm still grieving. When football was over and we said good-bye it was like a death."

Joseph expressed his love for his brothers, "[14] Then he fell on his brother Benjamin's neck and wept, and Benjamin wept on his neck. [15] He kissed all his brothers and wept on them, and afterward his brothers talked with him. Genesis 45:14-15

Paul and fellow believers expressed their love, "[36] When he had said these things, he knelt down and prayed with them all. [37] And they *began* to weep aloud and embraced Paul, and repeatedly kissed him, Acts 20:36-37

Of course, the greatest friend we have is the Lord Jesus Christ who is always ready to express His love for us.

I would love to tell you what I think of Jesus.
Since I found in Him a friend so strong and true;
I would tell you how he changed my life completely,
He did something that no other friend could do.

No one ever cared for me like Jesus,
There's no other friend as kind as He;
No one else could take the sin and darkness from me,
O how much He cares for me!

Con:

1. Marks of Friendship.

2. We may have trouble finding such a friend among men, but we have found such a friend in Jesus.

3. Abraham Lincoln said:

"I desire so to conduct the affairs of this administration that if at the end, when I come to lay down the reins of power, I have lost every other friend on earth. I shall at least have one friend left, and that friend shall be down inside of me!"

Chapter Twenty-Three

LEARNING TO LEAN

1 Sam. 21-22

Intro:

1. John Stallings was a pastor in Montgomery, Alabama. His world began to fall apart when one of his three daughters almost died of a serious illness; another was almost killed in a car accident. He was so distress that he resigned his church and moved. But things continued to go from bad to worse, coming to the end of his rope he sat down and wrote these words:

I'm learning to lean, learning to lean,
Learning to lean on Jesus.
Finding more power than I'd ever dreamed,
I'm learning to lean on Jesus.

About 7 months later he wrote some verses to go with it:

The joy I can't explain fills my heart,
Since the day I made Jesus my King;
His blessed Holy Spirit is leading my way,
He's teaching and I'm learning to lean.

There's glorious vict'ry each day now for me,
Since I found His peace so serene;
He helps me with each task, if only I'll ask;
Ev'ry day now I'm learning to lean.

2. That is the essence of what life is really all about – learning to lean on Jesus. And in order to make that happen the Lord has to remove some other things that we are depending upon. Swindoll noted:

"Gradually, David was losing all his support, everything he might have leaned on...David had a position and he lost it.

He had a wife and he lost her. He had a wise counselor, and he lost him. He had a friend, and he lost him. He had self respect, and he lost it...There might be centuries between us and David, but this man and his experiences are more relevant than ever, in our times. One of those, is the very familiar experience, of leaning on others – other people and other things rather than leaning on the Lord. David knew what it meant to have the crutches stripped away, and so do we."

I. FIRST, WE HAVE DAVID'S *CARNALITY.* 21:1-9

A. His *Fib.* 21:1-2

¹ Then David came to Nob to Ahimelech the priest; and Ahimelech came trembling to meet David and said to him, "Why are you alone and no one with you?" ² David said to Ahimelech the priest, "The king has commissioned me with a matter and has said to me, 'Let no one know anything about the matter on which I am sending you and with which I have commissioned you; and I have directed the young men to a certain place.' – Ahimelech was a great grandson of Eli the priest. David lied claiming to be on a secret mission for Saul. When we get in the flesh, honesty goes out the window. To tell a lie is clearly a violation of Scripture (Prov. 6:16-19/Col. 3:9-10).

B. His *Food.* 21:3-6

3 "Now therefore, what do you have on hand? Give me five loaves of bread, or whatever can be found." 4 The priest answered David and said, "There is no ordinary bread on hand, but there is consecrated bread; if only the young men have kept themselves from women." 5 David answered the priest and said to him, "Surely women have been kept from us as previously when I set out and the vessels of the young men were holy, though it was an ordinary journey; how much more then today will their vessels be holy?" 6 So the priest gave him consecrated bread; for there was no bread there but the bread of the Presence which was removed from before the LORD, in order to put hot bread in its place when it was taken away – they placed 12 loaves of bread in the Tabernacle, which symbolized the 12 tribes of Israel as being in the Lords presence. Only the priests were allowed to eat this bread (Ex. 25:30)/ Lev. 24:5-9). They were to be ceremonially clean (Ex. 19:15). Because of David's desperate situation Ahimelech sought the Lord's approval and it was given (22:10).

The Lord used this incident as a good example of how mercy is more important than rules (Mt. 12:2-4).

C. His *Foe.* 7

Now one of the servants of Saul was there that day, detained before the LORD; and his name was Doeg the Edomite, the chief of Saul's shepherds - his name means "anxious," "cared for" He was an Edomite, the position he held was described as that of "the chief" of Saul's shepherds (1 Samuel 21:7. The Septuagint reads: "tending the mules." Rabbinical legends speak of him as the greatest scholar of his time. The traditional title of Psalm 52 associates the composition of that Psalms with the events that led to the slaying of the priests (1 Samuel 21:7; 1 Samuel 22:9, 18, 22).

McGee, "There is a "Judas Iscariot" in the crowd that day at the tabernacle. His name is Doeg, and he is an Edomite. He is in Saul's service, and he is going to betray David and the high priest. David has a great deal to say about this man in Psalm 52."

[1] Why do you boast in evil, O mighty man? The lovingkindness of God *endures* all day long. [2] Your tongue devises destruction, Like a sharp razor, O worker of deceit. [3] You love evil more than good, Falsehood more than speaking what is right. Selah. [4] You love all words that devour, O deceitful tongue. [5] But God will

break you down forever; He will snatch you up and tear you away from *your* tent, And uproot you from the land of the living. Selah.
⁶ The righteous will see and fear, And will laugh at him, *saying,* ⁷ "Behold, the man who would not make God his refuge, But trusted in the abundance of his riches *And* was strong in his *evil* desire." ⁸ But as for me, I am like a green olive tree in the house of God; I trust in the lovingkindness of God forever and ever.
⁹ I will give You thanks forever, because You have done *it,* And I will wait on Your name, for *it is* good, in the presence of Your godly ones. Psalm 52:1-9

In England during World War II a war poster designed to warn against the unwitting disclosure of troop movements or other military secrets was displayed all over the country. It contained the words "Loose talk costs lives." Another saying was "loose lips sink ships." That is true spiritually as well. So instead of being people whose talk is undisciplined or loose, we should be people whose conversation is constructive and above all truthful.

D. His *Folly.* 8-9

⁸ David said to Ahimelech, "Now is there not a spear or a sword on hand? For I brought neither my sword nor my weapons with me, because the king's matter was urgent." ⁹ Then the priest said, "The sword of Goliath the Philistine, whom you killed in the valley of

Elah, behold, it is wrapped in a cloth behind the ephod; if you would take it for yourself, take it. For there is no other except it here." And David said, "There is none like it; give it to me." – this was foolish.

Lutzer, "He asked the priest to lend him a sword or a spear that he could use in self-defense…David should have remembered that this weapon had not delivered Goliath. Why should he now think that it would deliver him? Then he kept going until he came to Gath, the territory Goliath had come from! With Goliath's sword on! He depended on his enemy's sword and his enemy's territory for protection!"

One thing for sure, if David had been leaning on his integrity, that support was now gone. He is living in the realm of deception. While God does *not* want us to lie, He also does not want us to lean on our own integrity but on the imputed righteousness of Christ (Dan. 9:3-8/ Phil. 3:3-9).

Tozer speaking of the Christian notes:

"His interests have shifted from self to Christ. What he is or is not no longer concerns him. Christ is now where man's ego was formerly. The man is now Christ-centered instead of self-centered, and he forgets himself in his delighted preoccupation with Christ."

II. NEXT, HE ACTS *CRAZY.* 10-15

A. He goes to the enemies *Territory.* 10

Then David arose and fled that day from Saul, and went to Achish king of Gath – David fled 23 miles to the enemy city of Gath, the home of the Philistine giant Goliath (17:4). David has chosen to *fret* instead of place his *faith* in the Lord. Psa. 37 says, "Fret not..." The word means "to eat way, gnaw, gall, vex, worry, agitate, wear away."

H. Norman Wright said the word reminds him of what he sees when he hikes along the Snake River in the Grand Teton National Park in Wyoming. Colonies of beavers live along the riverbanks, and often he sees trees that are at various stages of being gnawed to the ground by them. Some trees have slight rings around their trunks where the beavers have just started to chew on them. Other trees have several inches of bark eaten away, and some have already fallen to the ground because the beavers have gnawed through the trunks. Worry has the same effect on us. It will gradually eat away at us until it destroys us.

B. He is recognized for his *Bravery*. 11-12

[11] *But the servants of Achish said to him, "Is this not David the king of the land? Did they not sing of this one as they danced, saying, 'Saul has slain his thousands, And David his ten thousands'?"* [12] *David took these words to heart and greatly feared Achish king of Gath* – David had a reputation for being a great soldier in battle.

C. He acted *Crazy*. 13-15

13 So he disguised his sanity before them, and acted insanely in their hands, and scribbled on the doors of the gate, and let his saliva run down into his beard. 14 Then Achish said to his servants, "Behold, you see the man behaving as a madman. Why do you bring him to me? 15 "Do I lack madmen, that you have brought this one to act the madman in my presence? Shall this one come into my house?"

Mattoones, "He is probably asking himself, "What was I thinking? Why am I here?" David changed his behavior to get out of this mess and ends up doing some things he probably never dreamed he would do. When you dance with the Devil's crowd, it will change your behavior and you will do things you never dreamed you would do. Such is the result of leaning upon your own understanding. Our ingenious plans, schemes, and falsehoods may seem to promote present security, yet, they can lead to future disgrace and problems. David is finding this out! David humiliates himself, dishonors God and acts like a madman. He lost all his self respect. When a believer dances with the Devil and his crowd, he is mad too... he is crazy because he loses his testimony, his effectiveness for Christ, and the respect of other believers."

This is not David's finest hour! He clearly loses his testimony. He had a reputation for being a great brave warrior but now he is going to be known as a drooling idiot! If David was leaning on his wonderful testimony – he isn't any longer! Truth is our testimony points to Him not us...

Barnhouse, "If you exalt God as He should be exalted, man thereby takes his true position of utter nothingness, and only then can he find real exaltation, for it will come to him through the grace of God in Christ. Man can thus reach the heights by taking the proper place of depth."

Lloyd-Jones, "Nothing so hurts the natural man's pride as the cross of Christ. How does the cross do that? It is because we are failures; because we are sinners...The Christian is not a good man! He is a vile wretch who has been saved by the grace of God."

That is our testimony! Paul testified toward the end of his life these words:

It is a trustworthy statement, deserving full acceptance, that Christ Jesus came into the world to save sinners, among whom I am foremost *of all.* 1 Timothy 1:15

III. THIRD, DAVID'S *COMPANY.* 22:1-5

A. He *Found* a place to *Stay.* 1

So David departed from there and escaped to the cave of Adullam... - Swindoll noted, "The cave of Adullam was no Holiday Inn. It was a dark vault on the side of a cliff that reached deeply into a hill. Huddled in this clammy cavern were 400 losers – a mob of miserable humanity. The original Mafia. They all had one thing in common – a bad record."

B. His *Frightened Family.* 1b, 3-5

1. They were *Reunited.* 1b

¹...and when his brothers and all his father's household heard of it, they went down there to him... - this must have given him some temporary comfort.

2. They were *Removed.* 3-5

³ And David went from there to Mizpah of Moab; and he said to the king of Moab, "Please let my father and my mother come and stay with you until I know what God will do for me." ⁴ Then he left them with the king of Moab; and they stayed with him all the time that David was in the stronghold. ⁵ The prophet Gad said to David, "Do not stay in the stronghold; depart, and go into the land of Judah." So David departed and went into the forest of Hereth - After David had secured the safety of his parents, he returned to Adullam and then moved his company to "the stronghold" or "fortress," which many students believe was at Masada by the Dead Sea, about 35 miles southwest of Adullam. The Hebrew word m*esuda* means "fortress" or "stronghold," and can refer to natural hiding places in the wilderness. The Prophet Gad warned David that the wilderness fortress wasn't safe and that he should return to the land of Judah, so he relocated in the forest of Hereth in the vicinity of the cave of Adullam. *Hereth* means "thicket."

C. His *Forgotten Society*. 2

² Everyone who was in distress, and everyone who was in debt, and everyone who was discontented gathered to him; and he became captain over them. Now there were about four hundred men with him – these are the dregs of society! The rejects and low-life's are attracted to him…

Trans: If David was leaning on his family – that was now only a past tense. His gang of oddities would hardly be anything on which one would or could lean on. We are living in days of *Focus on the Family* but we are called to be Christ centered not family focused.

"If anyone comes to Me, and does not hate his own father and mother and wife and children and brothers and sisters, yes, and even his own life, he cannot be My disciple. Luke 14:26

⁵⁹ And He said to another, "Follow Me." But he said, "Lord, permit me first to go and bury my

father." ⁶⁰ But He said to him, "Allow the dead to bury their own dead; but as for you, go and proclaim everywhere the kingdom of God."
Luke 9:59-60

Love your family but Lean on the Lord...

IV. FINALLY, SAUL'S *CRUELTY*. 22:6-23

A. Saul's *Discovery*. 22:6, 9-10

⁶ Then Saul heard that David and the men who were with him had been discovered. Now Saul was sitting in Gibeah, under the tamarisk tree on the height with his spear in his hand, and all his servants were standing around him.
1 Samuel 22:6

⁹ Then Doeg the Edomite, who was standing by the servants of Saul, said, "I saw the son of Jesse coming to Nob, to Ahimelech the son of Ahitub. ¹⁰ "He inquired of the LORD for him, gave him provisions, and gave him the sword of Goliath the Philistine." 1 Samuel 22:9-10

B. Saul's accusation of *Disloyalty*. 22:7-8

⁷ Saul said to his servants who stood around him, "Hear now, O Benjamites! Will the son of Jesse also give to all of you fields and vineyards? Will he make you all commanders of thousands and commanders of hundreds? ⁸ "For all of you have conspired against me so that there is no one who discloses to me when my son makes a covenant with the son of Jesse, and there is none of you who is sorry for me or discloses to me that my son has stirred up my servant against me to lie in ambush, as it is this day."

C. Saul acts *Disgracefully*. 22:11-23

1. The *Explosion*. 11-13

[11] Then the king sent someone to summon Ahimelech the priest, the son of Ahitub, and all his father's household, the priests who were in Nob; and all of them came to the king. [12] Saul said, "Listen now, son of Ahitub." And he answered, "Here I am, my lord." [13] Saul then said to him, "Why have you and the son of Jesse conspired against me, in that you have given him bread and a sword and have inquired of God for him, so that he would rise up against me by lying in ambush as it is this day?" - Never was Saul's paranoia more evident or more dangerous. Truth is, it was Saul who was trying to kill David, not David trying to kill Saul.

2. The *Explanation*. 14-15

[14] Then Ahimelech answered the king and said, "And who among all your servants is as faithful as David, even the king's son-in-law, who is captain over your guard, and is honored in your house? [15] "Did I just begin to inquire of God for him today? Far be it from me! Do not

let the king impute anything to his servant or to any of the household of my father, for your servant knows nothing at all of this whole affair." – Ahimelech didn't have a clue what Saul was talking about!

3. The *Execution* 16-19

a. The *Wise Refusal*. 16-17

16 But the king said, "You shall surely die, Ahimelech, you and all your father's household!" 17 And the king said to the guards who were attending him, "Turn around and put the priests of the LORD to death, because their hand also is with David and because they knew that he was fleeing and did not reveal it to me." But the servants of the king were not willing to put forth their hands to attack the priests of the LORD - This reminds us of the time Saul commanded the people to kill Jonathan for violating the oath, and they refused to obey him (14:41-46).

Wiersbe, "There was no evidence that Ahimelech had ever committed a capital crime, but Saul announced that he and his household must die. Even if the high priest had been guilty, which he was not, it was illegal to punish the whole family for the father's crime (Deut. 24:16). Their crime was knowing that David had fled and not reporting it to Saul. The things that Samuel had warned about the monarchy *and even more* were now taking place (1 Sam. 8:10-18). Saul had a police state in which each citizen was to spy on the others and report to the king anybody who opposed his rule. Israel had asked for a king "like the other nations," and that's what they received!"

b. The *Willing Rebel.* 18-19

18 Then the king said to Doeg, "You turn around and attack the priests." And Doeg the Edomite turned around and attacked the priests, and he killed that day eighty-five men who wore the linen ephod. 19 And he struck Nob the city of the priests with the edge of the sword, both men and women, children and infants; also oxen, donkeys, and sheep he struck with the edge of the sword – we can see here both the human and divine aspect of this.

- Human side: this demonstrates the sin of Saul, and demonstrated what Jesus said about lies being the father of murder (Jn. 8:44). This was unjust and illegal. And Saul was accountable and responsible for it.

- Divine side: this was actually fulfilling prophecy. It was part of God's plan. This slaughter of the priests was a partial fulfillment of the prophecy that had been given to unfaithful Eli (1 Sam. 2:27-36; 4:10-18), for God promised to replace the house of Eli with the house of Zado(1

Kings 2:26-27; 4:2). Everything that happens is ultimately part of God's wise, loving, and perfect plan (Eph. 1:11).

4. The *Exception.* 20-23

[20] But one son of Ahimelech the son of Ahitub, named Abiathar, escaped and fled after David. [21] Abiathar told David that Saul had killed the priests of the LORD. [22] Then David said to Abiathar, "I knew on that day, when Doeg the Edomite was there, that he would surely tell Saul. I have brought about the death of every person in your father's household. [23] "Stay with me; do not be afraid, for he who seeks my life seeks your life, for you are safe with me."

Trans: If David leaned on the fact that he had no past act of iniquity – that support was kicked out from under him. Look at verse 22! Now David has a skeleton in his closet and it will not be the last one. Paul consented to the death of Christians and he never really got over it. You open Peter's closet and it cried out "Beware a denier lives here!" John Mark's closet spoke of abandoning Paul when he needed him the most. I don't know about you, but I stopped leaning on a empty closet a long time ago. I just wish I had only one skeleton in mine. Now all I have to hang around the neck of that old skeleton is Rom. 5:20. The truth is it is *not* skeletons in our closet that's the problem but unconfessed sin in our lives.

In 1842, the first bathtub was denounced as a luxurious and democratic vanity. Boston made it against the law to bathe, except on a doctor's prescription. In 1843, Philadelphia made bathing illegal between November 1st and March 15th. In the spiritual realm we don't need a bath, the blood of Christ has cleansed us from all sin, but we do need a daily foot washing of confessing and forsaking sin.

Con:

1. It is best to lean on Jesus with integrity, a good testimony, a loving family, without any past iniquity. But if you're leaning on those things, one day God is going to remove them so you will learn to lean on Jesus alone. Prov. 3:5-6

2. In a BMW commercial during the recent big game, Bryant Gumbel and Katie Couric are seen (hilariously) arguing about the new-fangled "internet" in a 1994 clip from the *Today Show*. Think about it:

- 21 years ago, we didn't know what the Internet was.
- "Google" was just a number that mathematicians joked about,
- to find out if a restaurant was good, *you ate there or talked to somebody who had.*

- Your "wall"? Probably made of sheet rock, and if someone posted on it, then they'd better have used scotch tape.

It seems like our society's changed in a flash with the advent of connected computers. We couldn't have predicted it in 1994. What else is around the corner in the future, that for all our wisdom and knowledge we can't see coming? Who but God knows, and all of the uncertainty is designed to encourage us to lean upon the one who never changes.

Chapter Twenty-Four

HOW TO WALK THROUGH A SPIRITUAL WILDERNESS

1 Sam. 23

Intro:

1. There is a degree that God wants all of His children to earn – it's a B.D. Degree, *Backside of the Desert* degree!

- Abraham spent years in the backside of the desert before he learned to place his total trust in God.

- Moses spent 40 years in the backside of the desert learning the value of brokenness and humility.

- Jesus spent 30 years in virtual obscurity preparing for a 3 year ministry.

- Paul spent much time in the Arabian desert before being thrust into a successful ministry.

- David, the man after God's own heart, is going to spend much time in the backside of the desert before he is afforded the position of the king of Israel.

2. All of us are who desire to be used by God are going to have to spend some time in the backside of the desert, learning to walk by faith, getting spiritual eyes that see God, as bigger than every obstacle we face.

I. FIRST, DAVID'S *ENLIGHTENMENT.* 23:1-6, 9-13

A. The *Worry.* 1

Then they told David, saying, "Behold, the Philistines are fighting against Keilah and are plundering the threshing floors." – Keilah was located about 18 miles southwest of Jerusalem and belonged to the tribe of Judah. They had harvested their crops and stored them. But the Philistines were coming along and stealing their food supply.

In the second chapter of his book *Up from Slavery,* Booker T. Washington wrote, "I have learned that success is to be measured not so much by the position that one has reached in life as by the obstacles which he has overcome while trying to succeed."

David faced many obstacles on his way to the throne; we soon learn that life is overcoming one obstacle after another.

Soul Surfer. This film (2011) is based on Bethany Hamilton's book, Soul Surfer: A True Story of Faith, Family, and Fighting to Get Back on the Board (2004).

The film recounts the dramatic story of Bethany, who was born and raised on the island of Kauai, Hawaii. Naturally gifted, she was a talented surfer, winning competitions and obtaining endorsements even when she was a preteen. At the age of thirteen, in 2003, her promising future seemed over when a fifteen-foot tiger shark bit off her left arm below the shoulder in an attack soon picked up by the press nationwide. Amazingly, Bethany survived even though she lost 60 percent of her blood, her life saved only by an act of God. Less than one month later she returned to her board to surf again. Her testimony to the grace of God in performing this miracle, and the way she has thrived since the tragic accident, gives a wonderful illustration of how God gets us through the obstacles of life.

B. The *Word.* 2-4, 9-13

² So David inquired of the LORD, saying, "Shall I go and attack these Philistines?" And the LORD said to David, "Go and attack the Philistines and deliver Keilah." ³ But David's men said to him, "Behold, we are afraid here in Judah. How much more then if we go to Keilah against the ranks of the Philistines?" ⁴ Then David inquired of the LORD once more. And the LORD answered him and said, "Arise, go down to Keilah, for I will give the Philistines into your hand."

⁹ Now David knew that Saul was plotting evil against him; so he said to Abiathar the priest, "Bring the ephod here." ¹⁰ Then David said, "O LORD God of Israel, Your servant has heard for certain that Saul is seeking to come to Keilah to destroy the city on my account. ¹¹ "Will the men of Keilah surrender me into his hand? Will Saul come down just as Your servant has heard? O LORD God of Israel, I pray, tell Your servant." And the LORD said, "He will come down." ¹² Then David said, "Will the men of Keilah surrender me and my men into the hand of Saul?" And the LORD said, "They will surrender you." ¹³ Then David and his men, about six hundred, arose and departed from Keilah, and they went wherever they could go. When it was told Saul that David had escaped from Keilah, he gave up the pursuit – a quick review of Abiathar:

- Son of Ahimelech and only priest to escape the massacre at Nob (1 Sam. 22:20)

- Brought the Ephod from Nob to David and served him as priest (1 Sam. 22:20-22; 23:6,9)

- Later, helped to bring the ark to Jerusalem and served as one of David's counselors (1 Chron. 15:11; 27:34)

- Supported Adonijah's bid for the throne and was expelled from office by Solomon, ending Eli's priestly line (1 Kings 1-2)

The ephod was a sleeveless linen vest with a pouch containing two small objects, the Urim and the Thummim, these were somehow used to discover God's will.

Trans: Today we also face things that worry us, but we have something better than the ephod, we have the full and final written word of God (2 Tim. 3:16-17).

Samuel Chadwick, "I have guided my life by the Bible for more than 60 years, and I tell you there is no book like it! It is a miracle, a perpetual spring of wisdom, a wonder of surprises and an infallible guide and unspeakable source of comfort."

Our source book to get us through suffering is the Scriptures. Most people are not aware that Spurgeon's successful ministry was accomplished under great adversity. After giving birth to their twin sons, Spurgeon's wife

Susannah became a virtual invalid and seldom heard her husband preach. Spurgeon himself suffered from gout, rheumatism, and depression. Under these demanding circumstances, preaching often became a painful experience. These diseases eventually took his life at the age of 57. In addition to his physical suffering, Spurgeon endured undeserved public ridicule and slander. Newspapers called him vulgar and he was regarded as rude and rough; his ministry was dismissed as temporary. Probably the attacks by his fellow ministers were the most painful. Those on the left belittled him; those on the right doubted his salvation. When he withdrew from the Baptist union, because of doctrine integrity he was officially and publicly censured by it.

But Spurgeon continued faithfully preaching God's Word until the end.

II. FURTHERMORE, WE HAVE SAUL'S LACK OF ENLIGHTENMENT. 23:7-8, 19-23

A. Saul's faulty *Belief.* 7

When it was told Saul that David had come to Keilah, Saul said, "God has delivered him into my hand, for he shut himself in by entering a city with double gates and bars." – what we believe is only valid if it is according to truth. The truth was God had not delivered David into Saul's hands.

Reminds me of the religious leaders of Jesus day (Jn. 16:2).

What is sad is that Saul is a believer! Saul and David are on the same team! How sad when we waste our time fighting each other.

A recent gang fight in Chicago left one man dead and two injured. What made this so sad was that they were from the same gang. The stabbing was a case of mistaken identity, with deadly consequences. Here's how *The Chicago Tribune* described what happened:

A fight started when a car drove past a party. The people at the party threw a brick at the car, thinking it belonged to a rival gang. In the ensuing fight, one young man got stabbed and two young men got run over by the car. One of the victims died. It wasn't until the dust settled that those involved realized that they all were part of the same street gang."

How often do we set ourselves at odds with others without thinking that we may be fighting for the same team?

B. Saul's foolish understanding of a *Blessing*. 19-21

[19] Then Ziphites came up to Saul at Gibeah, saying, "Is David not hiding with us in the strongholds at Horesh, on the hill of Hachilah, which is on the south of Jeshimon?
[20] "Now then, O king, come down according to all the desire of your soul to do so; and our

part shall be to surrender him into the king's hand." [21] *Saul said, "May you be blessed of the LORD, for you have had compassion on me* – calling a curse a blessing, does not make it a blessing! It was sin and rebellion on Saul's part to seek David's life, and sin for the Ziphites to inform Saul where David was. And covering his sin with a *Praise the Lord* was foolish!

Flywheel is a film about Jay, a Christian used-car salesman who becomes convicted that he has been grossly overcharging his customers. In this scene, conviction begins to settle in Jay's heart when he manipulates the sale of a car to his pastor. As the scene opens, Jay is standing in the used car lot when he notices that his pastor is looking at a car. Jay walks over and says, "Well, the good Reverend came after all!" The pastor replies, "Jay, how's the car business today?" Jay says, "We're making ends meet. It's good to see you. Tell me what I can do for you?" Pastor says, "Well, I'm looking for a car for my daughter. She's our last one. I wish she were here, but she's out shopping for clothes with her mother. I'm just trying to find a good buy for her." Jay responds, "Well, let me commit to giving you a good deal."

The scene shifts to two salesmen that are sitting in the office that oversees the parking lot. Watching the interaction between Jay and the pastor, one salesman says to the other, "Hey, who is that guy with Jay? I think I've seen him before." The other salesman looks out the window and says, "He's a minister, isn't he? Jay will probably give him a deal." "Twenty bucks says he doesn't!" the other salesman fires back, knowing full well that Jay is a swindler. "Do you really think he's going to stiff a minister?" "Twenty bucks says he will!" "You're on," the other salesman replies, and both watch from the window. As they watch Jay and his pastor examining a Camry, they check the files to see its listed price. The Camry is worth $6,500. "Jay will sell it for $8,000," one salesman says. The other replies, "$7,000."

The scene shifts back to Jay and his pastor. Jay says, "I've got $8,500 in this car. If you want, I'll give it to you for $9,000." Thinking it over, the Reverend decides to take it for a test drive. When Jay comes into the office, one of salesmen asks, "Is he buying it?" "He might," Jay replies. "You think he will?" "I do." "How do you know?" "I sell cars for a living." "Ha! At what price?"

The next scene shows Jay's pastor signing on the dotted line. As Jay walks the minister to the Camry, the two salesmen check the bill on the desk. They're surprised to see that Jay sold the car for $9,000, and they argue over who won the bet.

When the scene shifts back to Jay and his pastor, the pastor says, "Jay, thanks. You've treated me so well today. I would like to do something for you. I'd like to pray and ask God to bless you and your business." Jay says, "I'd appreciate that..." "Let's pray." The minister puts his hand on Jay's shoulder, and says, "Lord, today I come before you and thank you for this day. I thank you for Jay and his business. I thank you for the car for Lindsay, and I ask that you protect her and give her grace as she drives this car. And Lord, I ask that you treat Jay just like he treated me today in this deal. In your name I pray, Lord, Amen."As the minister drives away, Jay says softly, "Amen,"

Saul's blessing upon the Ziphites, is as impossible as God blessing that used car salesman.

C. Saul's fantasy *Blaming.* 22-23

²² "Go now, make more sure, and investigate and see his place where his haunt is, and who has seen him there; for I am told that he is very cunning. ²³ "So look, and learn about all the hiding places where he hides himself and return to me with certainty, and I will go with you; and if he is in the land, I will search him out among all the thousands of Judah." – the word *cunning* here means "to be deceitful." But in reality it was Saul not David who was deceitful. The sad thing is Saul has lied so many times that his character is gone – he sold it for a pack of lies!

Did you ever see that movie *The Family Man* with Nicolas Cage? There's this scene where Nicolas Cage walks into a store to get a cup of coffee. And Don Cheadle plays the guy working at the counter. There's a girl in line before Nicolas Cage, and she's buying something for ninety-nine cents, and she hands Don a dollar. He takes nine dollars out of the till and counts it out, giving her way too much change. She sees that he is handing her way too much money, yet she picks it up and puts it in her pocket without saying a word. As she is walking out the door, Don stops her to give her another chance. He asks her if there is anything else she needs. She shakes her head no and walks out. So Don looks over at Nicolas Cage, and he says, 'Did you see that? She was willing to sell her character for nine dollars. Nine dollars!'"

When we tell lies about someone like Saul did about David, we are selling our character… cheap!

Trans: If our Belief's, Blessing, and Blame is not according to truth we are in danger of God's chastening hand. And, if like David we are on the receiving end of such lies, we need not worry about it, God knows the truth (1 Cor. 4:3-4).

Abraham Lincoln told reporter Francis Carpenter, "If I were to read, much less to answer, all the attacks made on me, this shop might as well be closed for any other business. I do the very best I know how – the very best I can; and I intend to keep doing so until the end. If the end brings me out alright, what is said against me won't amount to anything. If the end brings me out wrong, ten angels swearing I was right would make no difference."

III. THIRD, JONATHAN'S *ENCOURAGEMENT.* 14-17

A. His *Stubborn Father.* 14-15

[14] *David stayed in the wilderness in the strongholds, and remained in the hill country in the wilderness of Ziph. And Saul sought him every day, but God did not deliver him into his hand.* [15] *Now David became aware that Saul had come out to seek his life while David was in the wilderness of Ziph at Horesh –* Saul's heart was now hardened. He has made up his mind he is not going to repent and get right with God.

B. His *Strengthening* of his *Friend.* 16-18

1. He lifted up God's *Presence.* 16

And Jonathan, Saul's son, arose and went to David at Horesh, and encouraged him in God – many times we fail in our attempt to encourage people because we try everything but God. The only way to really strengthen anyone is to focus their attention back to God. It is His sovereignty, His strength, His love, His faithfulness, His wisdom and presence that enables us to keep on, keeping on.

2. He reminded him of God's *Promise.* 17

Thus he said to him, "Do not be afraid, because the hand of Saul my father will not find you, and you will be king over Israel and I will be next to you; and Saul my father knows that also." – David will be king because God has promised that he would be king.

Trans: The solution to all of our problems is God Himself, and the best friends we have constantly remind us of that truth. When friends or anything else becomes the focus, the supposed solution to our problems – we have a problem. The problem is that today many have traded God for human love itself - In the book *Love: A History*, Yale scholar Simon May calls *human love* our "new god." In his chapter "Love plays God" May writes:

"Human love ... is now tasked with achieving what once only divine love was thought capable of: to be our ultimate source of meaning and happiness."

May contends that we have changed the Bible's statement "God is love" to "love is god." Here are some of the core beliefs for this new "religion of love":

- Human love is the universal form of salvation available to all of us.

- We don't need "long and disciplined training" to learn how to love because most of us can love spontaneously and without effort.

- Human love is always benevolent and harmonious—a haven of peace.

- Human love transports us beyond the messy imperfections of the everyday world into a superior state of purity and perfection.

- Human love delivers us from all of life's losses and sufferings.

May writes, "These sorts of ideas saturate popular culture ... To its immense cost, human love has usurped a role that only God's love used to play."

IV. FINALLY, WE HAVE GOD'S *ENABLEMENT*. 24-29

A. His *Protection*. 24-26

²⁴ Then they arose and went to Ziph before Saul. Now David and his men were in the wilderness of Maon, in the Arabah to the south of Jeshimon. ²⁵ When Saul and his men went to seek him, they told David, and he came down to the rock and stayed in the wilderness of Maon. And when Saul heard it, he pursued David in the wilderness of Maon. ²⁶ Saul went on one side of the mountain, and David and his men on the other side of the mountain; and David was hurrying to get away from Saul, for Saul and his men were surrounding David and his men to seize them – God had given David a Rock of defense, most believe the reason he fled was not because they couldn't have defeated Saul but that David refused to harm God's anointed.

"Behold, this day your eyes have seen that the LORD had given you today into my hand in the cave, and some said to kill you, but *my eye* had pity on you; and I said, 'I will not stretch out my hand against my lord, for he is the LORD'S anointed.' 1 Samuel 24:10

But David said to Abishai, "Do not destroy him, for who can stretch out his hand against the LORD'S anointed and be without guilt?" 1 Samuel 26:9

"The LORD forbid that I should stretch out my hand against the LORD'S anointed; but now please take the spear that is at his head and the jug of water, and let us go." 1 Samuel 26:11

"The LORD will repay each man *for* his righteousness and his faithfulness; for the LORD delivered you into *my* hand today, but I refused to stretch out my hand against the LORD'S anointed. 1 Samuel 26:23

[14] Then David said to him, "How is it you were not afraid to stretch out your hand to destroy the LORD'S anointed?" [15] And David called one of the young men and said, "Go, cut him down." So he struck him and he died. [16] David said to him, "Your blood is on your head, for your mouth has testified against you, saying, 'I have killed the LORD'S anointed.'" 2 Samuel 1:14-16

B. His *Providence*. 27-29

²⁷ But a messenger came to Saul, saying, "Hurry and come, for the Philistines have made a raid on the land." ²⁸ So Saul returned from pursuing David and went to meet the Philistines; therefore they called that place the Rock of Escape. ²⁹ David went up from there and stayed in the strongholds of Engedi – Engedi means "The Spring of the Young Goat"; v. 29; Hb. 24:1). In this area David and his men had isolation, protection, and, because of the En Gedi spring, an adequate supply of fresh water.

Con:

1. Principles of how to walk through your spiritual wilderness:

- Find God's *Perspective* (DVP). 2 Tim. 3:16-17

When we went to Colorado some years ago on a hunting trip, one of the difficult parts was deciding what to bring, but in just one pocket I had "a guidebook, a lamb, a mirror, a microscope, a volume of fine poetry, a couple of biographies, a package of old letters, a book of songs, a sword, a hammer, and everything needed to be a godly hunter." Yes, it was my Bible!

- Focus on God's *Presence*. 1 Thess. 5:17

Bro. Lawrence, "In order to get in the habit of talking with God all the time, referring all we do to Him, we must first work hard at giving ourselves to Him. After concentrating on this a while, we find that God's love is inside us, helping us to easily commit ourselves to Him…The times of prayer should be no different from any other time…We can be just as conscious of God when engaged in ordinary activities as in prayer time…People delude themselves when they think that prayer time ought to be different from the rest of their lives…Prayer time is a time to sense God's presence and when this prayer time is over, nothing changes, because we still continue to be with God, praising and blessing Him with all our might…We should be pitied for being satisfied with so little. God has infinite treasures to give us – and yet we limit ourselves to brief, sensible prayers!"

- Place faith in God's *Promises.* Rom. 4:20-21

In Cleveland Ohio there is a 10 story bank building known as the "Society of Savings" it was built totally on unclaimed funds of people! People deposited money, and then, not hearing from them for years, the bank sent out several notices and after years of no response, the money was turned over to the building of that bank. God has given us a Bible loaded with promises, but many refuse to appropriate those promises by faith.

- Firmly stand on God's *Providence.* Rom. 8:28

We have a choice, we can look at circumstances or we can look to God's sovereign hand. If we fail to claim the promise of Rom. 8:28, then we will soon think, based on circumstances, that God is angry with us.

Thomas Brooks, "No man knows how the heart of God stands by His hand. His hand of mercy may be toward a man, when His heart may be against that man…And the hand of God may be set against a man, when the heart of God is dearly set upon a man, as you may see in Job…No man knows either love or hatred by outward mercy or misery; for all things come a-like to all, to the righteous and to the unrighteous. The sun of prosperity shines as well upon the brambles of the wilderness as upon fruit trees of the orchard; rain falls on the best garden as well as the stinking dunghill…God can appear to look sourly and chide bitterly and strike heavily, even where and when He loves dearly. The hand of God was sore against David when his heart was most set upon him."

Truth is God's heart is always for us (Rom. 8:31-), even when it appears that His hand is against us.

When everything seemed against Joseph – his brothers, his boss, his circumstances, his testimony was "You meant it for evil but God used it for good." So get ready to spend some time in the backside of the desert, it is the only place where we learn God's Perspective, Presence, Promises, and Providence.

Charles Stanley, "Dealing with Adversity [and we could add with spiritual wilderness] is like preparing for surgery. By putting our faith in what the doctor has said, we believe we will be better off if we have the surgery. That does not make it any less painful, but by submitting to the hand of a surgeon, we are saying that our ultimate goal is health, even at the cost of pain. Adversity [and spiritual dryness] is the same way. It is a means to an end. It is God's tool for the advancement of our spiritual lives."

Chapter Twenty-Five

EXAMPLES OF RESPECTING GOD'S DELEGATED AUTHORITY – EVEN WHEN THE PERSON IN THAT POSITION IS UNWORTHY

1 Sam. 24 and 26

Intro:

1. Several years ago the headlines in a newspaper caught my eye, it read Baptist Church Leaves Fold. The article went on:

"After 153 years, Raleigh's oldest Baptist church has broken away from the Southern Baptist Convention, in part because of the demonization's call on women to "submit graciously" to their husbands.

2. God has placed people in positions of authority:

- Husbands over wives.
- Pastors over congregations.
- Government over citizens.
- Parents over children.

To disregard and disrespect that delegated authority is to disregard and disrespect the God who gave them that authority.

I. FIRST, A *ROBE REMOVED*. 24

A. Saul's *Constant* desire to *Injure*. 24:1-2

¹ Now when Saul returned from pursuing the Philistines, he was told, saying, "Behold, David is in the wilderness of Engedi." ² Then Saul took three thousand chosen men from all Israel and went to seek David and his men in front of the Rocks of the Wild Goats – as soon as Saul deals with the Philistines he goes right back to trying to kill David. When we persist in sin, it becomes a Satanic stronghold.

The story is told of a certain African tribe that learned an easy way to capture ducks in a river. The tribesmen learned to go upstream, place a pumpkin in the river, and let it slowly float down into the flock of ducks. At first, the cautious fowl would quack and fly away. Then they'd float another pumpkin into the re-gathered ducks. Again they would scatter, and eventually return. Again, the hungry hunters would float another pumpkin. This time the ducks would remain, with a cautious eye on the pumpkin, and with each successive passing, the ducks would become more comfortable, until they finally accepted the pumpkins as a normal part of life. When the natives saw that the pumpkins no longer bothered the ducks, they hollowed out pumpkins, put them over their heads, and walked into the river. Meandering into the midst of the tolerant fowl, they pulled them down one at a time. What's for Dinner? Roast duck!

That's how Satan works, he seeks to get us familiar with sin – then before we know it sin has us in bondage.

B. The *Call* of *Nature*...or when nature calls! 3

He came to the sheepfolds on the way, where there was a cave; and Saul went in to relieve himself. Now David and his men were sitting in the inner recesses of the cave – here is the situation:

Saul arrives at a *sheepfold.* This was a large enclosure with a wall of thorn bushes around it to protect the sheep from wild animals or thieves. There was one entrance. The shepherd slept at the entry point for the shepherd was the door. Saul enters a cave to relieve himself! David and his men are watching - The caves were dark as midnight when you looked into them. When on the inside you see out easily and see anyone coming for miles around since it was high above the Dead Sea.

C. The *Counsel* of the *Culture.* 4a

4 The men of David said to him, "Behold, this is the day of which the LORD said to you, 'Behold; I am about to give your enemy into your hand, and you shall do to him as it seems good to you.' – his men were living by circumstances instead of God's Word. For us, we think if someone has wronged us, we have a right to get even. They may have hurt us or taken advantage of us and we think it is only right to get our pound of flesh!

This attitude might be popular but it is not Biblical (Rom. 12:19-21). You see if David had killed Saul, his heart would have become hardened like Saul's. When we play God and take vengeance into our own hands, we ultimately kill our own hearts.

According to Edward Barnes in *Time* (3/14/94), a Sarajevo man named Pipo is a Bosnian Serb sniper who has shot down 325 individuals for the sake of revenge. Before becoming a sniper, Pipo was a partner in a Sarajevo restaurant with a Muslim man. The two were friends as well as partners—until Pipo's mother was jailed and beaten by Muslims. Pipo recalls, "When she got out, she wouldn't talk about it. That's when I picked up a gun and began shooting Muslims. I hate them all." Killing for revenge has changed Pipo. "All I know how to do is kill, I am not sure I am normal anymore. I can talk to people, but if someone pushes me, I will kill them... In the beginning I was able to put my fear aside, and it was good. Then with the killings I was able to put my emotions aside, and it was good. But now they are gone." After shooting 325 people, Pipo has no more fear, no remorse, no feelings at all. He states plainly, "I have no feelings for what I do. I went to see my mother in Belgrade, and she hugged me, and I felt nothing. I have no life anymore. I go from day to day, but nothing means anything. I don't want a wife and children. I don't want to think."

D. The *Cutting* that was NOT according to *Scripture.* 4b

Then David arose and cut off the edge of Saul's robe secretly – of course for Saul to relieve himself he had to take off his robe and set it aside. Here David compromises, while he didn't take Saul's life, he did show disrespect for God's delegated authority. Again, we may not respect their person but we are supposed to respect their position.

Jesus said, "Render unto Caesar the things that are Caesar's" (Mt. 22:21). Part of that includes respect.

After Paul disrespected the High priest he apologized (Acts 23:2-5). See Rom. 13:1/ 1Pet.2:13-17).

E. The *Conscience* that was *Tender.* 5-7

⁵ It came about afterward that David's conscience bothered him because he had cut off the edge of Saul's robe. ⁶ So he said to his men, "Far be it from me because of the LORD that I should do this thing to my lord, the LORD'S anointed, to stretch out my hand against him, since he is the LORD'S anointed." ⁷ David persuaded his men with these words and did not allow them to rise up against Saul. And Saul arose, left the cave, and went on his way – the greatest thing we can have is a heart that is bothered by sin.

Twelve Kinds of Conscience:

1. Awakened (John 8:9)

2. Seared (1 Tim. 4:2)

3. Purged (Hebrews 9:9,14; Hebrews 10:2)

4. Pure (Acts 24:16; 1 Tim. 3:9; 2 Tim. 1:3)

5. Weak (1 Cor. 8:7,12,13)

6. Defiled (Titus 1:15)

7. Witnessing (Romans 2:12-15; Romans 9:1; 2 Cor. 1:12)

8. Good (Acts 23:1; 1 Tim. 1:5,19; 1 Peter 2:19; 1 Peter 3:16,21; Hebrews 13:18)

9. Convicting or healthy (Matthew 27:3)

10. Satisfied (1 Cor. 10:25-29)

11. Evil (Hebrews 10:22)

12. Perfect (Hebrews 9:9)

Tony Evans noted, "We have a built-in metal detector. When I go to the airport, I've got my keys in my pocket. I walk through security and beeps go off everywhere! The security guard will call me back and make me walk through again. When the machine beeps again, the guard will ask me to empty my pockets. So I'll reach in my pockets and pull out my keys, take off my watch, and put them on the side because the alarm has gone off, indicating that I've tried to walk onto a plane with metal in my pocket.

You have in your person, like a metal detector, a sin detector, called the Holy Spirit. So whenever you introduce sin in your life, you are going to hear a beep! There's going to be an alarm, and that's what your conscience is. That's where the Spirit of God pricks your conscience. It's like trying to fit a square peg in a round hole. If you keep twisting that peg and trying to force it, you will sooner or later cut down the square lines so that the square will become round like the hole, and it will eventually go in. That's what many of us do with our consciences."

F. The *Convicting Lecture.* 8-15

1. The *Humility* of David. 8

Now afterward David arose and went out of the cave and called after Saul, saying, "My lord the king!" And when Saul looked behind him, David bowed with his face to the ground and prostrated himself – these are signs of David's humility and brokenness. It takes far more power to respond in humility than to fight back in pride. *The Jackie Robinson Story* is the 1950 movie about the life, challenges, and achievements of baseball star Jackie Robinson. With the help of Brooklyn Dodgers general manager Branch Rickey, he broke the professional baseball color barrier. The movie depicts the prejudice and hatred Robinson had to endure and the depth of patience, courage, and self-control he displayed in the face of relentless adversity.

It is their first meeting. Rickey surprises Robinson by telling him he wants Robinson to try out for his team and possibly become the first black player in the major leagues. Rickey asks, "What do you think, Jackie? Do you got guts enough to play the game no matter what happens? They'll shout insults at you. They'll come into you spikes first. They'll throw at your head." Robinson replies, "They've been throwing at my head for a long time." Rickey says, "Suppose I'm a player on the eve of an important game. Suppose I collide with you at second base, and when I get up I say, 'You, you dirty black so-and-so.' What do you do?" Robinson asks, "Mr. Rickey, do you want a ballplayer who's afraid to fight back?" Rickey answers emphatically, "I want a ballplayer with guts enough *not* to fight back. You've got to do the job with base hits, stolen bases, and fielding ground balls, Jackie. Nothing else." Rickey is very happy with his answer. As Robinson is about to leave, Rickey tells him, "Remember one thing. No matter what happens on the ball field, you can't fight back. That's going to be the hard part. You can't fight back."

Robinson does turn the other cheek and becomes a model of courage and humility. That's the way David was in the face of unfair and relentless opposition from Saul (Isa. 57:15/Psa. 34:17-19).

2. David's *Inquiry.* 9

David said to Saul, "Why do you listen to the words of men, saying, 'Behold, David seeks to harm you'? – some men had poisoned Saul's mind against David with the lie that David wanted to harm the king. Truth is there are going to be people who are going to make false accusations about us. But God is like DNA He knows the truth. Reminds me of a Louisiana man who had been released from death row, becoming the 300th prisoner nationwide to be freed after DNA evidence showed he was innocent. Of those 300 prisoners, 18 had been on death row, according to lawyers from the New York-based Innocence Project.

3. David's *Opportunity.* 10-11

¹⁰ "Behold, this day your eyes have seen that the LORD had given you today into my hand in the cave, and some said to kill you, but my eye had pity on you; and I said, 'I will not stretch out my hand against my lord, for he is the LORD'S anointed.' ¹¹ "Now, my father, see! Indeed, see the edge of your robe in my hand! For in that I cut off the edge of your robe and did not kill you, know and perceive that there is no evil or rebellion in my hands, and I have not sinned against you, though you are lying in wait for my life to take it – David had proved that he meant Saul no harm, he just had the opportunity to kill him but refused to do so. The piece of Saul's robe in David's hand proved that.

4. David's *Maturity.* 12-13

¹² "May the LORD judge between you and me, and may the LORD avenge me on you; but my hand shall not be against you. ¹³ "As the proverb of the ancients says, 'Out of the wicked comes forth wickedness'; but my hand shall not be against you- in other words, David was willing to leave his case in God's hand.

5. David's *Inability* to harm Saul. 14

"After whom has the king of Israel come out? Whom are you pursuing? A dead dog, a single flea? – David posed no threat to Saul and his army!

6. The *Finality*. 15

"The LORD therefore be judge and decide between you and me; and may He see and plead my cause and deliver me from your hand." – again David leaves the whole thing in God's capable hands.

Trans: David has given us a wonderful example of how we should respond when we are mistreated. The key is to keep our eyes fastened on God.

St. Teresa of Avila. This renowned Spanish nun (1515– 82) once wrote, "Let nothing disturb thee; let nothing dismay thee. All things pass; God never changes: Patience attains all that it strives for. He who has God finds he lacks nothing: God alone suffices."

G. Saul's *Confession* of his *Failure*. 16-19

[16] *When David had finished speaking these words to Saul, Saul said, "Is this your voice, my son David?" Then Saul lifted up his voice and wept.* [17] *He said to David, "You are more righteous than I; for you have dealt well with me, while I have dealt wickedly with you.* [18] *"You have declared today that you have done good to me, that the LORD delivered me into your hand and yet you did not kill me.* [19] *"For if a man finds his enemy, will he let him go away safely? May the LORD therefore reward you with good in return for what you have done to me this day* – this all sounds good, but

they are empty words. Saul will soon go back to trying to kill David.

Fénelon (1651– 1715) was the archbishop of Cambrai, France, during the seventeenth and early eighteenth centuries. While holding office, he had the opportunity of becoming the spiritual adviser to a small number of devout people at the Court of Louis XIV. Under Fénelon's wise direction, these believers decided to live a spiritual life amid an immoral court. Fénelon wrote a number of spiritual letters to guide those under his tutelage. What follows is a portion of letter in modern paraphrase:

We can listen to endless sermons about Christian growth, and become perfectly familiar with the language, and yet be as far from its attainment as ever. Our great aim should be to be deaf to self, to listen quietly to God, to renounce every bit of pride and devote ourselves to living. Let's learn to talk less and do more..."

H. Saul's *Comforting* words about the *Future.* 20-22

[20] *"Now, behold, I know that you will surely be king, and that the kingdom of Israel will be established in your hand.* [21] *"So now swear to me by the LORD that you will not cut off my descendants after me and that you will not destroy my name from my father's household."* [22] *David swore to Saul. And Saul went to his*

home, but David and his men went up to the stronghold – Saul is finally confessing publically for the first time reality.

Trans: The bottom line is that David had an opportunity to kill Saul, it was refused *not* because of Saul's person but because of his position. Let's say we had John over at the Sushi House to cater one of our fellowship meals. And I looked out the window and saw that you parked right in front of the building. I send one of my grandchildren to say, "The Pastor asks you not to park here, because it is reserved for the caterers." What would you do? You could easily ignore or overpower a child, but out of respect for your Pastor I am sure you would honor the words of that grandchild. That grandchild would be delegated authority, and in the same way we show respect for God by submitting to His delegated authority in our lives.

II. FINALLY, A *SPEAR REMOVED.* 26

A. The *Spiteful.* 1-3

¹ Then the Ziphites came to Saul at Gibeah, saying, "Is not David hiding on the hill of Hachilah, which is before Jeshimon?" ² So Saul arose and went down to the wilderness of Ziph, having with him three thousand chosen men of Israel, to search for David in the wilderness of Ziph. ³ Saul camped in the hill of Hachilah, which is before Jeshimon, beside the road, and David was staying in the wilderness. When he saw that Saul came after him into the wilderness – second verse, same as the first!

B. The *Spies.* 4

David sent out spies, and he knew that Saul was definitely coming – this time David took the initiative, perhaps he could see where Saul was making camp for the night.

C. Saul was *Sleeping.* 5-7a

⁵ David then arose and came to the place where Saul had camped. And David saw the place where Saul lay, and Abner the son of Ner, the commander of his army; and Saul was lying in the circle of the camp, and the people were camped around him. ⁶ Then David said to Ahimelech the Hittite and to Abishai the son of Zeruiah, Joab's brother, saying, "Who will go down with me to Saul in the camp?" And Abishai said, "I will go down with you." ⁷ So David and Abishai came to the people by night, and behold, Saul lay sleeping inside the circle of the camp… - again Saul was vulnerable to an attack by David, and it was the result of God's sovereign power (v. 12b)

D. The *Spear.* 7-8, 11-12

with his spear stuck in the ground at his head; and Abner and the people were lying around him. ⁸ Then Abishai said to David, "Today God has delivered your enemy into your hand; now therefore, please let me strike him with the spear to the ground with one stroke, and I will not strike him the second time."

11 "The LORD forbid that I should stretch out my hand against the LORD'S anointed; but now please take the spear that is at his head and the jug of water, and let us go." 12 So David took the spear and the jug of water from beside Saul's head, and they went away, but no one saw or knew it, nor did any awake, for they were all asleep, because a sound sleep from the LORD had fallen on them - Saul's spear has been mentioned before: on two occasions he tried to kill David with it (18: 10–11; 19: 9– 10), and once he threw it at David's best friend, his own son Jonathan, for supporting David (20: 33).

David could have put Saul's spear throwing day to an end by merely picking up the spear and thrusting it through Saul's head - but David consistently left matters in God's hand.

E. The *Surety*. 9-10

9 But David said to Abishai, "Do not destroy him, for who can stretch out his hand against the LORD'S anointed and be without guilt?" 10 David also said, "As the LORD lives, surely the LORD will strike him, or his day will come that he dies, or he will go down into battle and perish – God will take care of Saul in His way and according to His timetable.

F. David's *Speech*. 13-25

1. The *Condemnation* of Abner. 13-16

¹³ Then David crossed over to the other side and stood on top of the mountain at a distance with a large area between them. ¹⁴ David called to the people and to Abner the son of Ner, saying, "Will you not answer, Abner?" Then Abner replied, "Who are you who calls to the king?" ¹⁵ So David said to Abner, "Are you not a man? And who is like you in Israel? Why then have you not guarded your lord the king? For one of the people came to destroy the king your lord. ¹⁶ "This thing that you have done is not good. As the LORD lives, all of you must surely die, because you did not guard your lord, the LORD'S anointed. And now, see where the king's spear is and the jug of water that was at his head." - Abner and his men had committed a capital offense by falling asleep on the watch. It was their job to make sure the king was safe.

2. The *Confusion* of why Saul is pursuing him. 17-19a

¹⁷ Then Saul recognized David's voice and said, "Is this your voice, my son David?" And David said, "It is my voice, my lord the king." ¹⁸ He also said, "Why then is my lord pursuing his servant? For what have I done? Or what evil is in my hand? ¹⁹ "Now therefore, please let my lord the king listen to the words of his servant… - David has declared his loyalty to Saul over and over again:

David addresses Saul as "my lord" three times (vv. 17– 19), calls him "king" six times (vv. 15– 17, 19– 20, 22), refers to him as the Lord's "anointed" twice in Saul's hearing (vv. 16, 23), and describes himself as Saul's "servant" twice (vv. 18– 19).

3. The *Consideration* that God is really behind it all! 19b-20

If the LORD has stirred you up against me, let Him accept an offering; but if it is men, cursed are they before the LORD, for they have driven me out today so that I would have no attachment with the inheritance of the LORD, saying, 'Go, serve other gods.' [20] *"Now then, do not let my blood fall to the ground away from the presence of the LORD; for the king of Israel has come out to search for a single flea, just as one hunts a partridge in the mountains."* – this seems strange to say the least. I think Chisholm makes a good point:

"Saul's unrelenting attempt to kill David is a sign of the Lord's disfavor with Saul. In other words, as an act of divine judgment, the Lord is prompting Saul to do this evil thing, as proof to everyone that the king is unfit to rule. If this is the case, David argues, then Saul should present an offering to God in an attempt to appease God's anger (cf. 3: 14)."

4. The *Confession* of Saul. 21

[21] *Then Saul said, "I have sinned. Return, my son David, for I will not harm you again*

because my life was precious in your sight this day. Behold, I have played the fool and have committed a serious error."

This is the third time in the story Saul confesses, "I have sinned." When he had been confronted by Samuel after his failure to wipe out the Amalekites, he twice acknowledged that he had sinned (15: 24, 30). His own son Jonathan warned him that taking David's life would be sin (19: 4– 5), and now Saul admits this truth out of his own mouth.

5. The *Commitment* of David. 22-24

22 David replied, "Behold the spear of the king! Now let one of the young men come over and take it. 23 "The LORD will repay each man for his righteousness and his faithfulness; for the LORD delivered you into my hand today, but I refused to stretch out my hand against the LORD'S anointed. 24 "Now behold, as your life was highly valued in my sight this day, so may my life be highly valued in the sight of the LORD, and may He deliver me from all distress." – just as God delivered David from Goliath, so the day would come when he would deliver him from the hands of Saul.

6. The *Conclusion.*

Then Saul said to David, "Blessed are you, my son David; you will both accomplish much and surely prevail." So David went on his way, and Saul returned to his place – we never know when we will see a person for the last time; this will be David's final encounter with Saul.

Trans: Again the main point is that David refused to harm Saul, not because of his worthy person but because of his position.

Con:

1. Examples of Respecting God's delegated authority – even when the person in that position is unworthy of it.

2. This is a needed message especially in our day, and the commercial says, "Defiance is in our bones!" Swindoll says it well:

"Let's face it, this generation is tough not tender: No longer is the voice of the parent respected in the home...the sight of the policeman on the corner a model of courage and control... the warning of the teacher in the classroom feared and obeyed...the older person treated with dignity and honor...the husband considered the head of the home. Ours is a talk-back, fight-back, get-even society that is ready to resist and sue at the slightest provocation. Defiance, resistance, violence, and retaliation are now our style...And those who resist authority become masters at rationalization. They develop an amazing disregard for the truth. They also re-define sin. And these people, who are often Christians, are so convinced that they are right, that they are shocked when they discover otherwise. When Cain curled his lip and stood tight-fisted in rebellion before his Maker, he was given a sobering warning, "If you do not do well, sin is crouching at the door; and its desire is for you, but you must master it." (Gen. 4:7b). Nothing has changed. The mark of Cain has been branded on this generation. Resisting authority still crouches like a beast at the door, ready to pounce on its prey, be it parent or policeman or teacher or employer or minister or president – whomever. Some never learn to "master it" and therefore spend their lives "under the smarting rod of God" as the old Puritans used to say, "Those who question authority face a hard future."

How about us? How do we relate to the authority that God has placed over us?

Chapter Twenty-Six

LESSONS WE CAN LEARN FROM THE BEAUTY AND THE BEAST

1 Sam. 25

Intro:

1. The Beauty and the Beast is a 1991 Disney movie. Belle's life is with her father Maurice, who is an eccentric inventor who has been prisoner in a strange castle owned by a hideous beast. His daughter, very concerned about the life of her father, decides to go to the rescue and she offers to take her father's place. The Beast accepts the offer and Belle sacrifices her freedom for love of her father. Before long she begins to develop feelings for the beast, and the beast for Belle. She also is able to see beyond the physical appearance and does everything possible to make her dreams come true.

2. In our story we have another Beauty and the Beast, only this time the Beast is just as ugly within as he is without!

I. FIRST, THE *REMARKABLE* MAN OF GOD. 25:1

Then Samuel died; and all Israel gathered together and mourned for him, and buried him at his house in Ramah. And David arose and went down to the wilderness of Paran – The death of Samuel reminds us of the end of the period of the Judges. Since the selection of Saul, the nation had become a monarchy. Saul has been rejected and David's descendants would occupy Israel's throne forever, Christ being the fulfillment of the promise. The mourning reveals the deep grief and respect that the nation had for Samuel. Now Samuel was dead, and all Israel had lamented him and buried him in Ramah, his own city…"

Samuel was in his 90's and finally going home. Reminds me of Billy Graham, he is waiting and looking forward to the day when he will head home.

"I am home in heaven, dear ones;
Oh, so happy and so bright.
There is perfect joy and beauty
In this everlasting light.
All the pain and grief is over,
Every restless tossing passed.
I am now at peace forever,
Safely home in heaven, at last."

Trans: For the saved one day you will enter Glory. Something every believer can amen. On October 24, 1852, Daniel Webster was lying in his bed on the verge of death. Dr. Jeffries had done all he could for his friend. The doctor picked up Daniel's hymn book and began reading every stanza of "There is a Fountain Filled With Blood." When the doctor got to the last verse, Webster's lips were moving, though no sound came: *When this poor lisping, stammering tongue, lies silent in the grave, then in a nobler, sweeter song, I'll sing thy power to save, I'll sing thy power to save.*

At that moment, the doctor looked at Daniel and their eyes met, and Webster faintly muttered three final words: Amen, Amen, Amen! and slipped into eternity.

II. FURTHERMORE, NABAL'S *RESUME.* 2-3, 36-38

A. He was *Wealthy.* 2

Now there was a man in Maon whose business was in Carmel; and the man was very rich, and he had three thousand sheep and a thousand goats. And it came about while he was shearing his sheep in Carmel – it is a sad combination when someone is wealthy but not generous.

Jim Walls noted, "The Bible doesn't mind prosperity; it just insists that it be shared."

B. He was a man of *Stupidity.* 3a

now the man's name was Nabal… - Nabal, whose name means "[intellectually and/or ethically] foolish,"

Boice, "Hebrew, like English, has quite a few words for describing those who are unwise. They correspond to words like simple, silly, simpleton, fool, and madman. The word used in this verse is *nabel*, which embraces the idea of a foolish but also an aggressively perverse personality. Folly expresses itself in evil acts."

C. His *Family.* 3b

and his wife's name was Abigail. And the woman was intelligent and beautiful in appearance… - reminded me of the boy coming home from Sunday School explaining to his mom how God made the first woman. He said, "Mom, God put the first man to sleep, and while he was asleep God took out his brains and made a woman out of them!"

Nabal's wife had all the brains in the family…

As one notes, "The Bible is a very balanced book. It warns about the demise and danger of beauty. The demise: "Beauty is vain" (Proverbs 31:30). The danger: "Do not desire [the adulterous woman's] *beauty* in your heart, and do not let her capture you with her eyelashes" (Proverbs 6:25). However, the Bible also notes (and likely values) beauty, especially feminine beauty. Abraham's wife Sarah was "a woman *beautiful* in appearance" (Genesis 12:11); she was "*very beautiful*" (Genesis 12:14). Isaac's wife Rebekah was also "*very beautiful*" (Genesis 24:16, NIV). Other women in the Bible who were called "beautiful" include Rachel (Genesis 29:17), Abigail (1 Samuel 25:3), Tamar (2 Samuel 13:1), Esther (Esther 1:11; 2:7), and the daughters of Job (Job 42:15). So, Biblically speaking, beauty is like a cut rose. It's worth beholding even though you know it is withering away. It's worth beholding even though its thorns can prick."

D. He was *Ungodly.* 3c

but the man was harsh and evil in his dealings, and he was a Calebite) – this man does not have many good qualities:

- The character of Nabal is described as "harsh and evil." It makes one wonder how he got his wealth in the first place?

"[3] ...was surly and mean in his dealings." (NIV)

"[3] ...was uncouth, churlish, stubborn, and ill-mannered." (TLB)

- He was from the tribe of Judah and the family of Caleb, an honorable man, one of the two spies who urged Israel to enter the Promised Land (Num. 13-14; Josh. 14:6-7).

But the name "Caleb" also means "a dog," so perhaps the writer was conveying this meaning as well. The man was like a stubborn vicious animal that nobody could safely approach.

- He was called a worthless man, by both his servants and wife (vv. 17, 25).

The term is literally, "a son of Belial" the Hebrew word *beliya'al* means "worthless-ness" and in the Old Testament refers to evil people who deliberately *broke the law and despised what was good*. (See Deut. 13:13; Judg. 19:22; 20:13; 1 Sam. 2:12.) In the New Testament, the word refers also to Satan (2 Cor. 6:15).

Trans: The reality, every lost person is a fool!

P. C. Craigie notes, "The fool is not a rare subspecies within the human race; all human beings are fools apart from the wisdom of God."

Dr. Joel Nederhood, was a radio preacher, he once told of being in Moscow and attending a booksellers' convention. At that time it was the age of *glasnost* (the openness in the last days of the Soviet Union), the American Bible Society was present and was giving away Bibles. A long line of people patiently waited to receive these Bibles, and the line stretched several hundred feet out into the display area, where it passed in front of a neglected booth manned by then seventy-year-old Madalyn Murray O'Hair, the most famous of American atheists. She must have been thinking, "What fools these Russians are to stand in line for Bibles. They should be buying books about atheism from me." But it was she, not they, like Nabal who was the fool.

III, NEXT DAVID'S *REQUEST* TO HIM. 4-9, 15-16

⁴ that David heard in the wilderness that Nabal was shearing his sheep. ⁵ So David sent ten young men; and David said to the young men, "Go up to Carmel, visit Nabal and greet him in my name; ⁶ and thus you shall say, 'Have a long life, peace be to you, and peace be to your house, and peace be to all that you have. ⁷ 'Now I have heard that you have shearers; now your shepherds have been with us and we have not insulted them, nor have they missed anything all the days they were in Carmel...¹⁵ "Yet the men were very good to us, and we were not insulted, nor did we miss anything as long as we went about with them, while we were in the fields. ¹⁶ "They were a wall to us both by night and by day, all the time we were with them tending the sheep – David was like the Mafia offering protection to business' for a little consideration.

Swindoll, "David and his 600 fighters had been behind the scenes, fighting various wild tribes in the wilderness of Paran. As such, they were also protecting these shepherds from the attack of wild tribes that would suddenly overrun an area, steal livestock, and assault small villages. According to customs of that day, at the time the sheep were sheared it was common for the owner of the animals to set aside a portion of the profit he made and give it to those who had protected his shepherds while they were out in the fields. It was kind of like tipping a waiter. There was no written law saying you had to do it, but it was a way of showing gratitude for a job well done."

- It's *Reasonable* – David had a legitimate need and made a reasonable request.

- It was *Right* – (1) If David had not slew Goliath in the first place, Nabal's wealth would have already been in the hands of the Philistines. (2) Had David not protected his sheep there would have been less sheep to shear!

Trans: Yet Nabal Refuses David's request! Lutzer notes:

"Obviously, Nabal knew who David was. After all David had gained national fame as the wonder boy who slew Goliath. But pride, power, and wealth filled Nabal with derision. This was his opportunity to stomp an important man into the dirt."

IV. NABAL'S *REFUSAL* TO FEED HIM. 10-11

10 But Nabal answered David's servants and said, "Who is David? And who is the son of Jesse? There are many servants today who are each breaking away from his master. 11 "Shall I then take my bread and my water and my meat that I have slaughtered for my shearers, and give it to men whose origin I do not know?" – MacArthur notes, "This pretended ignorance of David was surely a sham. The knowledge of the young king-elect was widespread. Nabal pretended not to know to excuse his unwillingness to do what was right."

When we have opportunities to help people we do well to take advantage of it. Which there is nothing to indicate that Nabal was a believer, it is easy for believers to become just as self-centered, with little or no concern for the ministry needs of others. It reminded me of something I read about, some missionaries in the Philippines set up a croquet game in their front yard. Several of their Agta Negrito neighbors became interested and wanted to join the fun. The missionaries explained the game and started them out, each with a mallet and ball. As the game progressed, opportunity

came for one of the players to take advantage of another by knocking that person's ball out of the court. A missionary explained the procedure, but his advice only puzzled the Negrito friend. "Why would I want to knock his ball out of the court?" he asked.
The missionary said, "So you will be the one to win!" The man shook his head in bewilderment. The game continued, but no one followed the missionaries' advice. And when a player successfully got through all the wickets, that player went back and helped his fellow player. When the final player finished, they joyously shouted, "We won! We won!"

V. FIFTH, DAVID'S *RAGE*. 12-13, 21-22

12 So David's young men retraced their way and went back; and they came and told him according to all these words. 13 David said to his men, "Each of you gird on his sword." So each man girded on his sword. And David also girded on his sword, and about four hundred men went up behind David while two hundred stayed with the baggage… 21 Now David had said, "Surely in vain I have guarded all that this man has in the wilderness, so that nothing was missed of all that belonged to him; and he has returned me evil for good. 22 "May God do so to the enemies of David, and more also, if by morning I leave as much as one male of any who belong to him."– David could have used a verse like Ja. 1:19-20 about this time!

Talk about overkill! It would be like killing cockroaches in your house with a shotgun! Reminds me of Steve Tran of California who placed 25 bug bombs in his apartment to get rid of the roaches. The spray reached the pilot light of the stove and caused an explosion – costing over $10,000 dollars in damage!

A fool always loses his temper, but a wise man holds it back. Proverbs 29:11

As we have said before vengeance belongs to the Lord not to us or David.

Prison Letters, by Corrie ten Boom. The story of Corrie ten Boom (1892– 1983) during World War II is well known. Corrie had suffered with a tremendous need for vengeance. After Corrie was released from prison following the war, she felt the need to write a letter to the man who had revealed her family's rescue operations to the Germans. She writes about that:

"I was free, and knew then as I know now it was my chance to take to the world God's message of the victory of Jesus Christ in the midst of the deepest evil of man."

Written on June 19, 1945, part of the letter to her betrayer reads:

Today I heard that most probably you are the one who betrayed me. I went through 10 months of concentration camp. My father died after 9 days of imprisonment. My sister died in prison, too. The harm you planned was turned into good for me by God. I came nearer to Him. . . . I have forgiven you everything. God will also forgive you everything, if you ask Him. He loves you and He Himself sent His Son to earth to reconcile your sins, which meant to suffer the punishment for you and me. You, on your part, have to give an answer to this. . . . Never doubt the Lord Jesus' love. He is standing with His arms spread out to receive you. I hope that the path which you will now take may work for your eternal salvation.

That should have been David's attitude toward Nabal.

VI. ABIGAIL'S *RESPONSE.* 14-31

A. Her *Receiving* a Report of what happened. 14-17

14 But one of the young men told Abigail, Nabal's wife, saying, "Behold, David sent messengers from the wilderness to greet our master, and he scorned them. 15 "Yet the men were very good to us, and we were not insulted, nor did we miss anything as long as we went about with them, while we were in the fields. 16 "They were a wall to us both by night and by day, all the time we were with them tending the sheep. 17 "Now therefore, know and consider what you should do, for evil is plotted against our master and against all his household; and he is such a worthless man that no one can speak to him."

B. Her *Resolve* to stop the bloodshed.

18 Then Abigail hurried and took two hundred loaves of bread and two jugs of wine and five sheep already prepared and five measures of roasted grain and a hundred clusters of raisins and two hundred cakes of figs, and loaded them on donkeys. 19 She said to her young men, "Go on before me; behold, I am coming after you." But she did not tell her husband Nabal. 20 It came about as she was riding on her donkey and coming down by the hidden part of the mountain, that behold, David and his men were coming down toward her; so she met them – As always we can see both God's Sovereignty and human responsibility.

- God's Sovereignty - Only a sovereign Lord could have arranged the timing of David's attack and Abigail's approach so that the two bands met.

- Human Responsibility - Our world today could use a few peace-makers like Abigail today. It seems many of our leaders want to keep people stirred up.

Truth is we are have the capacity to be as uncontrollably angry as David, but God working through people like Abigail can confront us with the need to change.

Dr. Ben Carson has become known throughout the world as a premiere brain surgeon, now running for President. The interesting thing is that Dr. Carson's career was almost over before it began. In his book *Take the Risk*, Dr. Carson writes:

"One day, as a 14-year-old in ninth grade, I was hanging out at the house of my friend Bob, listening to his radio, when he suddenly leaned over and dialed the tuner to another station. I'd been enjoying the song playing on the first station, so I reached over and flipped it back. Bob switched stations again. A wave of rage welled up. Almost without thinking, I pulled out the pocketknife I always carried and, in one continuous motion, flicked open the blade and lunged viciously right at my friend's stomach. Incredibly, the point of the knife struck Bob's large metal buckle and the blade snapped off in my hands. Bob raised his eyes from the broken piece of metal in my hand to my face. He was too surprised to say anything. But I could read the terror in his eyes. "I…I…I'm sorry!" I sputtered, then dropped the knife and ran for home, horrified by the realization of what I'd just done. I burst into our empty house, locked myself in the bathroom, and sank to the floor, miserable and frightened. I could no longer deny that I had a severe anger problem, and that I'd never achieve my dream of being a doctor with an uncontrollable temper. I admitted to myself there was no way I could control it by myself.

"Lord, please, you've got to help me," I prayed. "Take this temper away! You promised that if I ask anything in faith, you'll do it. I believe you can change me." I slipped out and got a Bible. Back on the bathroom floor, I opened to the Book of Proverbs. The words of Proverbs 16:32—["He who is slow to anger is better than the mighty, and he who rules his spirit than he who takes a city"]—convicted me, but also gave me hope. I felt God telling me that although he knew everything about me, he still loved me… That because he made me, he was the only one who could change me… And that he would. Gradually I stopped crying, my hands quit shaking, and I was filled with the assurance that God had answered my prayer.

Just as God worked through the friend of Ben Carson, so God worked through Abigail to hinder David from doing something that could have affected his whole life.

c. Her *Reasoning.* 23-31

1. Her *Humility.* 23-24

23 When Abigail saw David, she hurried and dismounted from her donkey, and fell on her face before David and bowed herself to the ground. 24 She fell at his feet and said, "On me alone, my lord, be the blame. And please let your maidservant speak to you, and listen to the words of your maidservant – she takes the blame.

2. Her *Honesty*. 25

"Please do not let my lord pay attention to this worthless man, Nabal, for as his name is, so is he. Nabal is his name and folly is with him; but I your maidservant did not see the young men of my lord whom you sent – while it is true that she does not show proper respect for her husband, it has to be kept in mind that what she said was true and her motive was to save his life.

3. Her counsel was *Heavenly*. 26, 28-31

[26] "Now therefore, my lord, as the LORD lives, and as your soul lives, since the LORD has restrained you from shedding blood, and from avenging yourself by your own hand, now then let your enemies and those who seek evil against my lord, be as Nabal...[28] "Please forgive the transgression of your maidservant; for the LORD will certainly make for my lord an enduring house, because my lord is fighting the battles of the LORD, and evil will not be found in you all your days. [29] "Should anyone rise up to pursue you and to seek your life, then the life of my lord shall be bound in the bundle of the living with the LORD your God; but the lives of your enemies He will sling out as from the hollow of a sling. [30] "And when the LORD does for my lord according to all the good that He has spoken concerning you, and appoints you ruler over Israel, [31] this will not cause grief or a troubled heart to my lord, both by having shed blood without cause and by my

lord having avenged himself. When the LORD deals well with my lord, then remember your maidservant." – everything she said focused on the Lord!

"*as the LORD lives…the LORD has restrained you…the LORD will certainly…fighting the battles of the LORD…of the living with the LORD your God…and when the LORD does…when the LORD deals well…*"

This is real counseling; too much counseling today is nothing more then psycho babble! It is self-centered and says very little about the Lord.

Reminds me of a restaurant in Atlanta, it is a true story you can find it listed in the Yellow Pages. If you call you will hear something like, "Hello! Church of God Grill!" What happened is they had a little mission and to make ends meet started selling chicken dinners after the Sunday morning church service. Well, people liked the chicken, and they did such a good business, they eventually closed down the church altogether and kept on serving the chicken dinners. They kept the name that we started with, and that's Church of God Grill."

Our counseling – and anything else for that matter should be focused on the LORD!

4. Her *Hospitality*. 27

"Now let this gift which your maidservant has brought to my lord be given to the young men

who accompany my lord – she in her wisdom met their needs.

Trans: I think one of the applications of this is this, if we're saved, thank God that He keeps us from living more Sinfully.

Abigail is a picture of God's restraining hand in our lives (Gen. 20:2-6/Heb. 7:25).

Davis, "The text teaches us how Yahweh rescues his servants from their own stupidity; how he restrains them from executing their sinful purposes, how sometimes he graciously and firmly intercepts us on the road to folly. With loving hands constructs the roadblocks to our foolishness. What mercy he sends that frustrates our purposes. What kindness builds hindrances in our path! We could hardly do better than to worship with David's own words, "Blessed be the Lord who has held back his servant from evil" (v. 39).

VII. DAVID'S *RESTRAINT.* 32-35

32 Then David said to Abigail, "Blessed be the LORD God of Israel, who sent you this day to meet me, 33 and blessed be your discernment, and blessed be you, who have kept me this day from bloodshed and from avenging myself by my own hand. 34 "Nevertheless, as the LORD God of Israel lives, who has restrained me from harming you, unless you had come quickly to meet me, surely there would not have been left to Nabal until the morning light as much as one male." 35 So David received from her hand what she had brought him and said to her, "Go up to your house in peace. See, I have listened to you and granted your request." - it is a blessing to think about how many times God has restrained us from ourselves!

Spurgeon, "We have not been so bad as others because we could not be. A certain boy has run away from home. Another boy remained at home. Is he, therefore, a better child? Listen! he had broken his leg, and could not get out of bed. That takes away all the credit of his staying at home. Some men cannot sin in a certain direction, and then they say to themselves, "What excellent fellows we are to abstain from this wickedness!" Sirs, you would have done it if you could, and therefore your self praise is mere flattery. Had you been placed in the same position as others, you would have acted as others have done, for your heart goes after the same idols."

I have sinned many times in my life, but I thank God that it has not been as many times as my old sin loving nature would like…to that I give all the praise to my sin restraining Lord!

VIII. NABAL'S DAY OF *RECKONING*. 36-38

[36] Then Abigail came to Nabal, and behold, he was holding a feast in his house, like the feast of a king. And Nabal's heart was merry within him, for he was very drunk; so she did not tell him anything at all until the morning light. [37]

But in the morning, when the wine had gone out of Nabal, his wife told him these things, and his heart died within him so that he became as a stone. ³⁸ About ten days later, the LORD struck Nabal and he died – God will take care of those who oppose us sooner or later.

Martin Luther confidently wrote:

"Our God will fulfill the promise of his word. He is on our side. No matter how the wicked strangle, imprison, and persecute, I am the more certain that God is my protection. Our doctrine must prevail: their doctrine must perish. God is our defense; he will see us through whether here or elsewhere. God is our refuge, to him we flee for safety."

Trans: For the lost it is not an advantage to die Wealthy (Lu.12:13-21). Charlemagne was the king of the Holy Roman Empire from 800 to 814 A.D. He instructed them that upon his death he should be placed upon his royal throne, with the imperial crown on his head and a Bible on his lap with his finger pointing to Mt. 16:26:

For what will it profit a man if he gains the whole world and forfeits his soul? Or what will a man give in exchange for his soul? Matthew 16:26

About 1,000 A.D. his tomb was opened by Emperor Otho. There was Charlemagne's skeleton remains, his skull still wearing the crown, a boney finger pointing to Mt. 16:26!

IX. DAVID'S UNBIBLICAL *ROMANCE.* 39-44

^{39} When David heard that Nabal was dead, he said, "Blessed be the LORD, who has pleaded the cause of my reproach from the hand of Nabal and has kept back His servant from evil. The LORD has also returned the evildoing of Nabal on his own head." Then David sent a proposal to Abigail, to take her as his wife. ^{40} When the servants of David came to Abigail at Carmel, they spoke to her, saying, "David has sent us to you to take you as his wife." ^{41} She arose and bowed with her face to the ground and said, "Behold, your maidservant is a maid to wash the feet of my lord's servants." ^{42} Then Abigail quickly arose, and rode on a donkey, with her five maidens who attended her; and she followed the messengers of David and became his wife. ^{43} David had also taken Ahinoam of Jezreel, and they both became his wives. ^{44} Now Saul had given Michal his daughter, David's wife, to Palti the son of Laish, who was from Gallim – He had already taken Ahinoam as his wife (27:3; 30:5; 2 Sam. 2:2). Whatever happened to his first wife Michal? Remember she is the one who had helped to save David's life? After David fled from home, Saul gave her to another man! Since there was no legal divorce, Saul essentially forced her into an adulterous relationship. Later David will demand that

Michal be returned to him (2 Sam. 3:13-16). What a mess!

There is no way to dance around this, this is polygamy pure and simple! The Bible never endorses polygamy (Deut.17:17/Mal.2:15/Mat. 19:4).

Trans: David confronts us with a Reality – we are all sinners! No matter how tall we think we stand the only one worthy of lifting up is the Lord Jesus Christ.

After WWI, General Pershing planned a series of victory parades. He gave two requirements to be in the parades: (1) One must have an unblemished military record; (2) they had to be at least 1 meter, 86 centimeters tall.

A group of American soldiers stated about 100 miles from Paris wanted to be in the parade but nobody knew how tall 1 meter, 86 centimeters was. But the tallest man in the group was a man they nicknamed Slim. He surely must be tall enough. But then they found out that 1 meter, 86 centimeters was 6 ft 1/5th inches tall. Slim was one-quarter of an inch too short! Truth is the very best among us – whether you be a David or a Daniel or a Paul...all fall short and must trust in the imputed righteousness of Christ to be acceptable in God's sight.

Con:

1. Lesson's we can learn from the Beauty and the Beast: It teaches us about Glory; the inadequacy of being Wealthy; the need for the hand of God to keep us from living more Sinfully; and the Reality that like David we all still fall short of the glory of God.

2. In the closing scenes from the Beauty and the Beast, the beast lies dying from a wound inflicted during combat with Gaston his enemy. Belle the beauty finally confesses her love for the beast and just in time gives him the kiss that breaks the curse. The beast is transformed back into a handsome prince and they live happily ever after. Beauty brought life to the beast, we could say.In our story the Beast Nabal dies, and in a sense, is replaced by a handsome king, David, and Abigail's life is transformed into a happier ever after.

Chapter Twenty-Seven

THE AMAZING PLACE OF GRACE

1 Sam. 27

Intro:

1. Dale Davis, "You must get a grip on grace. The Bible does not claim that God's servants are dipped in Clorox, so they will be infallible, sin-free and attractive to you. The living God does not have clean material to work with. Remember its only sinful clay the Potter works

with. We should not criticize the Potter because of the clay, but rather marvel that he stoops to work with such stuff. As long as we wallow in some idea of human worthiness, we will never understand the Bible, never tremble before this God, and never delight in this God. We must get a grip on grace."

2. Getting a grip on grace is not easy to do; we all have a hard time hanging on to the concept of God's unmerited, undeserved, unearned favor. We get a picture of God's grace in the chapter before us – just when David least deserves God's help and enablement, he gets it!

I. FOR STARTERS, WE HAVE DAVID'S CARNALITY. 27:1a

A. First, his lack of *Prayer.*

Then David said to himself... - why talk to ourselves, when we have the privilege of talking to God! He has shifted his focus from God onto himself, from prayer to self-counsel. Truth is ours is a generation that loves to talk *to* ourselves and *about* ourselves. Research has shown that on average, people spend 60 % of conversations talking about themselves—and this figure jumps to 80 percent when communicating via social media platforms such as Twitter or Facebook.

A recent study summarized in *Scientific American* reveals we talk about ourselves because it feels good.

Researchers from Harvard asked 195 participants to talk about themselves or other people. As they talked, the researchers scanned their brains. The results of the study showed that self-disclosure (or talking about ourselves) lit up the parts of our brain associated with motivation and reward—the same parts of the brain associated with pleasures like comfort food (fried chicken, pizza, or macaroni and cheese) or a hit from cocaine. The article put it this way:

"Activation of this system [in the brain] when discussing the self suggests that self-disclosure ... may be inherently pleasurable—and that people may be motivated to talk about themselves more than other topics (no matter how interesting or important these non-self topics may be)."

In other words, we love talking about ourselves because it feels good. It's a neurological buzz. The problem is that self cannot solve our problems and being self-absorbed always leads to depression and wrong thinking.

B. Second, he lost sight of the *Promise* of God. 1b-4

..."*Now I will perish one day by the hand of Saul. There is nothing better for me than to escape into the land of the Philistines. Saul then will despair of searching for me anymore in all the territory of Israel, and I will escape from his hand." ² So David arose and crossed over, he and the six hundred men who were with him, to Achish the son of Maoch, king of Gath. ³ And David lived with Achish at Gath, he and his men, each with his household, even David with his two wives, Ahinoam the Jezreelitess, and Abigail the Carmelitess, Nabal's widow. ⁴ Now it was told Saul that David had fled to Gath, so he no longer searched for him* – God had promised that David would one day be king of Israel. In fact, he had already anointed him and had reaffirmed this promise just recently!

Abigail encouraged David by saying, "²⁹ Someone might chase you to kill you, but the LORD your God will keep you alive. He will throw away your enemies' lives as he would throw a stone from a sling. ³⁰ The LORD will keep all his promises of good things for you. He will make you leader over Israel. 1 Samuel 25:29-30 (NCV)

Even Saul confessed this to be a fact, "Then Saul said to David, "Blessed are you, my son David; you will both accomplish much and surely prevail…" 1 Sam. 26:25

When we live in the flesh we no longer believe God's promises:

- We don't really believe everything is ultimately working for our good (Ro. 8:28).

- We stop praying because we no longer believe that God answers our prayers (Mt. 7:7-8).

- We no longer share the gospel because we do not believe God's promise that the gospel is the power of God (Rom. 1:16).

We quit in the face of delay and difficulty...We must believe God even when his promises seem impossible. Ro. 4:20-21

Did you know:

- Dr. Seuss' first children's books were rejected by 23 publishers before the 24th one sold six million copies.

- After being rejected by Hewlett-Packard and Atari, Apple microcomputers had a first year sales of 2.5 million dollars.

- During the first year of business, Coca-Cola sold only 400 Cokes.

- In his first three years in the car business, Henry Ford went bankrupt twice.

- Michael Jordan was cut from his high school basketball team.

For the believer, God's grace guarantees that His promises will be fulfilled in spite of our unbelief!

If we are faithless, He remains faithful, for He cannot deny Himself. 2 Timothy 2:13

Tozer, "You may have been serving God quite a while, but instead of getting better, you feel you're getting worse. You know what's happening to you? You're getting to know yourself better! There was a time when you didn't know who you were and you thought you were pretty fine. Then, by the good grace of God, He showed you yourself—and it was shocking and disappointing to you. But don't be discouraged, because He is faithful that calls you and He will also do it. God will finish the job. I've often wondered how a hen must feel about sitting for three weeks on an egg. My mother always put thirteen eggs under a hen and the old girl would sit right there. She might take a little coffee break once in awhile, but back she'd come again to the nest. For the first week, it was a novelty. Two weeks of it she might endure, but that last week must have been torture—just sitting there with nothing happening. Then about noon of the twenty-first day, the first little experimental peep is heard under her wings. And she smiles as only a hen can smile and says, "Thank God, they're here." After that it is just a question of time. One after the other, the chicks peck themselves out of their shells. I used to get down on my hands and knees as a boy and watch them picking themselves out. They're messy when they first appear, but give them about ten minutes in the sunshine and they're fluffy as can be, and lovely to look at. But they only come after twenty-one long days of waiting. God sometimes makes us wait. He made the disciples wait in Jerusalem for the Holy Spirit (Acts 1:4) and He may make you wait. But remember, God is faithful who called you, and He also will do it. This is our faithful God."

Trans: There have been many times in my carnality when I did not pray or claim the promises of God – but during those times the Lord Jesus still prayed for me and His promises still stood. That's grace!

II. NEXT WE SEE GOD'S *MERCY*. 27:5-9

A. God gave him a *City*. 5-7

5 Then David said to Achish, "If now I have found favor in your sight, let them give me a place in one of the cities in the country, that I may live there; for why should your servant live in the royal city with you?" 6 So Achish gave him Ziklag that day; therefore Ziklag has belonged to the kings of Judah to this day. 7 The number of days that David lived in the country of the Philistines was a year and four months – how cool is that! Actually Ziklag had *already* been given to Israel (Josh. 19:1-2, 5a). The only reason the Philistines had it was because Israel had failed to possess it. But it was theirs all the time.

We likewise have a city that is now ours, one that we will possess throughout eternity – the New Jerusalem (Rev. 21:10-14).

An Advertisement Of Heaven from the Bible:

FREE
BEAUTIFUL HOMES
to be
GIVEN AWAY
in a
PERFECT CITY!
with:
100% Pure Water Free
No Light Bills
Perpetual Lighting
Permanent Pavement
Nothing Undesirable
Everything New
Perfect Health
Immunity from Accidents
The Best of Society
Beautiful Music
Free Transportation
SECURE A CONTRACT TODAY FOR THE NEW JERUSALEM.
—*The Bible Friend*

This city can be entered into right *now* by faith!

But you have come [indic. Perf tense] to Mount Zion and to the city of the living God, the heavenly Jerusalem, and to myriads of angels, Hebrews 12:22

Again, Tozer notes:

"We must avoid the common fault of pushing the "other world" into the future. It is not future, but present. It parallels our familiar physical world, and the doors between the two worlds are open. "Ye are come," says the writer to the Hebrews (and the tense is plainly present)… All these things are contrasted with "the mount that might be touched" (12:18) and "the sound of a trumpet, and the voice of words" (12:19) that might be heard. May we not safely conclude that, as the realities of Mount Sinai were apprehended by the senses, so the realities of Mount Zion are to be grasped by the soul? And this not by any trick of the imagination but in downright actuality. The soul has eyes with which to see and ears with which to hear. Feeble they may be from long disuse, but by the life-giving touch of Christ they are now alive and capable of sharpest sight and most sensitive hearing. As we begin to focus upon God, the things of the spirit will take shape before our inner eyes. Obedience to the word of Christ will bring an inward revelation of the Godhead (John 14:21-23). It will give acute perception enabling us to see God even as is promised to the pure in heart. A new God-consciousness will seize upon us and we shall begin to taste and hear and inwardly feel God, who is our life and our all."

We both enter the city and look for it (Heb. 11:10, 13-16).

B. God also gives David *Victory.* 8-9

⁸ Now David and his men went up and raided the Geshurites and the Girzites and the Amalekites; for they were the inhabitants of the land from ancient times, as you come to Shur even as far as the land of Egypt. ⁹ David attacked the land and did not leave a man or a woman alive, and he took away the sheep, the cattle, the donkeys, the camels, and the clothing. Then he returned and came to Achish – keep in mind the Geshurites lived in a land that had already been given to Judah by God! God had already commanded Israel to eliminate the Amalekites. This was victories that God had given to David. Obviously these victories were not based on David's merit or worth but God's mercy.

but thanks be to God, who GIVES us the victory through our Lord Jesus Christ.
1 Corinthians 15:57

Our victory comes through our Lord Jesus Christ not our goodness or power. David who had crossed over to their enemies, the Philistines deserved to be defeated not victorious! Both the City and the Victory was an act of God's mercy and grace. And we have both also, but not because we deserve it.

Steve Brown tells of a father who caught his son smoking a cigarette. He told his son, "You deserve 3 hard licks from my belt." He put the boy over his knee and gave him one hard lick from his belt and sent him to his room. Several hours later he took him down to Dairy Queen and bought him a huge ice cream Sundae. He said, "Son, I want to teach you a lesson today, one that I hope you will remember. When I gave you one hit with the belt, when you deserved three that was mercy. And this ice cream you are now enjoying is grace!"

Our biggest problem is we lose sight of the mercy and grace that we receive on a daily basis.

III. FINALLY, WE HAVE DAVID'S *DISHONESTY*. 10-12

10 Now Achish said, "Where have you made a raid today?" And David said, "Against the Negev of Judah and against the Negev of the Jerahmeelites and against the Negev of the Kenites." 11 David did not leave a man or a woman alive to bring to Gath, saying, "Otherwise they will tell about us, saying, 'So has David done and so has been his practice all the time he has lived in the country of the Philistines.'" 12 So Achish believed David, saying, "He has surely made himself odious among his people Israel; therefore he will become my servant forever." – David was living a deceitful life. Deceit and dishonesty was wrong then and it is now.

Do not lie to one another, since you laid aside the old self with its *evil* practices, Colossians 3:9

When we were in Colorado, Ronnie shot a four point buck. Four of us were carrying it up a steep hill, someone said, "Hey, let's stop and pray!" I said, "Brother if you haven't been praying by now, I don't know what to tell you!" They were sort of embarrassed and shook their head in agreement. And then we proceeded onward. I came across spiritual that day, but the dark secret was, I had not been praying at all! Why did I say I was? I have no clue! And more importantly why didn't God strike me down for my deception? It was because of His mercy and grace!

Con:

1. Here we see David in the place of Carnality and Dishonesty – living without prayer or claiming the promises of God. Yet God blesses him with a city and victory.

Jerry Bridges, "One of the best kept secrets among Christians today is this: Jesus paid it all. I mean all. He not only purchased your forgiveness of sins and your ticket to heaven, He purchased every blessing and every answer to prayer you will ever receive. Every one of them – no exceptions…(Eph. 1:3)."

God is not keeping score, granting or withholding blessings on the basis of our performance. The score has already been permanently settled by Christ…We are sanctified by grace; we receive both temporal and spiritual blessings by grace; we are motivated to obedience by grace; and we will be glorified by grace. The entire Christian life is lived under the reign of God's grace."

2. Of course, the danger is to misunderstand the message of grace and think God is encouraging sin and disobedience.

Lloyd-Jones notes:

"There is a sense in which the doctrine he is talking about, the doctrine of grace is a very dangerous doctrine; I mean in the sense that it can be misunderstood. People listening to it may say, "Ah, there is a man who does not encourage us to live a good life, he seems to say that there is no value in our works, he says that all our righteousness are as filthy rags…Therefore what he is saying is that it does not matter what you do, sin as much as you like. [But] I say therefore, that if our preaching does not expose us to that charge and to that misunderstanding, it is because we are not really preaching the gospel. Nobody has ever brought his charge against the Church of Rome, but it was brought frequently against Martin Luther. They said, "This man is an antinomian [against the law] and that is heresy." The same charge was brought against George Whitefield two hundred years ago. Such a charge has always been brought against this startling, staggering message, that God justifies the ungodly and that we are saved not by anything we do, but in spite of it, entirely and only by the grace of God through our Lord and Savior Jesus Christ…I would say to all preachers: If our preaching has not been misunderstood in that way, then you had better examine your sermons again, and you had better make sure that you really are preaching the doctrine of grace."

I am not teaching that God's mercy and grace, in spite of your sin leads to an uncaring attitude about sin; but that God's grace and mercy flows to us, in spite of our sin, which releases the power of the Holy Spirit to make us as holy as we can possibly be in this life.

Chapter Twenty-Eight

THE DAY GOD MADE A SATANIC PSYCHIC SICK

1 Sam. 28

Intro:

1. In his book *Psychic Blues: Confessions of a Conflicted Medium*, psychic Mark Edward offers some fascinating thoughts on the hunger in our culture for community and spiritual truth. Edward admits that for decades he peddled what he called: "junkyard superstition … to the gullible, the lonely, the hopeful, and the dim." Among his many roles, he's been a dial-a-psychic with the Psychic Friends Network, a party psychic, a mentalist, a rent-a-psychic, a palmist, a fortune teller, and a graphologist.

Edward admits that he has no paranormal powers, and neither does anyone else. Edwards just relied on his intuition, common sense, and genuine empathy.

2. At best most Psychic hot lines are fraudulent and at worst demonic.

I. FIRST, ACHISH'S *CONFIDENCE* IN DAVID. 1-2

¹ Now it came about in those days that the Philistines gathered their armed camps for war, to fight against Israel. And Achish said to David, "Know assuredly that you will go out with me in the camp, you and your men." ² David said to Achish, "Very well, you shall know what your servant can do." So Achish said to David, "Very well, I will make you my bodyguard for life." – Chisholm notes, "bodyguard (Hebrew, "a guard for my head"). At this point Achish's words are dripping with irony. David, who once cut off the head of the hero of Gath and hauled it away as a trophy of war (17: 51, 54), will now be responsible for guarding the head of the ruler of Gath!"

David now faces a real dilemma, his deception and lies now come home to roost. He has led the king to believe he has been fighting his own people. Now he is between a rock and a hard place. Such is the cost of compromise with sin. It will put you, too, between a rock and a hard place. David can't tell the king he won't attack Israel without his life being in danger; and if he attacks Israel, he becomes a traitor to his own people, who he is destined to rule over. Such is the path of sin and compromise. You never know where sin will lead you and take you.

At Pier 39 in San Francisco, there is a section of pier that has been totally taken over by sea lions. In the beginning, there were only a few and now there are hundreds of them. Unconfessed sin is like that, it takes over and dominates our lives. When we compromise with sin and worldly living, we become like a rolling stone, heading downhill, and gaining momentum with every roll.

David is in a mess, and that is what happens when we get away from the Lord. So what does he do now?

Reminds me of one of those old TV episodes of the Lone Ranger where he and Tonto are hopelessly pinned down by Bad Bart and his men, the picture freezes and the announcer asks, "Will the masked man and his faithful companion survive? Will Bart kill him and terrorize the West? Stay tuned till next week for another thrilling episode!"

David's dilemma is suspended until chapter 29, where it reaches resolution.

II. NEXT, ISRAEL'S *CONTEMPLATION* OF SAMUEL. 3a

³ Now Samuel was dead, and all Israel had lamented him and buried him in Ramah, his own city… - this is to remind us that Samuel had been dead for some time. Saul has lost his prophetic source of divine guidance. We can also lose our prophetic source of divine guidance through neglect of God's Word.

We should lament on how our Government no longer consults God's Word. Mark Bauerlein, in *The State of the American Mind,* shared how a "stream of opinion surveys and widely reported anecdotes document an alarming decline in biblical literacy among Americans; that is, there is ignorance of key biblical texts, stories, characters, doctrines, themes, rituals, and symbols.

For example, when asked in January, 2004, to name his favorite book of the New Testament, presidential candidate Howard Dean, answered, "Job." At a November 2, 2011, briefing, White House press secretary Jay Carney elaborated on President Obama's invocation of God in rebuking the House of Representatives for not acting more quickly on a jobs bill. Carney said:

"I believe the phrase from the Bible is, the Lord helps those who help themselves'" The White House later issued a correction, noting, "This common phrase does not appear in the Bible."

On April 1, 2013, the *New York Times* issued the following correction of an article on Pope Francis's first Easter message:

"An earlier version of this article mischaracterized the Christian holiday of Easter. It is the celebration of Jesus' resurrection from the dead, not his resurrection into heaven."

There seems to be an ignorance of the Bible from every area, how many movie stars or popular singers had no clue about what the Bible really teaches.

In *It's a Long Story: My Life* by Willie Nelson, Willie recounts his time as a Sunday School teacher at Metropolitan Baptist Church— he shares about his "openness in exploring spiritual issues"—an openness that led to his eventual dismissal. But Willie claims his dismissal from the church was an "opportunity to delve deeper in the mystery of the Holy Spirit. More than ever, I sought to learn about the Lord."

One book that had a huge impact upon Willie was *The Aquarian Gospel of Jesus the Christ*, which taught that Jesus discovered and embraced the notion of reincarnation. Willie wrote:

From the first moment I considered the concept of reincarnation it made sense. The old paradigm was just too cruel, just too unchristian, to be believed: If you die in your sin, you spend eternity in hell. How could the compassionate God of mercy ever set up such a system? On the other hand, I was drawn to the idea that you keep coming back till you get it right. Reincarnation seemed merciful and completely Christ-like. Jesus got it right the first time around and was, after all, God incarnate, perfect man. But the rest of us would need several lifetimes to shed our sins and learn the lessons necessary to heal our troubled souls." [Willie Nelson with David Ritz, It's a Long Story: My Life (Little, Brown & Co., 2015), pp. 113-115; submitted by: Van Morris, Mt. Washington, Kentucky]

Well poor old Willie still doesn't have it right! And all because he refuses to simply believe what the Bible declares (Jn. 3:36).

III. THIRD, SAUL'S *CONDEMNATION* OF SPIRITISTS. 3b, 9

³...And Saul had removed from the land those who were mediums and spiritists... ⁹ But the woman said to him, "Behold, you know what Saul has done, how he has cut off those who are mediums and spiritists from the land. Why are you then laying a snare for my life to bring about my death?" – That was a good Biblical thing to do. Saul had obeyed the law (Lev. 19: 31; 20: 27; Deut. 18: 10– 11). It shows that Saul did not sin in ignorance but in a clear violation of what he knew was wrong.

- Mediums - These were people who deceived others by claiming to call up departed spirits. They used such means as ventriloquism to fool their clients.

- Spiritists - These were involved in casting spells, witchcraft, future telling, necromancy. They were idolatrous and used drug potions in their craft.

We should understand that reading one's horoscope, consulting a psychic, having one's palm read is sin and opens the door to satanic activity. An increase in such activity is a sign that we are living in the last days of the church (1 Tim. 4:1-2).

In 1692, the Salem witch hunt resulted in the execution of fourteen women and six men. Today, Salem has over 3000 registered witches. In fact, in the United States there are over 200,000 registered witches and many more not registered. A famous witch in Florida said in the New York Times that there are over eight million witches in the world today. People turn to palm readers, psychic friends, and horoscopes to know the future. As Christians, we are not to be worried about our future because our future is in God's hands. Research literature shows that the great majority of Americans who say they have "no religion" are still quite religious, or at least "spiritually inclined." Surveys support this.

In 2011, an Associated Press poll found that 8 in 10 Americans believed in angels—even 4 in 10 people who never went to church. In 2009 the Pew Research Center reported that 1 in 5 Americans experienced ghosts and 1 in 7 had consulted a psychic. In 2005, Gallup found that 3 out of 4 Americans believed in something paranormal, and that 4 in 10 said that houses could be haunted. More than 90 percent of those who do not belong to a church say that they pray, and 39 percent of them pray weekly or more often. Half of those who say they have "no religion" frequent New Age bookstores, and they are especially prone to believe in ghosts, Bigfoot, and Atlantis.

Stats like these led religion scholar Jeffrey J. Kripal to declare, "Americans are *obsessed* with the supernatural." In other words, people are rejecting the place where the Word of God is proclaimed and yet not the supernatural – that leaves the door wide open for Satanic deception! The world is being prepared for demon worship (Rev. 9:20-21).

[20] The rest of mankind, who were not killed by these plagues, did not repent of the works of their hands, so as not to worship demons, and the idols of gold and of silver and of brass and of stone and of wood, which can neither see nor hear nor walk; [21] and they did not repent of their murders nor of their sorceries nor of their immorality nor of their thefts. Revelation 9:20-21

The words from one Rock group go like this:

"Killer, intruder, homicidal man,
If you see me coming, run as fast as you can.
A bloodthirsty demon who's stalking the street,
I hack up my victims like pieces of meat.

I drink the vomit of the priests,
Make love to the dying whore...
I am decreed by Lord Satan's fine evil
To destroy what all mortals love most.
Satan, my master incarnate,
Hail praise to the unholy host.

IV. FOURTH, THE PHILISTINES *CONFRONTATION* WITH ISRAEL. 4

So the Philistines gathered together and came and camped in Shunem; and Saul gathered all Israel together and they camped in Gilboa – life always involves warfare. That is why we cannot afford to live in sin and expose ourselves to the enemies of our souls.

V. FIFTH, SAUL'S *CONSTERNATION*. 5-6

A. Because of the Philistines *Presence.* 5

When Saul saw the camp of the Philistines, he was afraid and his heart trembled greatly – or we might say because of God's absence. If we do not walk by faith we will be dominated by fear.

Nelson Study Bible, "Saul's persistent disobedience had left him completely without confidence in God's presence and protection."

B. Because of God's *Silence.* 6

When Saul inquired of the LORD, the LORD did not answer him, either by dreams or by Urim or by prophets – this verse catalogs the acceptable methods by which an Israelite can seek God's guidance: dreams, Urim and prophecy. God was silent because of Saul's unconfessed sin (Psa.66:9/Prov.1:24-30/Isa.59:1-2/Jam.4:3).

Torrey noted:

"Sin hinders prayer. Many a man prays and prays and prays and gets absolutely no answer to his prayer. Perhaps he is tempted to think that it is not the will of God to answer, or he may think that the days when God answered prayer, if He ever did, are over. So the Israelites seem to have thought . . . that the Lord's hand was shortened that it could not save, and that His ear had become heavy that it could no longer hear. . . . Many and many a man is crying to God in vain, simply because of sin in his life. It may be some sin in the past that has been unconfessed and unjudged, it may be some sin in the present that is cherished, very likely is not even looked upon as sin; but there the sin is, hidden away somewhere in the heart or in the life, and God "will not hear."

VI. SIXTH, SAUL'S *CONSULTATION* WITH A MEDIUM. 7-19

A. The *Request*. 7-8

1. To his *Servant*. 7

Then Saul said to his servants, "Seek for me a woman who is a medium, that I may go to her and inquire of her." And his servants said to him, "Behold, there is a woman who is a medium at Endor." – this is a capital offense (Lev. 20:6/1 Chron. 10:13-14).

2. Of a *Spiritist*. 8

Then Saul disguised himself by putting on other clothes, and went, he and two men with him, and they came to the woman by night; and he said, "Conjure up for me, please, and bring up for me whom I shall name to you."

Trans: Saul is acting totally inconsistent, on the one hand he gets rid of the Medium's and yet on the other hand goes and consults one.

Boa, "Human nature is a web of contradiction: we bear the image of God, but we are ensnared in trespasses and sin; we are capable of harnessing the forces of nature, but unable to rule our tongues; we are the most wonderful and creative beings on this planet, but also the most violent, cruel, and contemptible of earth's inhabitants."

Pascal noted, "Man is a reed, the most feeble thing in nature; but he is a thinking reed. The entire universe need not arm itself to crush him. A vapor, a drop of water suffices to kill him. But, if the universe were to crush him, many would still be more noble than that which killed him."

B. The *Restraint* removed. 9-11

⁹ But the woman said to him, "Behold, you know what Saul has done, how he has cut off those who are mediums and spiritists from the land. Why are you then laying a snare for my life to bring about my death?" ¹⁰ Saul vowed to her by the LORD, saying, "As the LORD lives, no punishment shall come upon you for this thing." ¹¹ Then the woman said, "Whom shall I bring up for you?" And he said, "Bring up Samuel for me." – Saul's promise cannot cancel out God's Word of punishment.

C. The *Result.* 12-15a

1. The *Surprise.* 12

When the woman saw Samuel, she cried out with a loud voice; and the woman spoke to Saul, saying, "Why have you deceived me? For you are Saul." - Did Samuel come back from the dead?" The answer appears to be that he did. Apparently, God intervened in this one case and truly raised up Samuel to deliver the message of doom and judgment to Saul. Notice:

- The witch is surprised (v. 12). She realizes Saul is with her.

- Saul identifies Samuel and he bows and speaks with him.
- The Bible says this is Samuel. (vv. 12, 15, 16)
- The message is clearly from God.

Merrill, "So startled was she by Samuel's appearance that she immediately realized that the work was of God and not of herself, and that Samuel's appearance, even in visionary form, was not the expected result clearly teaches that necromancers or mediums have no real power over the deceased, especially the righteous, but can only produce counterfeits."

2. The *Spirit.* 13-14

13 The king said to her, "Do not be afraid; but what do you see?" And the woman said to Saul, "I see a divine being coming up out of the earth." 14 He said to her, "What is his form?" And she said, "An old man is coming up, and he is wrapped with a robe." And Saul knew that it was Samuel, and he bowed with his face to the ground and did homage – This is fascinating! She sees what she perceives to be a divine being! Samuel had not yet received a glorified body (Dan. 12:1-2). Perhaps he had a temporary body? The point is that she was so impressed with Samuel that she called him divine. Of course, we do not turn into divine beings, at death, but this woman is simply reflecting her pagan belief that Samuel had become a "god." A belief that has no basis in the Scriptures. Coming out of the earth, because before the resurrection of the Lord Jesus, saints were in the paradise side of Hades (Lu. 16:19-31).

3. The *Supplication.* 15

15 Then Samuel said to Saul, "Why have you disturbed me by bringing me up?" And Saul answered, "I am greatly distressed; for the Philistines are waging war against me, and God has departed from me and no longer answers me, either through prophets or by dreams; therefore I have called you, that you may make known to me what I should do." – Samuel has no message about what he is to do, this is because Saul already knows what he is supposed to do – repent!

4. The *Separations.* 16-17

a. From the Lord's *Occupancy.* 16

Samuel said, "Why then do you ask me, since the LORD has departed from you and has become your adversary? – Saul no longer had the Holy Spirit indwelling him.

b. From his *Authority.* 17

17 "The LORD has done accordingly as He spoke through me; for the LORD has torn the kingdom out of your hand and given it to your neighbor, to David – Saul did not need to consult a psychic but to believe Biblical prophecy! God has already told him what was going to happen through the prophet Samuel.

c. From his *Body.* 18-19

18 "As you did not obey the LORD and did not execute His fierce wrath on Amalek, so the LORD has done this thing to you this day. 19 "Moreover the LORD will also give over Israel along with you into the hands of the Philistines, therefore tomorrow you and your sons will be with me. Indeed the LORD will give over the army of Israel into the hands of the Philistines!" – in less than 24 hours he would be dead! Notice this is another verse giving assurance of salvation, in spite of Saul's persistent rebellion he would still be "with" Samuel, in the paradise side of Hades! Jn. 5:24/Phil.1:6/1 Jn. 5:11-13.

"I have an insurance policy,
 Written in the blood of the Lamb,
 Sealed by the Cross of Jesus,
 Redeemable wherever I am.

The company will never go bankrupt,
 It is bounded by God's promise true;
 It will keep every word of its contract,
 Exactly what it says it will do.

I don't have to die to collect it,
 No premiums do I have to pay;
 It was paid on Calvary's tree;
 It insures me for living and dying
 And for all eternity."

VII. FINALLY, SAUL'S *CONTINUATION* IN THE FLESH. 20-25

[20] Then Saul immediately fell full length upon the ground and was very afraid because of the words of Samuel; also there was no strength in him, for he had eaten no food all day and all night. [21] The woman came to Saul and saw that he was terrified, and said to him, "Behold, your maidservant has obeyed you, and I have taken my life in my hand and have listened to your words which you spoke to me. [22] "So now also, please listen to the voice of your maidservant, and let me set a piece of bread before you that you may eat and have strength when you go on your way." [23] But he refused and said, "I will not eat." However, his servants together with the woman urged him, and he listened to them. So he arose from the ground and sat on the bed. [24] The woman had a fattened calf in the house, and she quickly slaughtered it; and she took flour, kneaded it and baked unleavened bread from it. [25] She brought it before Saul and his servants, and they ate. Then they arose and went away that night – eating in that day was a picture of fellowship.

Con:

1. There is much application here, but the main one is stay away from psychics!

2. As long as we keep silent about the gospel Satan is going to get his counterfeit out there.

3. Bill Arnold noted:

"Not many years ago, the practice of magic and participation in the occult were rare in North American society and were definitely seen as emanating from the fringes of society. All of that has changed with the rise of postmodernism and especially in the emphases of the New Age movement. A positive side of postmodernism is a renewed hunger and desire to experience the supernatural. But wherever Christianity has been slow or unprepared to meet the need, the New Age movement has rushed in to fill the gap with beliefs in channeling, crystals, horoscopes, paranormal psychology, and reincarnation."

But the truth is there is a real, lasting, eternal solution that should be found on the lips of every single believer in the Lord Jesus Christ. Maybe if we were not so busy giving our time and money to get someone in the White House, we could get people to God's House again.

Chapter Twenty-Nine

STRENGTHENING OURSELVES IN THE LORD

1 Sam. 29-31

Intro:

1. Moody's (1892) voyage with his son from Southampton, England, on board the North German Lloyd steamship Spree, was terrifying. Three days into the crossing, the propeller shaft on the ship broke, and it looked like the vessel was sinking. Moody wrote:

"That was an awful night, the darkest in all our lives! [Everyone was] waiting for the doom that was settling upon us! No one dared sleep...I was passing through a new experience." Moody continues, "I had thought myself superior to the fear of death. I had often preached on the subject and urged Christians to realize this victory of faith. During the Civil War I had been under fire without fear. I was in Chicago during the great Cholera epidemic, and went around with the doctors visiting the sick and dying...But on the sinking ship it was different...It was the darkest hour of my life! I could not endure it."

2. The greatest need we have is to learn to strengthen ourselves in the Lord, but such a lesson is only taught when we encounter the fiercest of storms in our lives.

I. FIRST, WE HAVE DAVID'S *REJECTION.* 29:1-10

A. The *Inspection.* 1-2

1 Now the Philistines gathered together all their armies to A'phek, while the Israelites were camping by the spring which is in Jezreel. 2 And the lords of the Philistines were proceeding on by hundreds and by thousands, and David and his men were proceeding on in the rear with A'chish – A'phek is where they had defeated Israel and captured the Ark ninety years earlier.

B. The *Indignation*. 3-5

³ Then the commanders of the Phi-lis-tines said, "What are these Hebrews doing here?" And A'chish said to the commanders of the Philistines, "Is this not David, the servant of Saul the king of Israel, who has been with me these days, or rather these years, and I have found no fault in him from the day he deserted to me to this day?" ⁴ But the commanders of the Philistines were angry with him, and the commanders of the Philistines said to him, "Make the man go back, that he may return to his place where you have assigned him, and do not let him go down to battle with us, or in the battle he may become an adversary to us. For with what could this man make himself acceptable to his lord? Would it not be with the heads of these men? ⁵ "Is this not David, of whom they sing in the dances, saying, 'Saul has slain his thousands, And David his ten thousands'?" – in reality their concerns were well founded (14:21).

C. The *Interaction* between A'chish and David. 6-10

1. A'chish *Praise* of David. 6-7

⁶ Then A'chish called David and said to him, "As the LORD lives, you have been upright, and your going out and your coming in with me in the army are pleasing in my sight; for I have not found evil in you from the day of your coming to me to this day. Nevertheless, you are not pleasing in the sight of the lords. ⁷ "Now therefore return and go in peace, that you may not displease the lords of the Philistines."

2. David's *Protest to A'chish.* 8-10

⁸ David said to A'chish, "But what have I done? And what have you found in your servant from the day when I came before you to this day, that I may not go and fight against the enemies of my lord the king?" ⁹ But A'chish replied to David, "I know that you are pleasing in my sight, like an angel of God; nevertheless the commanders of the Philistines have said, 'He must not go up with us to the battle.' ¹⁰ "Now then arise early in the morning with the servants of your lord who have come with you, and as soon as you have arisen early in the morning and have light, depart."

Trans: David's rejection is another illustration of God's mercy. What would David have done if A'chish had permitted David to go to battle with them against Israel? How many times has "goodness and mercy" followed us? The answer is "all the days of our lives!" In May of 2009, on the Haizhu bridge in China, a disturbed man in deep financial debt was poised on the edge of the bridge contemplating suicide. Police had closed the bridge, disrupting traffic for five hours. Suddenly a man pushed his way through the police cordons and walked up to the man considering suicide. He reached out and shook the hand of the troubled man. Then he pushed him off the bridge!

Later he explained why: "I pushed him off because jumpers like [him] are very selfish. Their action violates a lot of public interest. They do not really dare to kill themselves. Instead, they just want to raise the relevant government authorities' attention to their appeals."Fortunately, the police had spread an inflatable emergency cushion beneath the bridge, and as a result, the suicidal man was injured but not killed.

That man got what he deserved, but God is not like that! He does not push us even when it is exactly what we deserve.

II. FURTHERMORE, DAVID'S *RETURN* TO ZIKLAG. 11

So David arose early, he and his men, to depart in the morning to return to the land of the Philistines. And the Philistines went up to Jezreel – he returns back to the city that God had graciously given him.

III. NEXT, DAVID'S *RUIN.* 30:1-6

A. His City was *Torched*. 1

¹ Then it happened when David and his men came to Zik'lag on the third day, that the Amalekites had made a raid on the Negev and on Zik'lag, and had overthrown Zik'lag and burned it with fire – Amalekites, were sworn enemies of the Lord and of the Jews (Ex. 17:8-16; Deut. 25:17). All of this because of Saul's refusal to obey God and totally wipe them out (1 Sam. 15:1-11).

B. His wives were *Taken*. 2-5

² and they took captive the women and all who were in it, both small and great, without killing anyone, and carried them off and went their way. ³ When David and his men came to the city, behold, it was burned with fire, and their wives and their sons and their daughters had been taken captive. ⁴ Then David and the people who were with him lifted their voices and wept until there was no strength in them to weep. ⁵ Now David's two wives had been taken captive, Ahinoam the Jezreelitess and Ab'igail the widow of Na-bal the Carmelite.

C. His life was *Threatened*. 6a

⁶ Moreover David was greatly distressed because the people spoke of stoning him, for all the people were embittered, each one because of his sons and his daughters…

Trans: He sort of felt like D. L. Moody on that ship, it was one of the darkest days of David's life. Let us realize that being a believer does not exempt us from catastrophes (1 Pet. 4:12).

Steve Brown, "One of the great problems as believers is that some of us think nothing bad will happen to us when we begin to follow Christ. Some feel that God is in the business of preventing tragedy and are devastated when their rope breaks. They become bitter. You see, they have not prepared themselves by learning sound doctrine. Disney world Christianity may work in the world where everything is clean and fun and right. But it simply won't work in a world where there is disease, death, and heartbreak. You've got to have a tough faith for a tough world."

However, that is never the end of the story! "These things I have spoken to you, so that in Me you may have peace. In the world you have tribulation, but take courage; I have overcome the world." John 16:33

We must not forget the last part of that verse!

Lyle Arakaki of Honolulu, Hawaii, shares this insight:

"In Hawaii, because of the time difference with the continental U.S., the NFL Monday Night

Football game is played in midafternoon, so the local TV station delays its telecast until 6:30 in the evening. When my favorite team plays, I'm too excited to wait for television, so I'll listen to the game on the radio, which broadcasts it live. Then, because they're my favorite team, I'll watch the game on television, too. If I know my team has won the game, it influences how I watch it on television. If my team fumbles the ball or throws an interception, it's not a problem. I think, *that's bad, but its okay. In the end, we'll win!*

That is what Jesus was saying, you are going to go through storms in life, but never forget the final outcome is conquest.

IV. NOTICE DAVID'S *REACTION*. 30:6b-10

A. He *Focused* on God's *Presence*.
⁶*...But David strengthened himself in the LORD his God* – David could no longer say "my city, my family, my friends, my prosperity – he was reduced to My God! A blessed reduction!

Corrie ten Boom said this: "Look at the world—you'll be distressed. Look within—you'll be depressed. Look at Christ—you'll be at rest."

Thomas Brooks, "True grace will enable a soul to sit down satisfied with the naked enjoyments of Christ alone! The enjoyment of Christ without riches, the enjoyment of Christ without pleasures, and without the smiles of creatures...And though honor is not, it is enough that Christ is, that He reigns, conquers, and triumphs. Paul said, "Having nothing, and yet possessing all things (2 Cor. 6:10)."

Spurgeon notes, "Let us try to conceive of the way in which David would encourage himself in the Lord his God. Standing amidst those ruins he would say, "Yet the Lord does love me, and I love him. Though I have wandered, yet my heart cannot rest without him. Though I have had but little fellowship with him of late, yet he has not forgotten to be gracious, nor has he in anger shut up his bowels of compassion."

I have in my Bible the letters; DCFTE, they reminds me that I am:

- Deeply loved no matter what because God has been propitiated.

- Completely forgiven because the blood of Jesus Christ has cleansed me of all sin.

- Fully pleasing because the righteousness of Christ has been imputed to me because of Justification.

- Totally accepted because I have been reconciled to God.

- Entirely a new creature, one who cannot sin in my new self, because of regeneration.

B. He *Found* God's *Promises* through prayer. 7-10

⁷ Then David said to Abiathar the priest, the son of Ahim'elech, "Please bring me the ephod." So Abiathar brought the ephod to David. ⁸ David inquired of the LORD, saying, "Shall I pursue this band? Shall I overtake them?" And He said to him, "Pursue, for you will surely overtake them, and you will surely rescue all." ⁹ So David went, he and the six hundred men who were with him, and came to the brook Be'sor, where those left behind remained. ¹⁰ But David pursued, he and four hundred men, for two hundred who were too exhausted to cross the brook Be'sor remained behind – God has a promise for every problem.

Our Thinking vs. God's Promises:

- We say- It's impossible. God says- All things are possible with Me.

- We- I can't do it. God- You can do all things through Christ.

- We- I'm too tired. God- Come to Me, I will give you rest.

- We- I'm always worried and frustrated. God- Cast all your cares on Me.

- We- I can't go on. God- My grace is sufficient for you.

- We- I can't figure things out. God- I will direct your steps.
- We- I'm not able. God- I am able.
- We- It's not worth it. God- It will be worth it.
- We- I can't manage. God- I will supply all your needs.
- We- I'm afraid. God- I have not given you a spirit of fear.
- We- I don't have enough faith. God- I've given everyone a measure of faith.
- We- I'm not smart enough. God- I give you wisdom.
- We- I feel all alone. God- I will never leave you or forsake you.

Trans: God's Presence and Promise is the only foundation we need to build our lives upon.

V. FIFTH, GOD'S PROVIDENTIAL *REIGN*. 30:11-15

A. Their *Finding*. 11

11 Now they found an Egyptian in the field and brought him to David, and gave him bread and he ate, and they provided him water to drink – this Egyptian just happened to become sick; just happened to be left behind; he just happened to be able to survive the elements without food or water for 3 days; and just happened to be willing to tell David where the Amal'ekites were – right!

B. Their *Feeding.* 12-14

12 They gave him a piece of fig cake and two clusters of raisins, and he ate; then his spirit revived. For he had not eaten bread or drunk water for three days and three nights. 13 David said to him, "To whom do you belong? And where are you from?" And he said, "I am a young man of Egypt, a servant of an Amal'ekite; and my master left me behind when I fell sick three days ago. 14 "We made a raid on the Negev of the Cherethites, and on that which belongs to Judah, and on the Negev of Caleb, and we burned Ziklag with fire."

C. The *Following.* 15

15 Then David said to him, "Will you bring me down to this band?" And he said, "Swear to me by God that you will not kill me or deliver me into the hands of my master, and I will bring you down to this band." – it is extremely easy to get lost in the desert, so God in His providence gave them a willing guide to lead them to the enemy.

Trans: There is nothing more important that believing that God is always on His throne working everything out for His glory and our good.

VI. THEN WE HAVE DAVID'S *RETALIATION.* 16-17

¹⁶ When he had brought him down, behold, they were spread over all the land, eating and drinking and dancing because of all the great spoil that they had taken from the land of the Philistines and from the land of Judah. ¹⁷ David slaughtered them from the twilight until the evening of the next day; and not a man of them escaped, except four hundred young men who rode on camels and fled – one might object we are not supposed to retaliate! Right, we living in the Church Age are not allowed to retaliate, but David lived under the Law, which had an eye for an eye and a tooth for a tooth! This is why we spent the entire sermon Sunday looking at the dispensations.

VII. SEVENTH, THE GLAD *REUNION.* 18-20

¹⁸ So David recovered all that the Amal'ekites had taken, and rescued his two wives. ¹⁹ But nothing of theirs was missing, whether small or great, sons or daughters, spoil or anything that they had taken for themselves; David brought it all back. ²⁰ So David had captured all the sheep and the cattle which the people drove ahead of the other livestock, and they said, "This is David's spoil." – it all happened just as God had promised.

VIII. DAVID'S *RESOLUTION* TO GIVE GOD THE GLORY. 30:21-31

A. First, the *Victory* was not according to man's *Ability.* 21-23

²¹ When David came to the two hundred men who were too exhausted to follow David, who had also been left at the brook Be'sor, and they went out to meet David and to meet the people who were with him, then David approached the people and greeted them. ²² Then all the wicked and worthless men among those who went with David said, "Because they did not go with us, we will not give them any of the spoil that we have recovered, except to every man his wife and his children, that they may lead them away and depart." ²³ Then David said, "You must not do so, my brothers, with what the **LORD has given us,** *who has kept us and delivered into our hand the band that came against us* – how unlike our mentality today! We glorify our military and constantly give them the credit for keeping us safe…not so! Had David given the spoils only to those who actually fought in the battle, it would have been an acknowledgement that they were responsible for the victory.

B. Furthermore, this indicates that there is a variety of ministries – all important. 24-25

²⁴ "And who will listen to you in this matter? For as his share is who goes down to the battle, so shall his share be who stays by the baggage; they shall share alike." ²⁵ So it has been from that day forward, that he made it a statute and an ordinance for Israel to this day – we all do not have the same gifts, or same duties but all are important and used by God (1 Cor. 12:14-26).

C. Last, any *Prosperity* should produce *Generosity*. 26-31

26 Now when David came to Ziklag, he sent some of the spoil to the elders of Judah, to his friends, saying, "Behold, a gift for you from the spoil of the enemies of the LORD: 27 to those who were in Beth'el, and to those who were in Ra'moth of the Negev, and to those who were in Jat'tir, 28 and to those who were in A-ro'er, and to those who were in Siph'moth, and to those who were in Esh-te-mo'a, 29 and to those who were in Ra-cal, and to those who were in the cities of the Je-rah'me-el-ites, and to those who were in the cities of the Ken-ites, 30 and to those who were in Hor'mah, and to those who were in Bor-ash'an [Chor-ash-an], and to those who were in A-thach, 31 and to those who were in He-bron, and to all the places where David himself and his men were accustomed to go." – God always blesses us so that we might be a blessing to someone else (1 Tim. 6:17-18). Reminded me of something I read the other day. To most golfers, *a hole in one* is the ultimate, a miracle, a time for celebration. The interesting thing is that the Japanese believe those who receive good fortune have an obligation to share. So those who score *an ace* are required by custom to buy dinner, beverages, and other presents for club members and friends, all of which can easily add up to $10,000 or more! Noriaki Yamashita's tee shot on the 15th green bounced twice and plopped into the cup for a hole in one, he spent $13,000 on golf shoes, bags, sports towels, dinner, and beverages for his friends. That should also be our mentality – we are blessed by God to be a blessing to others.

III. FINALLY, THE *REMOVAL* OF SAUL. 31:1-13

A. The *Battle.* 31:1-6

¹ Now the Philistines were fighting against Israel, and the men of Israel fled from before the Philistines and fell slain on Mount Gil-bo'a. ² The Philistines overtook Saul and his sons; and the Philistines killed Jonathan and A-bin'a-dab and Mal-chi-shu'a the sons of Saul. ³ The battle went heavily against Saul, and the archers hit him; and he was badly wounded by the archers. ⁴ Then Saul said to his armor bearer, "Draw your sword and pierce me through with it, otherwise these uncircumcised will come and pierce me through and make sport of me." But his armor bearer would not, for he was greatly afraid. So Saul took his sword and fell on it. ⁵ When his armor bearer saw that Saul was dead, he also fell on his sword and died with him. ⁶ Thus Saul died with his three sons, his armor bearer, and all his men on that day together – Saul died just as God had predicted. God alone ultimately decides when we die (Heb. 9:27).

I read a true story about a patient with cancer; they gave him no hope of survival. The man decided he wanted to just go home and die.

They took him off all of his medication, off any support systems and let him go home to die – within weeks he was walking about with little pain, doing fine!

B. The *Brutal.* 7-10

⁷ When the men of Israel who were on the other side of the valley, with those who were beyond the Jordan, saw that the men of Israel had fled and that Saul and his sons were dead, they abandoned the cities and fled; then the Philistines came and lived in them. ⁸ It came about on the next day when the Philistines came to strip the slain, that they found Saul and his three sons fallen on Mount Gil-bo'a. ⁹ They cut off his head and stripped off his weapons, and sent them throughout the land of the Philistines, to carry the good news to the house of their idols and to the people. ¹⁰ They put his weapons in the temple of Ash-ta-roth, and they fastened his body to the wall of Beth-shan – sounds like something Isis would do!

Barber, "We know that an Amalekite had taken Saul's crown and bracelet from his body, so the king could only have been identified by the Philistines by his size and armor. When they found Saul, they showed their contempt for him by cutting off his head. In all probability it was placed on top of a spear and runner took it through the cities and villages of Philistia to give their people conclusive proof of Saul's death. Then Saul's armor was stripped off his headless form and placed in the temple of

Ashtarroth. Finally the naked bodies of the king and his sons were fastened to the wall of the city of Bethshan.. There, as people went in and out through the gate of the city, they saw the bloodstain corpses of those who had dared to stand against the united power of the Philistine armies."

C. The *Burial.* 11-13

[11] Now when the inhabitants of Ja'besh-gil-e-ad heard what the Philistines had done to Saul, [12] all the valiant men rose and walked all night, and took the body of Saul and the bodies of his sons from the wall of Beth-shan, and they came to Ja-besh and burned them there. [13] They took their bones and buried them under the tam-arisk tree at Ja-besh, and fasted seven days – he was cremated.

Ryrie, "Cremation was not the general Hebrew practice except in the case of criminals (Joh. 7:25). The bodies may have been burned because they had been so badly mutilated; even so, the bones were preserved and buried."

Con:

1. If we live long enough we are going to face many crises in this life, like D. L. Moody on that ship our first reaction might be panic and fear…But like David we must learn to strengthen ourselves in the Lord.

2. Here is the rest of the story related to D. L. Moody's experience:

After continuous prayer, Moody experienced renewed faith, and he slept more soundly than he could remember ever having slept before. He declared:

"I can no more doubt that God gave answer to my prayer for relief than I can doubt my own existence."

At about 3: 00 a.m., his son woke him up and told him to come on deck. There they saw deliverance as the steamer *Lake Huron* approached; its lookout had seen this ship's signals of distress. Moody later wrote:

"Oh, the joy of that moment, when those...passengers beheld the approaching ship! Who can ever forget it?...All fear was gone."

But for Moody the fear was gone *before* he had actually seen the rescue ship because he, like David, had strengthened himself in the Lord...so can we.

Gospel Presentation:

Let me ask you one of the most important questions you will ever ponder.

Have you come to a place in your life where you know for certain that if you died you would go to heaven?

The only answer to that question is, yes, no, or I don't know. Take a moment and think about it. A follow up question would be:'

If you were standing before God right now and He were to ask, "Why should I let you into my perfect heaven?"

What do you think you would say? You might say, "I go to church. I try to live a good life. I try to keep God's law." Such responses are sincere, and I appreciate your honesty. Most would probably say, "I don't know what I would say." Well, would you like to know? Then read the following carefully.

God Really Does Love You

"For God so loved the world, (put your name here), that He gave His only begotten Son, that whoever believes in Him should not perish but have everlasting life" (John 3:16).

It is natural to question this claim; we tend to wonder how God could love us with all of our problems and hang-ups, yes, you can say it – with all of our sins. My wife and I have had two children. When they were born they did nothing for us! And after they were born, for the first several months they kept us up all hours of the night; we had to change their diapers and feed them. I think most of you know what I'm talking about. However, we did love them. Why? I suppose it was because we had something to do with them being in this world. They are our children; they even looked a little like us – poor kids! You need to realize that God is the one who had everything to do with your coming into this world. Without God you would not even exist! He is the Creator and Sustainer of life. He, in fact, created you in His image and loves you even though you have done nothing to deserve it.

So What's a Fella to Do?

Have you ever felt that your life lacked purpose and meaning? Have these thoughts ever crossed your mind:

- Where did I come from?
- Why am I here?
- Where am I going?

God knows the answer to these questions. He created you with a definite purpose in mind.

"The thief does not come except to steal, and to kill, and to destroy. I have come that they may have life, and that they may have it more abundantly" (John 10:10).

An abundant life is a life of purpose, meaning, and fulfillment. That is what God offers you.

This brings up an unavoidable question—what happened! If He loves us and has this great purpose for our life, then why are both concepts so foreign to us? The answer is both profound and very simple.

Sin Separates!

We are all sinners, "for all have sinned and fall short of the glory of God" (Rom. 3:22). We are a sinner by birth. God created Adam and Eve and put them in a garden with only one commandment; they were not to eat of a certain tree. They disobeyed God by taking a bite, and thus they sinned. Now what kind of babies are two sinful people capable of having? It is the law of biogenesis—like produces like. This is why there is no need to teach children how to tell a lie, but only to teach them positive things like telling the truth. They know how to lie naturally!
The reason for that is that we are all born with a sin nature inherited from Adam.

"Therefore, just as through one man sin entered the world, and death through sin, and thus death spread to all men, because all sinned" (Rom. 5:12).

We are also sinners by behavior. Have you not sinned? The Bible commands us to love God with all our heart, mind, and soul. Have you always done that? Have you ever done that? Have you ever told a lie? Have you ever wanted to? God not only looks at our deeds but at our desires. The Bible clearly declares we have all sinned.

So What?

Here is the answer to the so-what question.

"For the wages of sin is death, but the gift of God is eternal life in Christ Jesus our Lord" (Rom. 6:23).

What we have earned from our sin is death. Death means separation.

- There is spiritual death—the separation of the spirit/soul from God. "And the LORD God commanded the man, saying, 'Of every tree of the garden you may freely eat; but of the tree of the knowledge of good and evil you shall not eat, for in the day that you eat of it you shall surely die'" (Gen. 2:16–17). The day they ate of it they did not physically die; that took place many years later. But God said *in the day* you eat of it you will die. They died spiritually that very day.

- There is also physical death—the separation of the spirit/soul from the body. "And as it is appointed for men to die once, but after this the judgment" (Heb. 9:27). The fact that everybody dies physically is proof positive that everyone is spiritually dead. If we were not sinners, we would not die. The statistics are rather impressive; one out of every one person dies!

- If you die physically while you are spiritually dead, you will die eternally. Eternal death is the eternal separation of the spirit/soul/body from God's goodness, grace, mercy, and blessings. It is to be fully conscious and live in a place the Bible calls the lake of fire. "Then Death and Hades were cast into the lake of fire. This is the second death. And anyone not found written in the Book of Life was cast into the lake of fire" (Rev. 20:14–15).

Question: How can you say one moment that God loves me and then in the next that He condemns me?

Well let us imagine putting on a judge's robe and sitting on the bench. Then the unthinkable happens. Your son, whom you love very much, is brought before you, guilty of a capital offense! The penalty for his crime is death, and the evidence is clear as to his guilt. Would you sentence him to death? If you were a just judge, you would, not because you no longer love him, but in spite of your great love for him. God is holy, righteous, and just, as well as a God of love. This looks like bad news!

However, the very word *gospel* means good news, so where is this good news?

Jesus Christ Is God

"In the beginning was the Word, and the Word was with God, and the Word was God" (John 1:1).

This is a great mystery, but the Bible teaches that God became God/man. "And the Word became flesh and dwelt among us, and we beheld His glory, the glory as of the only begotten of the Father, full of grace and truth" (John 1:14).

Jesus Christ the Substitute

The Lord Jesus Christ lived a perfect life and then died in your place. "But God demonstrates His own love toward us, in that while we were still sinners, Christ died for us" (Rom. 5:8 NKJV).

Let us put our judge robe back on for a minute. Imagine after sentencing your boy to be executed, taking off your robe and then voluntarily offering to die in his place. That would make you just and loving at the same time. That is what Jesus Christ actually did for us. We do not understand all of this but must accept it by faith. I do not understand electricity, but I still do not live in the dark. I do not understand how the digestive system works, but I still eat. I do not understand how a brown cow eats green grass and produces white milk. You do not have to understand everything to be saved—just that you are a sinner and that Jesus Christ died for your sin.

He Is Not Here, He Has Risen

"For I delivered to you first of all that which I also received: that Christ died for our sins according to the Scriptures, and that He was buried, and that He rose again the third day according to the Scriptures, and that He was seen by Cephas, then by the twelve. After that He was seen by over five hundred brethren at once, of whom the greater part remain to the present, but some have fallen asleep" (1 Cor. 15:3–6).

By rising from the dead, He proved that He paid for all of our sins. If He had not, death would have held Him. It also proved that He had no sin of His own. If He had, He would have stayed dead like everybody else.

One Way Only

We have all seen *One Way Only* signs, and so it is with the way of salvation. There is only one person who can save. "Jesus said to him, 'I am the way, the truth, and the life. No one comes to the Father except through Me'" (John 14:6).

You can line up every one of us on the West Coast with plans to swim to Hawaii, and no doubt, some would swim a lot farther than others. Nevertheless, we would all have one thing in common: nobody would make it! It is impossible for anybody to swim from the West Coast to Hawaii. And it is just as impossible for sinful man to make his way to a Holy God on his own without experiencing God's wrath. What one needs is a boat to get them from the West Coast to Hawaii. Moreover, the only salvation boat is the Lord Jesus Christ. That Jesus is the only way to be saved is as true as $2 + 2 = 4$. There is only one answer to that equation, and there is only one way to be saved.

"Nor is there salvation in any other, for there is no other name under heaven given among men by which we must be saved" (Acts 4:12).

Facts

These are only facts. Giving mental assent to these facts is not enough to save anyone. It is not enough to give intellectual assent to these facts. We must believe and thus receive Christ.

"But as many as received Him, to them He gave the right to become children of God, to those who believe in His name" (John 1:12).

Faith

Facts must be wedded to faith. So, what do we mean when we say believe or place your faith in Christ?

Faith involves mind, emotion, and will.

Years ago, a tightrope walker named Charles Blondin, went across Niagara Falls, walking on a wire. He went back and forth. He even filled a wheelbarrow with bricks and took that across. A crowd gathered, and he asked one of them, "Do you believe I could do that with you?" The man agreed that he could. Then Blondin said, "Hop on in, and I'll carry you across." The man said, "No way!" You see, he did not really believe. He believed in his mind that Blondin could take him across; he wanted him to in his emotions, but he would not commit himself to Blondin and trust him to take him across. Saving faith involves our mind, emotion, and will.

Amazing Grace

You likely have heard the song, "Amazing Grace." We are saved by grace through faith in Jesus Christ. Now faith is not a work—faith is to believe in the work of another. "For by grace you have been saved through faith, and that not of yourselves; it is the gift of God, not of works, lest anyone should boast" (Eph. 2:8–9).

Dr. Gerstner: "Christ has done everything necessary for his salvation. Nothing now stands between the sinner and God but the sinner's good works. Nothing can keep him from Christ but his delusion that he does not need Him—that he has good works of his own that can satisfy God. If men will only be convinced that all their righteousness is as filthy rags; if men will see that there is none that does good, no, not one; if men will see that all are shut up under sin—then there will be nothing to prevent their everlasting salvation. All they need is need. All they must have is nothing. All that is required is acknowledged guilt. But alas, sinners cannot part from their virtues. They are imaginary, but they are real to them. So grace becomes unreal. The real grace of God they spurn in order to hold on to the illusory virtues of their own. Their eyes fixed on a mirage; they will not drink real water. They die of thirst in the midst of an ocean of grace."

Repentance is a synonym for faith; it is like heads and tails of *one* coin. Repentance is not making a vow you will stop sinning, nor is it a change of life. You cannot stop sinning or change your life until God saves you! I have fished most of my life and I have never cleaned a fish before I caught it. Repentance is a *change of mind*, about who you are, a sinner; and about the Lord Jesus Christ, the only one who can save you based on His death, burial, and resurrection.

Good Enough Is Not Good Enough

The religious leaders of Jesus' day prayed three times a week, fasted twice a week, never missed going to the house of worship, and memorized the Old Testament (Luke 18:9–12). Yet, Jesus said that if you are not more righteous then they, you are not going to make it!

"For I say to you, that unless your righteousness exceeds the righteousness of the scribes and Pharisees, you will by no means enter the kingdom of heaven (Matt. 5:20).

Then he says something rather startling:

"Therefore you shall be perfect, just as your Father in heaven is perfect" (Matt. 5:48).

Did you know Jesus said it takes perfect righteousness to get to heaven? We all know that nobody is perfect! How then can we be perfectly righteous before a perfectly righteous God?

"For He made Him who knew no sin to be sin for us, that we might become the righteousness of God in Him" (2 Cor. 5:21).

The truth is, there is only one person who lived a perfect life, and that was Jesus Christ. You see, the good news is that not only did Jesus die on the cross in our place, to offer us forgiveness of all our sins, He also offers us His

perfect righteousness, placed on our account! The only sin Jesus ever knew was ours; the only righteousness we will ever know is His.
Never the Same!

Salvation is not an external thing. When you receive Jesus Christ as your Savior, He makes you a new creature within!

"Therefore, if anyone is in Christ, he is a new creation; old things have passed away; behold, all things have become new" (2 Cor. 5:17). And the Holy Spirit takes up permanent residence within you.

"And because you are sons, God has sent forth the Spirit of His Son into your hearts, crying out, 'Abba, Father'" (Gal. 4:6).

Thus, you now have the desire (new nature) and the power (indwelling Holy Spirit) to live for God. You are positionally changed from being in Adam to now being in Christ, and experientially changed because the inner transformation of regeneration and salvation begins the process of progressive sanctification, which ultimately leads to glorification.

"For it is God who works in you both to will and to do for His good pleasure" (Phil. 2:13).

While we still have an old sin nature though Satan is opposing us every step of the way, we must grow in the grace and knowledge of the Lord Jesus. It is also true that our entire life is different! If we are what we've always been, we are not saved. I know that I am saved because on the seventh of May, 1974, I received the Lord Jesus Christ as my Savior and also because I have never gotten over it! And it is not that we are trying to be saved. If I asked you, "Are you an elephant?" You would not say, "Well, I'm trying to be!" You either are an elephant or you're not. No one who is trying to be saved understands salvation. *You are either saved or you're not!* You are saved because you have had a personal, life-changing encounter with the Lord Jesus Christ at a point in time. It is a matter of trusting not trying.

So Are You Ready to Be Saved?

If this is something you want to do, then here is a suggested prayer; the words are not what's important but what's in your heart. If God is dealing with you, then cry out to Him:

Lord Jesus, I need you. Thank you for dying on the cross for my sins. I cannot save myself. I cannot even help you save me. But the best I know how, I confess that I am a sinner and believe that the Lord Jesus Christ died on the cross for my sins and rose from the dead. I open the door of my life and receive you right now as my Savior. Come in and make me the kind of person you want me to be.

If you just received the Lord Jesus Christ as your Savior, then you are saved! This promise is based on the authority of God's Word.

"But as many as received Him, to them He gave the right to become children of God, to those who believe in His name" (John 1:12).